Working Women into the Borderlands

CONNECTING THE GREATER WEST SERIES

Sterling Evans, Series Editor

Working Women

INTO THE BORDERLANDS

Sonia Hernández

Foreword by Sterling Evans

TEXAS A&M UNIVERSITY
College Station, Texas

First edition

Connecting the Greater West Series

Manufactured in the United States of America
This paper meets the requirements of ANSI/NISO, Z39.48-1992 (Permanence of Paper).
Binding materials have been chosen for durability.

Library of Congress Cataloging-in-Publication Data

Hernández, Sonia, 1976- author.
Working women into the borderlands / Sonia Hernández ; with a foreword by Sterling Evans.—First edition.
pages cm.—(Connecting the greater west series)
Includes bibliographical references and index.
ISBN 978-1-62349-040-9 (cloth : alk. paper)—
ISBN 978-1-62349-041-6 (pbk. : alk. paper)—
ISBN 978-1-62349-139-0 (e-book)
1. Women in the labor movement—Mexico, North—History—20th century. 2. Women in the labor movement—Mexican-American Border Region—History—20th century. 3. Women labor union members—Mexico, North—History—20th century. 4. Mexican American women labor union members—Mexican-American Border Region—History—20th century. 5. Economic development—Mexico, North—20th century. 6. Economic development—Mexican-American Border Region—20th century. I. Title. II. Series: Connecting the greater west series.
HD6079.2.M6H47 2014
331.40972'1—dc23
2013043168

To three generations of *norteñas:*

Senorina Morado Véliz,

Eustolia Véliz Hernández,

Camila Chávez Hernández

Contents

Foreword

IMPORTANTLY, AND I WOULD ADD, very proudly, Sonia Hernández's *Working Women into the Borderlands* is the first book in the Connecting the Greater West series. In so many ways, Hernández's work embodies the very essence of the series, to explore the changing and growing ways that historians and others are coming to view the North American West, a West that includes the American West, northern Mexico, western Canada, and the borderlands areas between the regions. Subject areas of books in the series will include transnational history, borders and borderlands, immigration, environment and agriculture, and indigenous negotiations of bordered regions. Thus, the book before you here examines the bordered region between the northeastern Mexican states of Nuevo León, Tamaulipas, and south Texas—an area characterized by robust agricultural development (tobacco, cotton, ixtle fiber), and later, industrialization (textile and garment factories, industrial bakeries), on both sides of the Rio Grande that separates the United States from Mexico in this part of the continent.

Working Women into the Borderlands also makes a welcome contribution to the ever-growing literature on borderlands history, and adds important research and analysis to the understudied gender history of the region. Indeed, Hernández "works" women into the Tamaulipas/Texas boundary region, but her book is also about "working" women, those *norteñas* who provided essential agricultural and industrial labor there in the late nineteenth and early twentieth centuries. You will read in this book how gender fits neatly into other themes to tell a more complete story of the agricultural and industrial history of the lower Rio Grande Valley. As she explains in the Introduction, "The process of negotiating the making of the borderlands involved the articulation of gender, racial and class ideologies, as well as ideas of modernization." And you will get to meet many of these women, as Hernández through meticulous binational research has uncovered their voices via archival sources, and has interviewed others so that their memory of these times and places can be preserved and used to help us understand borderland labor history more thoroughly. So, you get many things with this book! Borderlands history, agricultural and industrial history, gender history, and labor history all blend here to relate a social history of this lower Rio Grande Valley region.

Speaking of which, the northern Tamaulipas/southern Texas borderlands are among the least studied area along the long US-Mexico boundary. While certainly this literature is growing, it still lags behind that of the Arizona/Sonora or California/Baja California borderlands historiography. *Working Women into the Borderlands* helps to correct this lacuna and hopefully will stimulate other scholars to view the area as an important borderlands region worthy of historical inquiry. Other scholars may want to launch into comparative borderlands analysis, contrasting the labor or gender or agricultural history of Hernández's study to that of other regions along the US-Mexico line. For the lower Rio Grande Valley, Hernández shows how women's work and their labor activism helped to transform the region—helping in a big way to make it more productive, and therefore more modern.

The transformation of the region that Hernández tracks was characterized by a change from smaller, light industries in Tamaulipas to larger, heavy industries that developed in regional cities. As she evidences here, women workers played an integral role in this process. But the industrial development was also dependent on capital investment from north of the border. That kind of investment flow illustrates once again the transnational nature of this story that played out in a borderlands region. The work environments, however, were gender-based, based on notions of expectations of "women's work" and what their place in society should be. But instead of victims, many women you will meet here became activists and fought for their and their fellow women workers' rights. Some responded by crossing into Texas to add their work skills to industries there, adding yet another transboundary dimension to this fascinating history. Combined, all of these dimensions show how women shaped the economic development of a dynamic borderlands region, and add to our understanding of the Greater West.

—STERLING EVANS
Series Editor

Acknowledgments

THERE WERE MANY TIMES I THOUGHT this book would never come to fruition. It did, partly due to several people who believed in me and kept encouraging me. I owe a great debt to people who took the time to carefully review my work and provide critical and constructive criticism. Many provided valuable assistance in various phases of the project. The idea for the book began to develop in a Mexican history seminar taught by Professor John Mason Hart at the University of Houston (UH). Our class regularly met at one of Houston's top Vietnamese restaurants; I always looked forward to listening to Professor Hart discuss the origins of peasant and urban workers' discontent and uprisings, his detailed descriptions of Mexican archives, and his encyclopedic knowledge of American investments in Mexico since the days of Benito Juárez. His passion for archival research, his love for labor history, and his deep respect for Mexican and Mexican American people motivated me to further investigate my parents' homeland—Tamaulipas and Nuevo León. Moreover, the absence of women in monographs on the region's development during the late nineteenth and early twentieth centuries made little sense to me, as I knew that they too had built these *norteño* borderlands.

The research journey that has culminated in this manuscript was a long but enriching experience. A Murray Miller Research Grant from the History Department at the University of Houston provided the resources to spend time in the Archivo General de la Nación in Mexico City and the Archivo General del Estado de Nuevo León (AGENL) in Monterrey. A fellowship from the Center for Mexican American Studies at UH allowed me to take time off work and focus on research—I thank Professor Tatcho Mindiola and his wonderful staff. A Lily Endowment–Hispanic Scholarship Fund Research Grant allowed me to do research at the Archivo Histórico de Tampico. A College of Arts and Humanities Faculty Research Grant and a Faculty Research Council Grant from the University of Texas–Pan American (UTPA) provided the time and resources to conduct further research at the AGENL and the Archivo Histórico de Tampico and to visit the Archivo General del Estado de Tamaulipas (AGET), Archivo Municipal de Reynosa, the Mary Norton Clapp Library at Occidental College, the National Archives, the Library of Congress, and the Wagner Labor Archives at New York University. I utilized travel funds from the Department of History & Philosophy at UTPA to conduct research at the Nettie Lee Benson Latin American Collection at the University of Texas at Austin and the Woodson Research Center at Rice University. César Morado Macias and his staff at the AGENL provided invaluable assistance over the course of several trips. I thank the staff at the AGET and my good friend Carlos Rugeiro, now director of that archive. I am indebted to my friends at the Instituto de Investigaciones Históricas at the Universidad Autónoma de Tamaulipas; special thanks go to the great staff, including Laura Montemayor, Juan Díaz, Oscar Misael Hernández, now at the Colegio de la Frontera Norte–Matamoros, and Jesús Jaimes Hernández, now at the Universidad Nacional Autónoma de México (UNAM). I am indebted to Susie Porter for her invaluable comments on earlier drafts of the chapter on *cigarreras* in Nuevo León. I am also grateful for the constructive criticism by Teresa Fernández Aceves of an abbreviated version of that chapter, presented at the Conference on Gender and Mexican Women's History in Oaxaca in 2009, and to Mary Goldsmith Connelly for sharing insight on the records of the Junta de Conciliación y Arbitraje. Parts of chapter 3 were presented at a Newberry Seminar in Labor History, where Jim Case provided insightful comments; the Writing across the Curriculum group at UTPA read several drafts of chapters 3, 5, and 6 over the course of three years. I also thank my colleagues Brent Campney and Stephanie Alvarez for their editorial assistance with an abbreviated version of chapter 6. I thank Guadalupe San Miguel Jr. for his encouragement and support and La Colectiva–UH members for their camaraderie and encouragement. My good friend Diana Méndez, from the Colegio de México, graciously shared research findings from her own work on Mante, Tamaulipas, that helped me clarify many doubts I had on my own research. I thank Sterling Evans, Mary Lenn Dixon, and the great staff at Texas A&M University Press for their support, encouragement, and patience.

Sections of chapters 4 and 5 appear in Arnoldo De León's edited anthology, *War along the Border,* and were carefully edited by both Arnoldo and Guadalupe San Miguel Jr. Some of my research assistants over the course of this project include Rodolfo "Chico" Arriaga and David Robles, and I thank them for their assistance with transcriptions. Students in my graduate Borderlands History seminar helped me understand what I was writing about when I got off track. Special thanks go to Trinidad González for his constant encouragement, for his willingness to engage in lengthy conversations about my work and provide critical feedback, and for sharing research with me. The Department of History & Philosophy at UTPA offered much-needed encouragement; many thanks go to

Michael Faubion, Michael Weaver, Russ Skowronek, Linda English, and the late Juanita Garza. My Mexican American Studies colleagues deserve a big thank-you for encouraging me and allowing me time off from our very busy agenda to complete this manuscript. *Gracias a* Edna Ochoa, Marci McMahon, Stephanie Alvarez, and Emmy Pérez. I also thank colleagues Maritza de la Trinidad and Cynthia Paccacerqua for their support. Many thanks also go to George Gause and Janette Garcia from Special Collections at the UTPA library. Gracias al profesor Roldolfo Rocha for planting the seed of historical curiosity and thanks to Ala Qubbaj, vice provost for faculty affairs, for his support. Staff members of the Mary Norton Clapp Library at Occidental College were very patient and provided invaluable assistance.

I am grateful for the assistance I received from Patricia Hernández Reyna during several visits to the Archivo Histórico de Tampico. I also thank Claudia Sorais Castañeda García from the Instituto Tamaulipeco para las Artes y Cultura and the people of Río Bravo who graciously opened the historic *casco antiguo,* the actual structural shell of the main Casa Grande headquarters, of the Hacienda Sauteña to hear me speak about *norteñas* who fought for the ideals of the Revolution. Meeting several of the now aged first *ejidatarios,* or communal landholders, of Río Bravo brought me much joy and kept my passion for the study of this region alive.

My late grandmother, Senorina, a strong-minded *ranchera,* and my uncle, Felipe, shared numerous stories about ranch life on the outskirts of Río Bravo; the Hernández-Véliz family always supported and encouraged me. My father taught me the value of work and respect as I grew up watching him work cutting other people's lawns. He also instilled in me a love and respect for *corridos* and *norteño* music. My mother provided insight into the everyday life of a ranch girl who made *tortillas* on a daily basis and later grew up to be a *costurera* who worked for more than twenty years sewing other people's clothes. Special thanks go to Lisa, my little sister, whose editorial assistance proved invaluable and whose company alone helped me through those rough times. I thank Oscar for his encouragement since my days in graduate school, even when he did not understand what I was doing, and for sharing stories of his life as an immigrant and carpenter and about cotton culture in Vallehermoso. I also thank him for the countless times he took care of our home and our little Cami when I could not.

And so the history of this expansive homeland—Ramones, Nuevo León, Río Bravo, Tamaulipas, and the Rio Grande Valley—to both my parents as well as scores of other *norteños,* takes center stage in this book. I hope that I have done a good job and that the great-grandchildren of the *norteños* who worked as *campesinos* and *obreros* read it one day. This book is the product of years of encouragement and support, and it is so much better because of it.

Working Women into the Borderlands

Introduction

Norteño *History as Borderlands History*

> On his knees, hands swollen sweat flowering on his face his gaze on the high paths the words in his head twinning cords—tossing them up to catch that bird of the heights. Century after century swimming . . .
>
> GLORIA ANZALDÚA, "A SEA OF CABBAGES," 1987

> Given the fact that most of my *compañeras* feel that they are restricted at work, that we feel we do not have any liberties [at the factory,] . . . I have chosen to denounce the factory for violation of my work contract . . . violation of our rights as workers.
>
> ANA MARÍA SÁNCHEZ, MONTERREY, NUEVO LEÓN, 1937

AS PORFIRIO DÍAZ EMBARKED upon his second decade as dictator of Mexico in 1892, Teodora Cepeda, a local *campesina* from a hacienda in the Nuevo León countryside, traveled to Monterrey in search of a local scribe to assist her in labor matters. Resolved to voice her demands, Teodora presented a labor complaint to none other than the governor of the state of Nuevo León. By way of the local scribe, Teodora petitioned the governor, Bernardo Reyes. She explained that despite the fact that her husband had paid off debts to the hacienda where they both worked, he had not been granted permission to leave the estate. According to practice, workers could leave if they did not owe the estate any money. Teodora had wished to relocate her family once her husband cleared his debt. She further explained that, "with my husband's permission," she had directed her complaint to the governor because her husband could not endure the "bad treatment" of his *patrón* any longer, and she pleaded with the governor to intercede on her behalf. Governor Reyes's office responded by offering to find the family a "poor people's lawyer."[1]

Teodora and her family had witnessed employers increase their control over campesino workers because of the limited size of the workforce, migration to the growing urban areas offering higher industrial wages, and competition for workers on the Texas side of the international border. These turn-of-the-twentieth-century processes, fueled by an alliance between American and regional capital and access to cheap Mexican labor, converted the northeastern part of Mexico into a "modern and progressive" region—qualities that altered the lives of thousands of *norteños* (northerners) such as the Cepedas. In the same way, like the Cepedas, residents and transient migrants shaped this transformation by directly engaging a state that had become increasingly concerned with economic development based on the privatization of land and high levels of foreign investment, as well as the expansion of commercial agriculture.[2] Workers' engagement with the state was shaped by their view of the central role of the community, their need for arable land, and a growing awareness of worker rights. Workers engaged the state through petitions, collective organizing, and, by 1910, outright contestation and rebellion.

Working Women into the Borderlands recounts the story of ordinary people such as Teodora, cigar makers, *ixtle* workers (who processed agave fibers), and other norteños who, as they sold their labor and attempted to negotiate their respective local socioeconomic conditions, were anything but ordinary as they assumed a central role in the transformation of the Mexican northeastern borderlands. This work pays close attention to the various ways in which workers sought to voice their concerns to local, state, and even national authorities. Ideas of mutual reciprocity, grounded in colonial practices, helped people deal with change. On the one hand, this change was defined and promoted as "modernization" by state representatives and investors but seemed disruptive to the majority of working-class residents. This book also heeds the call for a gendered investigation of the borderlands.[3] The process of negotiating the making of the borderlands involved the articulation of gender, racial, and class ideologies, as well as ideas of modernization.[4] Working women in the region, despite lacking voting rights and being barred from certain male-controlled mutual-aid societies and unions, contributed to the emerging industries and commercial agriculture. They demanded labor rights by claiming *vecino* status and its accompanying community rights. They held strongly to cultural practices that directly clashed with newer perspectives on the uses of land and labor. By claiming such community rights, women became key players in this contested terrain. Their power came from belonging to a community that helped them negotiate conditions in the workplace.[5] This idea of community belonging was grounded in ideas of mutual reciprocity, collectivity, and *cooperativismo*.[6] These were not new ideas. Such community-based practices had been quite common on the northern frontier since the early settlement period and had survived waves of socioeconomic change that began with the Bourbon reforms and continued throughout the Díaz period as efforts to consolidate national power and bring the nation's periphery under the purview of the state took place.

As urban centers attracted campesinas such as Teodora, hacienda management used labor control mechanisms to retain the labor force. As the historians Miguel Angel González Quiroga and Juan Mora-Torres have shown, laborers could and did cross into Texas in search of higher wages, thus forcing landowners in Mexico to develop more creative ways to retain labor. Norteño families like the Cepedas would find some room to maneuver and negotiate their way through difficult labor conditions. Further, that Teodora's petition was "approved" by her husband reveals gendered notions of power and authority. While it is important to note that not all petitions for *amparo* (petitions for aid, in the broadest popular sense) were granted, the deeper, more significant aspect of such requests reveals the persistence of pre-industrial cultural practices in the region.

During the American Civil War a mature norteño bourgeoisie emerged and dominated commerce well into the Porfiriato. With the last of the rebellious indigenous groups controlled through the use of military force by the 1890s, merchants extended their economic ties across the border. By the late nineteenth century Mexico was well on its way to becoming a unified nation-state. The efforts to tame the border region in order to attract foreign investment and make the region and its resources "consumable," as the historian Samuel Truett has explained for the Arizona-Sonora borderlands, succeeded.[7] The Mexican northeastern borderlands would epitomize this transformation, and the people of the region would come to represent some of the most resilient and active participants in the Mexican Revolution.

Inspired by European and American ideas of modernity and progress, national, regional, and local elites sought to transform their nation through industrial development and commercial agriculture. The capital and technological know-how could be imported from more "advanced" countries to make the transformation of Mexico possible. According to national and regional elites, the solution to economic and social problems in the country was industrial development and commercial agriculture, which would provide employment for restive peasants and result in higher levels of productivity. As one Mexican writer observed, Mexico had what was needed to facilitate capital investment: peace, stability, and a people with a strong desire to work.[8]

From 1880 through the Mexican Revolution, the Northeast transitioned from a sparsely populated region into a highly capitalized borderland, with Monterrey emerging as its industrial nucleus. Here, I employ the term *borderland/s* as a space and process whereby cultures, ideas, and capital clash and mesh. This particular borderland emerged as a "crossroads" between two expanding nation-states and became a contested space that has remained in constant flux (up to this day) and serves as the only borderland where the most industrialized country meets a "developing" country. The borderlands were a product of the rise of two nation-states, not the drawing of a geopolitical line. The rise of the nation-state, as the historian Friedrich Katz has explained, also involved economic reorganization and widespread free wage labor.[9] However, the boundary helped to shape certain political economic developments. In very basic terms, the borderlands experienced a process of incorporation that I argue was never completed. While Katz employs the term *frontier,* as have other historians who focused on the period before the Porfiriato, the term implies a certain emptiness, a certain sense of past and not present, and ascribes a sense of linearity to a complex and profound transformation. It was not that the frontier then became a borderland, that one replaced the other. The borderlands of the Northeast have gone through cycles of change that both resident and transient peoples have helped to shape on an ongoing basis.[10]

While Elliott Young and Samuel Truett have warned students of the borderlands to avoid "bounding [the] terrain too tightly" and have suggested that they "recognize diversity of narratives" in their collection of essays, they recognize that it was nonetheless important to delineate "turning points" in the history of the borderlands.[11] The turning point this book examines is the rise of industrial capitalism and its accompanying effects, which have often been defined as "modern" or associated with "modernization." Several scholars have examined this transition but have done so, with some exceptions, to explain the region's shift to industrial development and have not acknowledged and critically examined the impact of women's labor and the larger process of borderland making. Further, there is little in the way of research that examines how entrenched ideas of gender and societal expectations were renegotiated and the effect these expectations had on nation and border making. *Working Women into the Borderlands* thus argues that the development of the region was not fueled solely by male labor in the smelters, railroads, and oil and mining sectors. Women's work in cordage (ixtle) and brown sugar (*piloncillo*) haciendas, *tabacaleras* (cigar factories), and textile and garment factories, as well as in other industries, helped to build the borderlands. Women toiled at haciendas as *jornaleras* (day laborers)—working as *tallanderas* (extractors of agave/ixtle fiber) and *piloncilleras*—but they also owned *fábricas de tallado de ixtle* and tabacaleras. This book supports the findings of Francie Chassen López, who studies Oaxaca and has shown how "the growth of women's role in the agricultural proletariat was clearly prerevolutionary."[12] Moreover, as the majority of women in the region worked as tallanderas, seamstresses, and cigar makers, their work fell within the limits of "light industries." Most studies on the Mexican Northeast focus on heavy industries, including steel, oil, and smelters, yet, as this book shows, light industries complemented the growth of heavy industries and played a key role in addressing the basic consumer needs of both an expanding regional population as well as those living across the Río Grande. An analysis of women's labor in these sectors reveals a more complex and inclusive story of how borderlands are made. An analysis of gendered forms of labor activism within what has been traditionally a male-centered norteño history reveals hidden aspects of the history of unionism in the North and further contradicts the long-held view of norteño society as highly egalitarian and as a place where higher wages prevailed.[13]

Working Women into the Borderlands also reveals other, more adverse aspects of modernization, industrial development, and labor relations that tend to be glossed over in popular norteño histories. It points to how rampant physical abuse was at haciendas in both Tamaulipas and Nuevo León. While wages were certainly higher in such industries as smelting, glass making, beverage production (mainly beer), and cigar making, they were anything but high on the commercial estates. Day laborers and tallanderas in the countryside received some of the lowest wages in the country. Also, the level of American investment in the region was higher than what has been documented until now. The making of the norteño borderlands was possible through US capital, and it involved exploitative conditions in the form of physical abuse and depressed wages. While norteños demonstrated a high level of cultural resiliency through the use of colonial-era practices, including the *petición* and collective organizing, it would be direct action in the form of multiple uprisings in the early 1900s that would effect structural change.

Through the combined efforts of military *mestizo* soldier-colonists, pacified Indians, the Mexican army, and the US government, rebellious Indians, or "*indios bárbaros*," had finally been controlled or entirely eliminated by the 1880s.[14] With the "Indian problem" cleared and regional *caudillos*, or strongmen, controlled, Díaz's state centralization project was successful. Mexican modernization then was rooted in land and tax concessions to wealthy foreigners to entice them to invest the capital that Mexico lacked. Land that appeared "unproductive" was labeled "*baldía*" and granted, sold, or auctioned to the highest bidder. With the financial support of American and other foreign capitalists and cooperation from regional merchants and elites, Díaz showed the world that Mexico was now up to par with the modern and industrialized countries of the world. Along the northeastern border of Mexico, the push to make the country modern resulted in far-reaching changes at the community level that provoked strong reactions from the peasant and *ranchero* populations. The borderlands became primed for investments and for eventual "progress," and the making of the borderlands as envisioned by pro-Díaz state and regional elites in cooperation with American capitalists reveals much about the development of Mexico as a nation-state.

The words *modern* and *progress,* at least for regional and state elites, meant linking the region and the nation via railways, building factories, privileging private ownership over communal land ownership, and expanding commercial agriculture to make land productive by using modern irrigation technology. For the majority of norteños, this progress translated into increased labor control and a push toward creating a permanent labor force, widespread wage labor, and land loss. For many it also meant daily encounters with Americans, who came to own more than five million acres of the Northeast. This made the borderlands a highly contentious site; the everyday forms of negotiation and resistance that developed point to how, despite living on the periphery of two nations, norteños were all but peripheral.

Records from US and Mexican municipal, state, and national archives helped to document norteños' active role in the transformation of the region. Among the key sources used to create the narrative were petitions to state and national authorities by peasant women and men asking for financial aid, as well as records of intervention in labor disputes concerning physical abuse, higher wages, employment assistance, and general grievances against management and supervisors. Petitions found in the Archivo General del Estado de Nuevo León (AGENL) reveal strategies of negotiation and resistance such as walking off the job, abandoning haciendas and ranches to migrate to Mexican urban centers or Texas, and creating all-female or all-male collectives. Labor complaints from the Junta Local de Conciliación y Arbitraje and Junta Central de Conciliación y Arbitraje in the AGENL and the Archivo General del Estado de Tamaulipas (AGET), respectively, spanning from 1917 to 1936, form an indispensable body of data. Even though the first labor dispute was presented in 1917, the eyewitness reports and testimonies by men and women offer rich background information on labor conditions, community developments, and family disputes in the pre-1917 period. Complaints submitted by both women and men related to "*injurias*" (abuse and slander cases) and "*falta de respeto a la autoridad*" (lack of respect for authority), and related collections pertaining to judicial matters in the AGENL (in the Archivo de Juzgado del Primer Distrito con sede en Monterrey, or AJPDM) contain valuable documents that at first glance seem to have little to do with labor. Complaints vary, from accusations of tainting a person's reputation to lack of respect and theft. Yet, in the testimony provided by all of the parties involved, there is detailed information on residents' occupations, wages, and occasionally place of origin. These documents supplement government records on women's occupations and wages.[15]

This book tells the story of women's place in the rise of industrial capitalism and widespread commercial agriculture by stressing three themes as necessary points of investigation: the concept of region (the Northeast) and its function as a borderland, the role of women and gender in it, and the various ways in which workers engaged the state to negotiate labor relations.

Conceptualizing and Positioning the *Norteño* Borderlands

The conceptual framework of *Working Women into the Borderlands* draws from various histories of the Mexican North in general and on the northeastern part of this expansive region more specifically. The historian Friedrich Katz's multinational research laid the foundation for an understanding of the political and economic processes that unfolded along the northern borderlands, particularly in Chihuahua. Katz's *The Secret War in Mexico: Europe, the United States, and the Mexican Revolution* examines the Mexican Revolution within a larger global context. Besides the groundbreaking contributions that book made in terms of international research, Katz's analysis of the transition of the frontier resonates with the history of the greater Mexican Northeast. The region's long tradition of political autonomy, beginning with the wars of independence, came under attack with Díaz's ascension to power and the onset of centralization. Díaz's tough rule and oppressive tactics served to "close the frontier" and pacify rebellious indigenous and mestizo groups just as the United States confined indigenous peoples to reservations. As the threat of rebellions subsided, regional elites and *políticos* primed the region for foreign investment, which eventually paved the way for the consolidation of the nation-state. This shift that Katz identifies, from "frontier to borderlands," which echoed Frederick Jackson Turner's "frontier thesis," was facilitated with the influx of American capital. In Katz's view, the process of growth and development from North to South was possible only through an unequal alliance between US capital and Mexican labor. This accumulation of American capital has been meticulously studied by historian John Hart, who has demonstrated that foreign investments in Mexico served as a testing ground for future US investments across the globe.[16] In the Mexican Northeast, particularly in Tamaulipas, US capital played a substantial role in altering the lives of both residents and transients.

In examining *la frontera norte,* the economic historian Mario Cerutti has proposed the idea of an *ámbito regional,* or a regional sphere of influence, for nineteenth- and early twentieth-century Mexico. While Cerutti's main objective is to examine capital formation and the emergence of the Monterrey bourgeoisie, he nonetheless acknowledges that, to do so, it is necessary to analyze the process within the context of an *ámbito.*[17] According to Cerutti, the *ámbito regional* most appropriate for the study of capital formation in Monterrey was one that included the greater Northeast. Industrial development ultimately required large amounts of capital and reliance on a more permanent labor force, which had begun to develop in the seventeenth century in mining sectors dispersed throughout the region. Explaining the economic history of Monterrey through neither a "political-administrative jurisdiction, state-province, or . . . municipality, nor by a purely geographic framework, nor, for that matter, by an international border," Cerutti proposes for the study of capital formation a methodology based on region. This approach refers to a space that was "recognizable by its marked internal coherence, a system of relations that stood out against the backdrop of its time."[18] According to Cerutti, the "Chicago of Mexico," as Monterrey became known, had operated within a larger economic context. Its historic ties with the Gulf of Mexico ports—Matamoros and Tampico—and its commercial networks with norteño cities such as Victoria, Montemorelos, and Nuevo Laredo, as well as its interdependence with American and European markets, gave the region considerable economic power, which laid the foundation for the capital accumulation that fueled industrial development, urbanization, and modernization during the Porfiriato.

As Cerutti was expanding his "*ámbito regional*" approach to the study of capital formation in Monterrey, historians were reshaping Herbert E. Bolton's "Spanish Borderlands."[19] In the 1980s there emerged new scholarship grounded in social and cultural history, demography, and gender and shaped by the social atmosphere of the aftermath of the Cuban revolution, the American civil rights movement, Vietnam, the women's movement, and other global social movements. Scholars such as David J. Weber and Ramon Gutiérrez expanded the field by examining the growth of the present-day US Southwest within the context of the larger history of the United States and incorporated indigenous histories, as well as gender and social relations.[20]

The history of industry and merchants (as told by Cerutti), as well as labor relations, became the focal point of many studies published in the 1980s that dealt with the eastern portion of the expansive northern region.[21] The active role of workers, principally in the cities of Monterrey and Tampico, has occupied a central role in the recent historiography of the Mexican Northeast. Studies on Monterrey and Tampico as leaders in the production of steel and oil emphasized working-class issues. As the historian Javier Rojas Sandoval pointed out in the early 1990s, "the almost two decades of General Bernardo Reyes' tenure as governor has been recorded as the era of great industry in the historiography of the region. . . . However, little is known as to what this meant for the workers—the '*jornaleros*' and the labor conditions endured by those *obreros* who made Nuevo León's modernization possible."[22] The push by historians like Rojas Sandoval to incorporate workers' perspectives continued. Like Rojas Sandoval, other historians, including Oscar Flores Torres, examined the rise of the working class and its resistance to and contributions to industrialization.[23] As scholars' interest in workers grew, studies on laborers from other parts of the Mexican Northeast appeared.

Perhaps one of the best studies on obrero culture and the sociocultural composition of the working class is Leif Adelson's work on Tampico. Building on Carlos González Salas's early narratives on the diverse working-class and port life of Tampico, Adelson meticulously probed the Tampico municipal archives to compile a history of oil workers. Focusing on the *petroleros* employed at the Compañía Mexicana de Petróleo El Aguila and Mexican Petroleum Company (and its subsidiary Huasteca Petroleum), Adelson identifies several factors contributing to the formation of a unique working-class consciousness. He notes the workers' changed environment, principally material changes that resulted from capital accumulation. The shift to industrial capitalism and the discovery of oil introduced a scientific approach to the production process, increased dependence on free wage labor, and introduced ideas of individuality, transmitted through foreign workers and supervisors alike. As a response, the workers collectively resisted and negotiated certain terms set forth by foreign and domestic enterprises. Ultimately, the workers identified with each other, despite some occupational and background differences, because they shared a hostile environment in which employers disregarded their rights as workers. Adelson's study remains the definitive work on the male oil workers of Tampico.[24]

Save for Tampico and Monterrey, the cities of the Northeast (including Matamoros, Nuevo Laredo, Victoria, Linares, and Montemorelos) have not received adequate historiographic attention regarding the rise of industrialization and specifically the way in which gender shaped this transition.[25] Monterrey has captured the most attention from scholars. Alex Saragoza, Juan Mora-Torres, and Michael Snodgrass published groundbreaking studies on Monterrey. Saragoza re-creates the history of elite ruling families who controlled industries in Monterrey through a series of intermarriages and paternalistic practices in the workplace and who were able to maintain control during the Revolution. Through an examination of labor-capital relations, Snodgrass details the story of the emergence of industrial paternalism and union militancy in the steel, beer, glass, and smelting industries of the city.[26] Juan Mora-Torres outlines the emergence of Monterrey as an industrial leader and explains the development of a border labor market, all while examining the decline of the countryside. Building on Miguel Angel González Quiroga's work on labor and migration in the mid- to late nineteenth century, Mora-Torres recounts the history of the Nuevo León working class both at haciendas and in factories. While Mora-Torres's focus is on Monterrey, his examination of the decline of the countryside vis-à-vis the emergence of the city as a powerful industrial center sheds light on conditions for the entire region. His discussion of a border labor market increasingly dependent on migrant Mexican labor provides a broader in-depth analysis of the effects of capitalism and widespread free wage labor. His treatment of labor conditions in the northern areas due to competition over Mexican labor from both sides of the border builds on Katz's findings and complements my own findings with regard to women workers.[27]

This book builds on the aforementioned worker-based studies, as well as those that have given a voice to community-based resistance and negotiation. Of particular significance is Florencia Mallon's *Defense of Community in Peru's Central Highlands.* The socioeconomic transition from early manufacturing, industrialization, and, eventually, capitalism in Peru's highland region was strongly resisted by peasant households, and in some cases the old ways coexisted with the new economic system. Peruvians defended their community as far-reaching changes unfolded with widespread free wage labor, the increased presence of foreign capital, and migration and urbanization. A similar process occurred in the Mexican Northeast. As the railroad linked the cities with the countryside and as major oil and steel/smelter operations began to form part of the landscape, socioeconomic differentiation among norteños increased. Like the Peruvians, norteños encountered *enganchadores* (labor contractors), experienced significant wage discrepancies vis-à-vis foreign workers, and became increasingly dependent on hourly wages.[28]

More recently, studies by Elliott Young, Casey Walsh, Jerry Thompson, and Samuel Truett have not only expanded the literature on the Mexican Northeast (and South Texas), as well as northern Mexico more generally, but have also underscored the pivotal role *fronterizos* played in the construction of the nation-state and of the border itself. Young's analysis of the ethnic Mexican Catarino Garza and his failed attempt to overthrow Díaz takes into consideration how residents from both sides of the border shaped, through their participation—directly or indirectly—this "crossroads." That same region where Garza garnered support for his revolution witnessed the emergence of commercial agriculture, particularly in Vallehermoso, between Matamoros and Reynosa. Walsh's historical-anthropological approach has advanced our understanding of how residents viewed regional and local development and how places such as the *región valle del Río Bravo,* along Mexico's northern periphery, played a central role in the making of the Northeast. Further, Thompson's detailed study on Juan Cortina, as well as Samuel Truett's examination of how regional elites and industrialists primed the Sonora-Arizona borderlands for investments, demonstrates the importance of binational archival research in the writing of borderlands history. Taken together, these studies provide a solid historiographical and theoretical framework in which to situate the history of norteños within the larger narrative of how borderlands are created. As the Northeast became a bordered region serving as one of several "crossroads" of Mexico and the United States, the Mexican state, in unison with US capital, was strengthened and expanded. The border then became a central site and symbol of state power.[29]

Despite the aforementioned studies that illuminate the cultural dimensions of industrial development, examine the relationship between the city and countryside, and place workers at the forefront, women have been essentially absent from these studies.

Gendering the Norteño Borderlands

While particular attention has been given to women belonging to the landed elite in studies by Juan Fidel Zorilla and in the memoir-based book by Sara Aguilar de Belden Garza (a member of the Monterrey elite herself), there is little analysis and no discussion of working-class women in them.[30] More recently, there have been research efforts to examine campesinas, though most studies focus on the post-1940 period, after the span of this study. Nonetheless, they are useful in providing a comparative context across various time periods. The scholar Veronika Sieglin has examined rural women who labored in the citrus-growing region of southern Nuevo León and their role in the regional agricultural economy.[31] Similarly, Maria Zebadúa has examined campesinas' reproductive role in agricultural regions and their daily life during the post-1940 period. Both Sieglin's and Zebadúa's studies have laid the foundation for the history of working-class women in the Northeast, although their focus is on Nuevo León.[32]

Several monographs include sections or entire chapters on urban women workers. Michael Snodgrass's *Deference and Defiance in Monterrey* includes a chapter on women in the brewery there, Cervecería Cuahectémoc. His interviews with several retired women workers shed light on how women perceived their role in the industry and on the relationship between work and family.[33] Jocelyn Olcott's *Revolutionary Women in Postrevolutionary Mexico* includes several examples of women's labor activism in Tampico and Monterrey in the 1920s and 1930s, and her treatment of the relationship between citizenship and gender ideologies sheds light on women's organizations and labor reforms that addressed women's issues.[34] Further, Mary Goldsmith's work on Tampico domestic workers, based on records from the Junta Central and the Junta Local de Conciliación y Arbitraje, is essential because it focuses on the labor of women workers in domestic service, hotels, and commercial laundry establishments while underscoring the challenges that these workers faced as they organized and demanded labor rights.[35] More recently, Myrna Santiago has examined women's work in oil labor camps in Tampico and northern Veracruz. She expands the history of oil and Mexican-foreign relations by analyzing the contributions of women to the emerging petroleum industry.[36] While both Goldsmith's and Santiago's research is limited to Tampico and its vicinity, these are studies that have broadened the historiography of Tamaulipas and the role of women in labor.

Research on women's labor in the field of Mexican, Chicana/o, and Latin American history illuminates our understanding of the role of norteñas in industrial capitalism and how they negotiated gender and class ideologies. The research by Heather Fowler-Salamini, Susie Porter, Carmen Ramos Escandón, and Vicki Ruiz has helped to provide shape and meaning to the story of norteña workers. Fowler-Salamini's work on the coffee sector in Veracruz in the post-1920 period demonstrates the heterogeneity of the female working class and shows how a unique worker identity was constructed and how it "reconfigured provincial conceptions of gender and class."[37] Women put differences aside based on a shared work environment facilitated through ideas of class and gender. Similarly, Carmen Ramos Escandón's work on the formation of a unique "feminine labor consciousness" in the textile industry expands our understanding of women's labor. Women's everyday associations as fellow workers helped to create a unique female work consciousness grounded in ideas of gender solidarity to deal with changes associated with factory work.[38] Susie Porter has shown how women's participation in wage work eventually influenced labor legislation and helped construct female citizenship. Further, Porter's inclusion of women workers outside the factory walls sheds light on the unevenness of industrialization.[39] This book is similarly influenced by the arguments put forth by Veronika Sieglin and Jocelyn Olcott, which I take up in the chapters on rural women's work on haciendas and ranchos and women's work in the tabacaleras.

Equally, the work on Chicanas by Vicki Ruiz, particularly her discussion of social bonds and fictive social networks to cope with everyday challenges such as assimilation policies and racial discrimination, has given shape to my analysis of norteñas' everyday forms of survival. Ruiz notes the cultural resiliency of women as they successfully organized themselves. Despite socioeconomic and political changes, women managed to retain a sense of community and a collective identity. The strategies norteñas used, which included collective forms of organization, using the family as a source of support, and the successful organizing of all-female *cigarrera* and *costurera* unions in the post-1920 period, resemble the varied strategies implemented by *mexicanas* and Chicanas just across the border in Texas. These commonalities point to the way in which Mexican cultural practices, particularly ideas of collectivity rooted in Mexican *cooperativismo* and the practice of submitting written petitions, survived and crossed the border along with Mexican women. These traditions became cross-generational, given their use by later generations of Chicanas. Similarly, Deena González's work on Spanish and Mexican women in Santa Fe during the transition to US control of the region reminds us that women were active and participated in such monumental changes.[40] In short, the history of Chicanas not only helps illuminate norteño history but is also part of it.[41] Moreover, studies on rural women's work in various parts of Latin America, mainly the groundbreaking work of Carmen Diana Deere and Francie Chassen López, have proven crucial to our understanding of the work of campesinas. The research by the historian María Teresa Fernández Aceves on women's labor and activism in the tortilla industry in Guadalajara, a city that underwent a transformation comparable to that of Monterrey, sheds light on obrera mobilizations and the formation and renegotiation of class and gender ideologies. Heather Fowler-Salamini's discussion on *trabajadoras de confianza* (trustworthy employees), as well as Emilio Zamora's work on South Texas labor, have provided shape and meaning to this particular history of norteñas' negotiation of their gendered class status and their greater role in labor.[42]

Valuable to our understanding of local communities are the various microhistories of towns, including Linares and Ocampo, by local *cronistas* or town historians. These brief works include rich information from municipal archives and oral histories from older community members.[43] These histories have often been overlooked because they were published in Spanish, have not been accessible in the United States, or were written by local schoolteachers or nonacademics. Nonetheless, these brief studies of local communities offer rich detail on the everyday lives of norteño residents.

Given the focus here on the various forms of contestation and negotiation initiated by residents, this book has benefited from the work by Cynthia Radding and Christina Jiménez. While Radding's work focuses on the western part of what became northern Mexico and examines colonial processes, her treatment of the use of community-based ideas of political representation and of the idea and practice of vecino privilege is applicable to the Northeast. While the focus of this book is on the last years of the Porfiriato and the first decades of the twentieth century, evidence indicates that norteños engaged pre-industrial colonial practices that emphasized the privileged position of vecinos or inhabitants of *rancherías* and pueblos or as permanent workers on haciendas. The idea that those in higher positions of authority had a responsibility to community members resonated with norteños and further confirmed their roles and their right to engage an ever-expanding nation-state. Jiménez's work on residents of Morelia, in the southwestern state of Michoacán, and their use of the written petition to support infrastructure projects demonstrates how ordinary residents engaged the state to reject, accept, or negotiate changes in their respective communities. Norteños, too, addressed the state directly, thus shaping the very nature of industrial development.[44]

Ultimately, worker negotiations helped to shape the contours of what became one of the most dynamic borderlands in the world. The northeastern borderlands of Mexico developed into a unique corner of the country that had extensive economic ties to the United States, that had possessed a market based on cross-regional trade since the early nineteenth century, and that, by 1910, was a highly contested site.[45] Disparate wages on commercial haciendas and ranchos, limited access to resources, abusive working conditions, and general discontent with regard to access to arable land led to a cross-class coalition that would take part in the country's bloody revolution.

Working Women into the Borderlands heeds the call for binational research and incorporates archival documents that have never been consulted, particularly those that highlight the voices of peasant women. It treats the region encompassing the border states of Nuevo León and Tamaulipas as a "crossroads" bypassing state and national boundaries while acknowledging women's labor contributions to the very development of the region. Collectively, the chapters in this book place people's responses and their subsequent roles in the rise of industrial capitalism at the heart of its analysis. The chapters underscore norteños' direct engagement with the state when their communities, their social relationships, and, in short, their livelihoods were altered by widespread wage labor, foreign investment, physical abuse, loss of land, wage discrimination, and generally substandard working conditions. From the periphery, norteños took an active role in shaping the outcome of the Mexican Revolution, used the institutions created by the Revolution to effect change, and ultimately helped to shape the development of the nation-state. While by the end of the 1930s women's efforts to organize had been largely co-opted by the new revolutionary state, their long journey to demand what the Revolution had promised them served as evidence of their crucial role in labor and the labor activism that helped to build the borderlands. It is through the study of borders that we can learn a great deal about nation-states. It is my goal in this book to "work women into the borderlands," placing their contributions at the forefront of the profound transformations occurring at the turn of the twentieth century.

Chapter One

Selling the *Norteño* Borderlands

Capital, Land, and Labor

I was in Monterrey on the 23rd . . . expecting the pleasure of meeting you in person; but having a party of capitalists with me, I could not await your arrival. In my opinion the Monterrey and Gulf RR. will open up a garden spot in your country, and I expect to locate along its line some solid enterprising capital, in mining and other enterprises.

A. W. GIFFORD TO GOV. ALEJANDRO PRIETO, 1889

THE MODERNIZATION AGENDA carried out by state elites, politicians, and a pro-foreign investment climate fostered by the Díaz regime helped bring to fruition A. W. Gifford's prediction of a "garden spot" in Tamaulipas. Gifford's Imogene Mining Company, as well as scores of other foreign enterprises, found a welcoming environment and pro-business climate in Tamaulipas and in neighboring Nuevo León during the Porfiriato. Gifford, the president of Imogene Mining, envisioned the creation of a zone between Monterrey and Tampico that would produce *piloncillo, ixtle,* and other products for a global market. Like many investors, Gifford built a solid relationship with regional and state elites and politicians to exploit the natural resources of Tamaulipas and Nuevo León by relying on the relatively inexpensive labor of resident *norteños* and transient migrants. Regional elites, state representatives, and foreign investors venturing in Mexico led the effort to develop the Northeast through the linking of towns and ports via railroads, infrastructure development, a capitalized banking system, the exploitation of old mines, and the commercialization of agriculture.

The last decades of the nineteenth century marked the onset of the modern Mexican nation-state. The process of modern nation building and border making in the far northeastern reaches of Mexico was rooted in the privatization and commercialization of land, the decline of communal forms of subsistence, an increase in free wage labor, and a more permanent labor force. The borderland region did not, as Juan Mora-Torres rightly explains, develop when the geopolitical border was established in 1848. Regional elites and mid-size *rancheros,* as well as foreign investors—primarily American—would reap the benefits of norteño free wage labor. The concentration of arable land in the hands of few individuals and corporations had begun during the Benito Juárez period. This process and the eventual commercialization of land gradually tore at the communal foundation of the *municipio libre* (autonomous village/pueblo), *poblados,* and *rancherías* that made up the majority of the settlements. During the colonial period, land in the northern fringes of Mexico had been allotted and divided up either as large grants (*porciones*), rancherías, or military colonies, or it was under the purview of missionaries—Jesuits and Franciscans who had been granted lands by the king of Spain for missionary purposes and settlement. Gradually, the more sedentary indigenous populations such as the Indios Olivos were integrated into missions, and ethnic groups from other parts of the republic headed to the North and assisted in the pacification of more rebellious groups. *Mestizos* and other groups received land grants to form military colonies. Some indigenous groups survived the intrusion, especially those who lived in hard-to-reach places such as the Sierra Huasteca, in the present-day states of Tamaulipas and San Luis Potosí, and areas farther south.

In southern Tamaulipas, the Jesuits controlled enormous portions of land that would become some of the first great haciendas in the Northeast. With secularization, government officials confiscated much of the land belonging to the Jesuits. A decade after the newly organized Mexican government implemented the Colonization Law of 1823, intended primarily for the province of Tejas, German immigrants led by the Baron Racknitz set up colonies in Tamaulipas.[1] Further, an expansive tract of land, covering almost two-thirds of southern Tamaulipas, was confiscated from the Jesuits, and by 1842 the land had been sold to a tobacco entrepreneur named Felipe Neri del Barrio. In 1865, José Domingo Rascón, father of José Martín Rascón, purchased the land.[2] Secularization increased the number of landholdings in private hands, and it intensified in the 1850s and 1860s with the Leyes de Reforma, promulgated by Benito Juárez. Although the process of land privatization began during the Juárez period, it was during the Porfiriato that this process accelerated and further reorganized communities.

In the 1860s, as Americans fought against each other in the Civil War, norteño merchants, taking advantage of the strategic location of their region, engaged in extensive trade with the Confederacy. The rupture between the US North and the South and the subsequent blockades of vital southern ports forced the Confederacy to seek alternative ports in order to continue exporting cotton. The new cotton- and weapons-based trade relationship between the Confederacy and merchants from Matamoros and Monterrey further expanded the economy of the Mexican borderlands.[3] With a strong financial base developed during the Civil War, the region witnessed its second economic boom of the nineteenth century. This time, however, the economic resurgence resulted in profound social and economic repercussions for the growing border population. The changes that took place during the 1880s were driven by a strong regional and national desire to keep up with modernized countries.[4]

Principal economic activities consisted of livestock ranching, agriculture, maritime trade (in the ports of Matamoros and Tampico), and mining in the Sierra de San Carlos, as well as in the central-western region of neighboring Nuevo León. The region frequently supplied raw materials to markets in the United States, England, and Cuba. A manufacturing sector emerged in central Nuevo León but remained small until the 1890s. Local manufacturing was limited in scope, so norteños regularly obtained finished goods from the United States.[5]

The nineteenth century would prove especially harsh for a variety of indigenous groups whose homes were situated throughout the borderlands. As Gen. Gerónimo Treviño, military commander of the Linéa del Bravo and regional elite, eloquently put it to his American audience in a reunion along the border in 1877, "the *lipanes* are a constant threat to our security and safety with their depravations on the left banks of the *Bravo*. . . . I ordered Coronel Nuncio to apprehend them and keep them jailed." He continued, "In my opinion[,] once apprehended, they should be taken to the interior, [and] placed in *talleres* and *casas de beneficiencia* where they will be educated and taught how to work based on their age and sex."[6] Such state-sponsored views of Indian peoples as disposable, uneducated *ociosos* (lazy/idle persons), shared also by recruited mestizo nonnative *colonos* and local mestizo *vecinos,* lent credibility to the idea of Indians as obstacles to progress, as impediments to the process of clearing land to make it productive and eventually attract foreign investment. Bold investors such as the oil giant Edward Doheny noted how "there was no greater menace, except as far as Indians were concerned, from 1875 to 1910," and in this way he justified how "we went with impunity wherever we desired to go in Mexico."[7]

After Díaz launched his revolution from the Río Bravo region and took power in 1876 he implemented a program to eliminate or transplant uncooperative Indians and to recruit able-bodied colonists to populate the region. Like the Mexican officials who had planned to entice settlers to Tejas in the 1820s, in the 1870s and 1880s Díaz offered land to prospective colonists who were Mormon, Russian, Anglo American, Chinese, and African American. In some cases, the Mexican government profited from these land offers; one hundred miles

Northeastern Mexico and the greater south Texas region.

southwest of Ciudad Victoria, Tamaulipas, in 1903, Hacienda del Chamal was organized via the Blalock Mexico Colony, which attracted American settlers from Texas, Oklahoma, and midwestern states. The Banco Mercantil Hipotecario de México recorded the sixty-six-thousand-peso transaction.[8] In late 1893 Governor Prieto authorized a Mr. McKastle, an American colonization agent in Monterrey, to establish an agricultural colony in Tamaulipas.[9] By 1910 foreigners controlled more than 70 percent of the coastal frontiers and borders. The number of foreign-owned tracts of land (often comprising more than one hundred thousand acres) was significant, and the fact that Americans owned "the largest and best conditioned bearing orchard[s]" further revealed the growing socioeconomic chasm between norteño laborers and Americans in the Northeast.[10]

Acquiring land from the government was fairly easy, particularly after the passage of the Ley sobre Terrenos Baldíos in 1883 under Pres. Manuel González, who essentially followed Díaz's orders. *Companías agrícolas* and *companías colonizadoras* (commercial agriculture corporations and land settlement companies) came to facilitate the transformation of norteño land—owned by military colonos, rancherías, and *poblados en común* or *tierras comunales* (communal villages) since the colonial period and now claimed as "vacant lands" under the "terrenos baldíos" designation for "unoccupied" land. This uncultivated land, labeled as "unproductive" by government surveyors, was thus, in their view, in need of "transformation." Land and labor served as strategic incentives for regional elites and *caudillos* to acquiesce to Díaz's centralizing efforts. In this manner, President González acquired the Hacienda El Cojo, extending from Tampico to Victoria and including the following haciendas within its borders: La Palma, El Carrizal, El Barco, Chocoy, Opichan, El Rosario, Las Flores, Tancasneque, Alamitos, Montaña de Galul, Santa Juana, Tierras Blancas, Rayón, Timas, Cuestecistas, Acuña, La Panocha, and El Pretil, among others.[11] This process of privatizing land took aim at the very foundation of pueblo and village life, even among scattered communities and sparsely populated villages. This transformation forever altered the lives of residents and would serve as the basis for claiming community autonomy and workers' rights and for fostering *cooperativismo* and, eventually, uprisings. In towns and villages across the Northeast, norteños demanded an end to the "*maltratamiento por parte de mayordomos y hacendados*" (abuse from supervisors and landowners).[12]

In implementing the new land law, government surveyors, assisted by land developers and regional elites, declared desirable lands to be "terrenos baldíos" and began to employ large numbers of workers from nearby villages and from the interior of the country to clear the tracts. By 1876 the government had made the surveying of these "vacant" areas mandatory and thus provided economic opportunities for land surveying companies, which were allowed to retain one-third of the surveyed lands as compensation.[13] Thus began the rise of powerful land surveying companies or *compañías deslindadoras.* Land surveying companies such as Gen. Gerónimo Treviño's Compañía Deslindadora de Terrenos Baldíos allowed regional elites to acquire sizable tracts of land. Treviño's La Babia property comprised more than a million acres and had increasing numbers of cattle.[14] Treviño, as explained later, would come to represent a type of transnational cultural broker who persuaded American capitalists to invest in Mexico. As lands were cleared, the Díaz government extended tax and land concessions to railroad companies to link urban centers with remote villages and rancherías, which solidified a burgeoning transnational market.[15] The original goal of the law was to populate the "*enormes extensiones del territorio*" to fend off any foreign threats. However, the government, with little faith in its own people, advocated populating the land with "practical and hardworking agriculturalists from Europe" to avoid another War of 1846.[16] Yet, the Europeans did not come—at least in the numbers that the government expected. Instead, land became privatized and concentrated in the hands of a few whose estates or *latifundios* were among the largest in the country, thanks in great part to the surveying companies. As the historian Raul Rangel Frías writes, "the *compañías deslindadoras* produced great *latifundios* that ended up in the hands of prominent men such as . . . Treviño . . . or foreigners who rented lands or became owners of property that became public due to the surveys and that should have remained under ownership of states' treasury or [the] federal government."[17] The expansion of existing estates and the creation of new ones altered the geographic landscape of the Mexican Northeast. "Following the American tradition," such estates began to use barbed wire to enclose haciendas and ranches. These estates would focus on the production of a variety of goods that not only addressed the needs of the local border population but were among the main exports, destined for international markets.[18]

In many cases, making land "productive" coincided with curbing any threats or quashing any local rebellions that jeopardized the centralizing mission of Díaz. In certain instances, the same regional elites who collaborated with Díaz and his efforts to bring the northern periphery into closer scrutiny assisted with curbing such threats. Díaz also offered tracts of land to those who had extended support to him during the Revolution of Tuxtepec, which had secured him control of the region and eventually the entire country. Treviño, for example, served as Díaz's point person in negotiations with Americans such as Brig. Gen. Edward O. C. Ord in "combating *bandolerismo* along the border" when Díaz launched the border revolt that paved his way to the presidency. It was Treviño who collaborated with General Ord to rid the border of the rancher and revolutionary Juan Cortina. As Jerry Thompson has argued, Ord believed that "peace could never be restored to the region as long as Cortina remained on the border." Mexican regional elites in support of Díaz would come to help the "Mexican government remove Cortina."[19] As rebellions such as Cortina's and others were quelled, the process of land privatization could resume.

As in other places in Latin America, a small landowning class came to control expansive tracts of arable land, thus displacing communities that had for centuries worked the lands *en común* (as a collective). As sharecroppers and temporary or transient laborers, these workers moved in search of better wages and available work and formed the bulk of the norteño labor force during the transitional effort to modernize the borderlands.

Porfirio Díaz and his cohort of *científicos* shaped the future of Mexico through a series of transportation, communication, trade, and land concessions to foreigners. Government agents promoting investments in banking, railroad, telegraph, tourist, and agricultural industries assured investors that the "progressive" climate of Mexico "protected" them and their properties. Mexican boosters wrote that the "climate and soil are rich" and "offer tremendous opportunities for growers," and "Mexico's new regime, for the first time, [is] able to offer small tracts of land to purchasers."[20] Moreover, foreigners were "guaranteed safety" and could travel to Mexico "with the utmost degree of confidence and hope."[21]

Financiers and entrepreneurs from various countries embarked on a journey into Mexico driven by descriptions of "a rapidly developing country, [with] mining regions, the richest in the globe, and cheap labor."[22] Supporters of the Díaz agenda argued that foreign investments would create job opportunities for thousands of Mexicans, and thus modernization would benefit everyone. Foreign investors "traveled the entire country in search of mines, raw materials, and shortly thereafter petroleum."[23]

The social differentiation rooted in the long and turbulent history of conflict over land rights in Mexico was exacerbated with the carte blanche offered to foreigners to virtually control the country economically.[24] By the eve of the Mexican Revolution, more than nine million Mexicans out of a population of fifteen million had no land, and half of the country "belonged to less than three thousand families."[25] Many of the foreign investors who would come to own extensive tracts of land were considered absentee landowners who placed fellow Americans in supervisory positions to oversee their commercial operations.

Pamphlets produced by American boosters promoting business ventures in Mexico made it clear that what Mexico "offered to the [foreign] settler" [land, specifically] did not belong to anyone. The relative ease with which investors could set up shop was further facilitated by the availability of cheap labor. As one such brochure published in Chicago put it, "in Mexico there are good things that are yet to be obtained. In more developed countries the good things have already been taken up by people who intend to keep them."[26] The publication stated further that "a very important factor to take into account is the price of labor. Here in Mexico labor costs only about one-half of what is paid for in the United States. The foreign settler or investor finds his capital at once multiplied by two."[27]

Boosters advertised Mexican land as abundant and available, its resources as rich and abundant, and its people as primitive, exploitable, disposable, and cheap to hire as laborers. Literature published by the state of Tamaulipas underscored the agricultural potential of the region, encouraging capitalists to invest in its lands. One section described *zapupe,* a fiber-producing plant similar to the *henequen* grown in Yucatán. Indigenous peoples used the plant to make ropes, rough sacks, and similar products. The writers touted the advantages of cultivating zapupe: the highly productive plant yielded numerous large leaves—some seventy-five to eighty leaves per plant—which would then be combed for large amounts of fiber. The authors of a magazine sponsored by the Tamaulipas Agriculture and Ranching Expo boasted of the low wages offered in the region (fifty centavos was the standard *jornal* or daily pay) and pointed out that the cost to produce one pound of zapupe fiber averaged two centavos and that it could be exported to New York and other American cities and valued at up to nine centavos per pound.[28] Tamaulipas boosters argued that the fifty-centavo jornal was quite generous given that peons were generally paid around thirty centavos. Wages were considerably higher for males, as compared to the national average wage for peons. The magazine writers reminded both foreign and native potential investors that zapupe could remain up to three weeks in the field without being harvested. They explained that "this is of great benefit to growers because[,] in the event laborers refused to work or if they demanded higher wages," growers would not lose profits and could use the extra weeks before harvesting to persuade workers to return to the fields.[29] It was literature such as this state-sponsored magazine that encouraged investors like A. W. Gifford to envision productive and lucrative projects. Yet, this literature also served as a reminder that laborers were reluctant permanent workers.

Mexican elites and foreign investors held their own ideas about regional development and the laborers they were to hire. These ideas correlated to an existing hierarchy based on race, class, and gender. Their ideologies about women and men were rooted in social Darwinist thought, eugenics, and nineteenth-century ideas about female virtue and morality. Peasant men were described as "little brown m[e]n," "unclean," and basically untouched by the "refinements of modernization."[30] A representative peasant woman appeared as "outwardly, at least, more cleanly than a man . . . [a] good housewife, [and] an affectionate mother."[31] And most literature referred to her constant "display [of] feminine fondness for fripperies . . . and a love of hoarding the heavy, fat silver dollars." This reflected the general sentiment at the time, as Edward Doheny stated in 1918, that Mexicans were "kindly people of primitive habits, not overly energetic or industrious."[32] As chapter 2 will show, these deeply held perceptions of Mexicans would create tensions between laborers and both native and foreign landowners.

Developing the borderlands into a productive industrialized space also meant hiring women as wage laborers. As reported in the 1895 and 1910 censuses, close to six thousand women worked as *jornaleras* in the country while more than fifty-six thousand were considered *peones de campo,* or field laborers. With a shortage of laborers in the North, women from the countryside, particularly from San Luis Potosí and the south-central part of the country, migrated in search of work and ended up clearing much of the land that would be labeled "unproductive" and offered to investors.[33] Women made up much of the labor force in *haciendas ixtleras, piloncilleras,* and *tabacaleras,* and many worked in commercial laundries and hotels and as domestic servants throughout the region. The drawn-thread work sector employed large numbers of women. In the case of Matamoros, more than two hundred women and girls produced handkerchiefs, doilies, and short-waist patterns, "toil[ing] early and late on this work in their homes."[34] The total production of "home industry" in the region was valued at approximately five thousand US dollars, and some women sold their products in Mexico City and across the border.[35]

Because laborers were in short supply in the region, women often filled the demand for labor, particularly in less desirable work. As a report by a British diplomat explained, "the work of gathering and scraping the lechugilla [*sic*] leaves is both hard and disagreeable . . . and the owners of ixtle lands have considerable difficulty in securing sufficient men used to the work."[36] Besides the view of women as necessary hires, they were perceived as passive laborers. A state-sponsored magazine highlighted the high crop-yielding Hacienda San Pedro Los Saldañas, in Jaumave, Tamaulipas, which hired large numbers of women. The writers noted that the hacienda owner, "the progressive engineer" José R. Montesinos, imported the modern American Winfield *desfibradora* (shredder), thus "modernizing the region." They also argued that, besides commanding only low wages, these workers "were easily manipulated."[37] Women were described as docile and perceived as "evincing very little desire to exceed the narrow limits of . . . daily life."[38]

Compared to other regions of Mexico and Latin America more generally, women from northern Mexico had greater economic opportunities because of the persistent labor shortages. Women could earn more than men in certain sectors and would come to dominate selected industries. While there was no real concerted effort to oust women from the workforce during the period under examination, there was an effort to keep women in certain sectors in the hope of maintaining their femininity during the postrevolutionary period.

With claims of a cheap and docile labor force, regional elites hoped to realize their vision for the borderlands. Although a cheap and docile workforce was convenient and could be used to entice foreign investment, the discourse on modernization was justified specifically to "improve communities" through extensive industrial ventures. Yet, "improving communities" in most cases meant increasing land values and profit for only a small segment of the population.

Governor Prieto, a pro-Díaz engineer and landowner himself, rallied his constituency to support the construction of a railroad line connecting Ciudad Victoria to the Gulf port of Tampico in the south-central part of his state. Prieto came from a wealthy landowning family from southern Tamaulipas, near San Antonio Rayón, and he represented the elite and progressive thinkers of the Mexican Northeast. With extensive experience gained while working on railroad construction projects in Guatemala, Costa Rica, and Panama, Prieto was determined to carry out the Porfirian agenda of modernization in his native Tamaulipas. In 1891 Prieto assured residents that a railroad would "awaken the city [Ciudad Victoria] from prolonged lethargy and stagnant commerce, [and renew] agricultural industries, mining, and textiles."[39] He explained the need for "development" in a speech he gave in Ciudad Victoria: "I believe that a railroad from Ciudad Victoria to Tampico would be of enormous advantage because the railroad would provide an outlet for exporting *fibras textiles* from Jaumave and Palmillas, pine and cedar woods from the Sierras of Victoria and Gómez Farias, mineral products from the *vetas* [mines] of Llera y Revillagigedo, and agricultural goods grown along the Guayalejo and Tamesí Rivers."[40]

Prieto represented the increasingly intimate economic relationship with foreign investors in the Northeast and was the sort of "agent of transnational corporate power" about whom historian Samuel Truett writes in his study of the Sonoran borderlands.[41] After his second term as governor ended in 1896 (first term lasted from May 1888 to May 1892, when his second term began), he became the engineer for the port of Tampico. By 1901 he had finalized a contract with two American capitalists, Markus W. Conkling and William Astor Chanler. The agreement between the norteño and the two New York men would result in a major water supply system for some fifty thousand people in the port city, and those living in "the better neighborhoods" would have access to a modern sewer system. In 1903 Prieto wrote to Pres. Porfirio Díaz that the sanitation project in Tampico should be showcased at the upcoming world exposition in Saint Louis, Missouri, so that all "civilized nations" could appreciate the progress being made in Mexico.[42] The alliance between American capitalists and regional elites grew even stronger as Díaz and his supporters continued extending benefits.[43]

For many, the arrival of the railroad embodied modernity and represented the dawn of a new era. The Northeast had maintained strong economic ties with the United States since before the American Civil War, and the railroad accelerated this commercial relationship by placing the region firmly within the US and global economic orbit. By 1910, with more than twenty-four thousand kilometers of track laid by thousands of workers, "Mexico [had] established the basic infrastructure needed to navigate the modern international economy."[44] Undeniably, the advent of the "iron horse" revolutionized society. At the national level, the construction of railroads solidified commercial ties between cities, pueblos, and haciendas, particularly those with connections to main rail lines. In the Northeast railroad tracks connected the industrial hub, Monterrey, with large haciendas producing cattle, fruit, corn, and wheat near the municipalities of Padilla and Güémez in Tamaulipas, which "seemed to expand their boundaries on a daily basis."[45] The railroad extended out to haciendas devoted to agricultural production near the towns of Casas, Llera, and Xicotencatl, thus increasing land values and accelerating the growth of regional, national, and transnational markets.[46] The rail line connecting Monterrey with Tampico crossed through the outlying towns around Tampico, including Ciudad Madero and Altamira, and made stops in El Fuerte, Esteros, Manuel González, Rosillo, Calles, Ignacio Zaragoza, Ciudad Victoria, La Misión, Caballeros, Santa Engracia, and Estación Cruz, as well as Carrizos.[47]

Merchants had relied on *arrieros* (muleteers) and *fleteros* (freighters) to transport goods over land, yet this traditional transportation network was far too costly and slow. The largest *carretones* (carts) often required fourteen mules and carried up to fifty tons.[48] During the rainy season the roads connecting Matamoros with Laredo, Nuevo Laredo, Monterrey, and Tampico became difficult to cross, prolonging trips. If a trip to Monterrey from Matamoros normally took two days, heavy rains could turn it into ten days. The problems associated with inclement weather, activities prior to and during the American Civil War in the 1850s and 1860s, contraband, high tariffs, and robberies all impeded long-distance road commerce. The arrival of the railroad was gladly welcomed and solved many of the commercial problems merchants encountered. In addition, the railroads dramatically reduced both transportation costs and travel time for freight and passengers.[49] The Mexican railroad in the Northeast would consist of two major routes: the Ferrocarril Central Mexicano (Mexican Central Railway) and the Ferrocarril de Monterrey al Golfo.[50] In the summer of 1882 the railroad reached Monterrey, carrying families from Laredo, Nuevo Laredo, Lampazos, and Villaldama.

By the early 1900s the Central Railway had acquired the Monterrey al Golfo, giving the Central strategic power over the Gulf of Mexico region.[51] The Central then extended from Chihuahua to Tampico via Monterrey, boosting the commerce of cities along the route, such as Ciudad Victoria. Tracks also extended to mining centers and textile factories farther south, reaching the fertile citrus region of Montemorelos by the late nineteenth century.[52]

Consolidated in 1905 and by then employing more than twenty thousand laborers, the Central became a division of the National Railways of Mexico, with its financial center in New York and a board in Mexico City overseeing daily operations. It became the largest private enterprise in the nation. The contract drawn up between the Díaz government and the Central, through the National City and Morgan Banks of New York, reflected the enormous advantages and benefits extended to foreign corporations. One major land concession included a ninety-nine-year contract for building a rail line connecting Mexico City to the border at Nuevo Laredo (and later Laredo) via Saltillo.[53]

As railroads linked the cities and towns of the region together, mining activity increased. Among the mines founded early on were the Minas de San Gregorio, El Carmen, Mineral de San Nicolas, and the Real de Minas de San Carlos de Vallecillo, the last one being owned by the American capitalist James Stillman.[54] Several of the mines boosted production at the famed Fundidora de Fierro y Acero. Mario Cerutti notes that Fundidora de Fierro y Acero was "perhaps the best representation of the industrial process occurring in Monterrey between 1890 and 1910. . . . [It was] founded by the most prominent of the local bourgeoisie, those from other Mexican regions, and representatives of the bourgeoisie from the most advanced countries."[55] A driving component of industrialization in the Northeast, Fundidora de Fierro y Acero actively participated in the global economy and accelerated the specialized division of labor pervasive in capitalistic economies. As the smelting industry expanded, so too did the relationship between foreign investors and regional elites. This alliance converted Nuevo León into a metal-producing state, and, along with Coahuila, Chihuahua, and other northern states, it became part of an expanding global economy.[56]

Discoveries of *chapapoteras* (oil seeps) in southeastern Tamaulipas, particularly in Tampico, further accelerated the economic transformation in the region. Relying on geological reports of petroleum finds in Tamaulipas, foreign companies soon began negotiations with the Mexican government to invest their time, technology, and capital in the region.[57] In partnership with investor John F. Dowling, Adolfo A. Autry organized the Compania Exploradora del Golfo de Mexico, an American company based in Mexico City. Producing only four thousand gallons of kerosene, Exploradora soon abandoned the operation and Autry relinquished the property and machinery in 1880.[58] Efforts to secure petroleum, however, did not cease. One of the first foreign concessions for oil production was in 1880 and involved Henry Clay Pierce's Waters Pierce Oil Company, which planned construction of an oil refinery in Arbol Grande in the Tampico area. The same law that stimulated mining and smelting activities also spurred foreign investments in Mexican oil fields. Waters Pierce, directed by Pierce, had established partnerships with John D. Rockefeller's Standard Oil and other petroleum companies. In 1908 the Díaz government extended a concession to the Weetman Pearson (later, Lord Cowdray) Trust, which established the Compañía Mexicana de Petróleo El Aguila. Pearson's oil enterprise and combined interests in Mexico reached a value of $59 million by 1910. President Díaz's son served on the El Aguila board of directors, but perhaps of more significance to the Mexican Northeast was American Edward L. Doheny's Mexican Petroleum firm.[59] With the financial help of American oil giants Charles Adelbert Canfield, Michael Benedum, and Joseph Clifton Trees of South Penn Oil, Doheny acquired more than four hundred thousand acres of land near El Ebano in the Tampico vicinity. El Ebano became Doheny's first Mexican oil field. As he gained access to larger tracts of land, total production from the wells of Mexican Petroleum surpassed eighty-five million barrels a day. The expansion of commercial activities led Doheny to seek more investments, particularly from William Solomon, who had close ties to financial giants Edward H. Harriman and Marcellus Hartley Dodge; all were members of the International Banking Corporation. Doheny, together with other petroleum companies operating in Mexico, invested $50 million in petroleum operations.[60]

Along the northern border in Nuevo Laredo, the railroad boosted production in three brick factories that had been operating since the 1880s; their annual production reached five million units. The Guadalupe Mining Company of Philadelphia installed a *concentrador,* or large mineral processor, that handled up to three hundred tons per day. With this brief industrial boom, Nuevo Laredo joined Matamoros and Reynosa in becoming important points of commercial contact with Monterrey, Victoria, and Tampico. The links between these towns, strengthened by the railroad, formed the complex web of trade and social relationships that glued the Northeast together.[61]

With railroad access to the Gulf of Mexico via Tampico, Monterrey held a position as a commercial and industrial driving force that grew ever more important. In the words of the American entrepreneur Joseph A. Robertson, "Not a single city of equal size in the North American continent demonstrated potential for progress and development as [great as that of] Monterrey." Not surprisingly, Monterrey was called the "Chicago of Mexico."[62] Despite the commercial power and potential for progress Monterrey possessed, it could not function in isolation.

Robertson, like other Americans in Mexico, created alliances with Mexican regional elites from neighboring states to pave the way for investment opportunities. Robertson epitomized the foreign investor in Mexico at the turn of the twentieth century. He enjoyed close ties with prominent business leaders such as Thomas S. Bullock and Victor A. Wilden, both stockholders of the Ferrocarril de Monterrey al Golfo. He also created a partnership with the local elite and lawyer Emeterio de la Garza, Governor Prieto, and Gen. Gerónimo Treviño.[63] He was also, for the most part, an absentee landowner. His multiple businesses made it difficult for Robertson to remain in the Northeast for prolonged periods, so he placed his American friend Ricardo Mitchel in charge of overseeing his lucrative orchards in Montemorelos, Nuevo León.[64]

A longtime ally of President Díaz and Governor Reyes, Gen. Gerónimo Treviño was one of the strongest advocates of industrialization in Nuevo León.[65] Treviño's relationship with Díaz went back to the days of the French intervention in Mexico during the 1860s. He was under the military orders of Díaz and Mariano Escobedo, and when Díaz launched the Revolution of Tuxtepec from Brownsville, Texas, Treviño became the commander of the northern Mexican forces.[66] Like Prieto in Tamaulipas, General Treviño was a member of the Nuevo León oligarchy and had extensive connections with American financiers. Treviño's second marriage was to none other than General Ord's daughter, Roberta "Bertha" Augusta Ord. Their wedding in San Antonio, Texas, proclaimed to be "of great national importance," was attended by elites from both sides of the border: "This marriage is of great national importance, because the union between a military favorite with the daughter of a distinguished American general has formed a close alliance between both nations[,] . . . and there is no doubt that such [a] union will produce great things. Treviño is a major figure in five Mexican states."[67]

The marriage turned out to be of great *trans*national importance; it solidified Díaz's administration with the support of key military figures such as Ord. Treviño was not the only Mexican elite who married an American woman. Ramón Corona (who served as minister plenipotentiary in Madrid, Spain), Matías Romero (former minister of war), and Ignacio Mariscal (the Mexican consul in

New York who was also campaigning for supreme court justice in Mexico) all married "*señoritas americanas*."[68]

In 1884 Roberta Ord died, and Treviño remarried into the prominent Zambrano family.[69] His third marriage would also reap great benefits. The Zambranos, a foreign family, had investments in textile, steel, and mining. Treviño, like Robertson, was stockholder of the Monterrey al Golfo railroad and invested in some of the most lucrative industries in the region: banking, mining, and glass making. It was through a partnership of Treviño, de la Garza, Robertson, Frank R. Brown of San Antonio, and other American investors, including the National City Bank, that construction of the Monterrey al Golfo line was completed.[70] As the noted historian Israel Cavazos has argued, Treviño "intervened in industrial projects in Monterrey and played a role in encouraging American businessmen to invest in Nuevo León."[71]

Partnerships that produced heavy investments led to increased land values, ultimately resulting in the concentration of large tracts of land in the hands of a small number of Mexican elites and foreigners. Investors such as William Kelly, of the Companía de Terrenos y Minas del Estado de Tamaulipas, profited due to the growth in land values as the railroad crisscrossed his properties in the Northeast. Kelly, like many foreigners involved in business ventures in the region, hired agents, who submitted daily reports on conditions in the region. Through reports from W. F. Cummins, an American geologist, Kelly received information on the potential for railroad construction in the region. The impact of the railroad on renewed growth in mining, smelting, and other industrial operations led to land concentration and increases in land values, as the following correspondence from Cummins to Kelly reveals: "There is no sort of doubt, if a railroad . . . from Tampico to Matamoros or [the] vicinity within the near future would be built, the line would give a shorter route by about 300 miles between the City of Mexico and St. Louis or Chicago than the present line. When such a line is built it will necessarily pass not far from this land [Hacienda El Sacramento] and will add largely to the development of this part of the state [Tamaulipas] as well as enhance the value of lands."[72]

Kelly's business ventures had begun in the Rio Grande Valley of Texas. During the 1880s he involved himself in the steamboat and railroad businesses in the region. Kelly aligned himself with the "antimonopolists," a group of merchants who sought to limit the steamboat monopoly of James Stillman, Richard King, and Mifflin Kenedy. While Kelly and others won limited victories, including the rights to a short railroad near Point Isabel, Texas, the monopoly of Stillman, King, and Kenedy would survive as rights were secured to build a railroad connecting Laredo to Monterrey and eventually Mexico City. The traffic created by railroad construction via Laredo–Nuevo Laredo left the Brownsville-Matamoros sector in economic decline. By 1902 Kelly had sold four thousand acres of land to Henrietta King of the King Ranch and was unable to economically compete with the big merchants of the area. While Kelly's investments fared better south of the border, his experience with land development projects, railroad construction, and regional politics in South Texas equipped him with the necessary business acumen to navigate similar conditions in Mexico.[73]

Investments in the area of smelting, oil, and railroads spurred economic activity in other sectors and created a demand for laborers. Smaller foreign and native corporations engaged in shipping and dock work received concessions from railroad and petroleum companies and began to send their *enganchadores* to the countryside in search of laborers.[74] Thousands of laborers went to work in the mines, steel plants and smelters, railroads, and oil fields, and this demographic shift, coupled with industrial development, led to the growth of Tampico and Monterrey as major urban centers in the region. On the other hand, the countryside lagged behind, losing its population to these emerging sites of employment.

If the norteño borderlands were to be showcased to the world to encourage investments to make the land "productive," free wage labor and indebted free wage labor would facilitate this transformation. Since the colonial period, residents had moved freely in search of higher paying work given the scarcity of labor. As was customary, workers provided their services to private commercial estates during harvest time and spent the rest of the year tending their own gardens or sharecropping at different haciendas or ranchos. While free wage labor had been prevalent in northern Mexico since the eighteenth century, particularly in the mines, it increased with the industrial boom. Workers typically received daily wages in smelters, *petroleras,* railroad work sites, and steel factories. Haciendas and ranchos also drew from a historically transient labor force that sold its labor as it pleased.

Hacienda management found it difficult to retain laborers full-time precisely because of the tradition of independent labor and the proximity to Texas, where, despite similar working conditions, higher wages prevailed. In Nuevo León at haciendas and larger ranchos, laborers were for the most part *peones acasillados* (resident peons or peasants).[75] While haciendas could count on these resident peons, the labor pool often was *flotante,* or transient. By the early twentieth century, as Casey Walsh has noted, "the pattern of land tenure in northern Tamaulipas was changing from an earlier system marked by a somewhat communitarian use of unfenced grazing lands and water sources to one in which private ownership of clearly delineated agricultural land was more important."[76]

The process would take on a similar character in neighboring Nuevo León, with the emergence of heavy industries complicating such changes in land tenure.

Inquiries about investment opportunities in land continued to pour in. During Alejandro Prieto's tenure as Tamaulipas senator, Americans contacted his office on numerous occasions inquiring about investment opportunities. Julio Guerrero, a close friend of Prieto, wrote from Mexico City that "an individual from Texas sought land in Tamaulipas in the size of about 2 or 3,000 acres for a commercial milk establishment."[77] Throughout his tenure as senator and during his two terms as governor, Prieto received many other inquiries on the potential of his state for business ventures. He graciously granted requests using the "terrenos baldíos" law.[78]

State-sponsored literature promoted investment opportunities in Mexico, encouraging outsiders to come to Mexico. The consolidation of the land privatization program that had begun during the Juárez period radically changed the course of norteño history. Once land was consolidated and privatized and labeled "baldía" it could be offered to the highest Mexican bidder or to foreign investors and either priced at a reduced rate or offered as a concession; investors, via *enganchadores,* could then recruit laborers and eventually create garden spots like that envisioned by A. W. Gifford. This process culminated in the monopolization of land, lucrative railroad concessions, the arrival of foreigners setting up productive colonies, and increasing commercial production at haciendas and ranchos. It also involved the introduction of modern machinery that women would come to use as companies such as the Singer Manufacturing Company "established numerous branches" throughout Tamaulipas.[79]

Resident women and men, as well as a growing population of migrants considered a *población flotante,* formed the basis of the labor force that fueled the growth of the region. On a very basic level the majority population of campesinas and campesinos and a small number of workers with some industrial work experience were reduced to labor-selling, landless persons. This population would take part in some of the first uprisings that culminated in the Mexican Revolution.

By 1910, in a cross-class alliance, campesinos had in some cases joined forces with *pequeños propietarios* (small landowners), who likewise felt the growing pressure from large native and foreign landowners. Joining them too would be sharecroppers, small merchants, and campesinas and campesinos, as well as industrial workers from the urban centers. They would come to lead the revolutionary movement in 1910. At the heart of the norteño struggle were calls for the right to a dignified way of life, access to arable land, a living wage, an end to physical abuse at haciendas, and the right to organize. Their struggle was firmly rooted in the idea that pueblos or the free village (the *municipio libre*) had rights. This historical memory of an autonomous, liberal northern frontier whose basic foundation was the community and its survival would come to shape residents' views of their role in the transformations occurring at the turn of the twentieth century. They acknowledged that their community formed part of a much greater entity—an expanding nation-state, but they saw this relationship as one based on mutual understanding, obligation, and reciprocity. The state had an obligation to them as vecinos—members of a community—just as they had a responsibility to it. This perceived obligation would become evident in the way in which laborers, particularly women, directly petitioned representatives of the state to negotiate the changes wrought by increased wage labor and an increased foreign presence, as well as factory work and its associated effects.

Chapter Two

Peasant Women's Work in a Changing Countryside during the Porfiriato

The Americans come here to take advantage of Mexicans.

MARÍA GÓMEZ, TAMPICO, APRIL 20, 1896

María and [her] mother came in and called me some name they have for Americans, *gringa*.

MRS. H. A. WOOLMAN, TAMPICO, APRIL 20, 1896

IN 1896, AS ALEJANDRO PRIETO was completing his first term as governor of Tamaulipas, two *campesinas* from the southern part of the state left their village in search of work. Residents relied on an extensive social network of communication among area *norteños* for employment opportunities, and the two campesinas and sisters, María Gómez and Altagracia Gómez, took advantage of this system. A local domestic worker who labored on a nearby hacienda informed the sisters that her *patrona* (boss) wished to hire several *costureras* (seamstresses). The sisters left their small village near the Tamaulipas–San Luis Potosí border and headed to the large hacienda near Tampico. What the campesinas did not know was that they would come to labor for *americanos* whom Prieto had encouraged to come and invest in the state. María and Altagracia would eventually secure employment at the hacienda owned by the American investor Hester Woolman. Mrs. Woolman had accompanied her husband to Mexico, and, given that she had been trained in the "modern, scientific-method of dress-cutting," she decided to pursue a business venture of that nature in northeastern Mexico.[1] As explained earlier, pro–foreign investment policies at the federal level, supported locally by regional elites, enticed foreigners like Mr. Woolman and his dress-cutter instructor wife to explore capitalistic ventures in Mexico.

Rural women's work such as that of the Gómez sisters—largely understudied and unacknowledged in the historiography of the region—would take center stage as commercial agriculture, large-scale ranching, and the expansion of factory-based work altered the socioeconomic landscape of the borderlands. María and Altagracia, like other rural women, labored in a region that witnessed an increased presence of foreigners, expansion of commercial agriculture, and, by the first decades of the twentieth century, a rapid demographic growth in urban centers while the countryside lagged behind. This chapter examines rural women's labor at haciendas and factories in the countryside within this historical context. It examines female-owned agro-industries, as well as race relations between campesinas and foreigners in haciendas within the larger context of women's working conditions during the Porfiriato. While the Mexican Northeast as a region experienced uneven industrial development, with the bulk of projects being undertaken in Monterrey and Tampico, research reveals that those working in the countryside nonetheless shaped industrialization.

While there has been little in the way of analyses of women's labor contributions to industrialization, save some studies of women in Monterrey's glass and brewery sectors, norteñas' work has been largely ignored.[2] This lack of attention is surprising given that in sectors such as the *tallado de ixtle* (cordage production), *tabacaleras* (cigar factories), *piloncillo* (brown sugar), and haciendas (where women primarily did domestic work but also were *jornaleras*) women formed part of the labor force. Women played a crucial role in the transition from "an agrarian republic to [an] industrialized nation-state," as the historians who have studied rural *mexicanas* have argued.[3] Further, as research on this corner of the periphery of Mexico reveals, both rural resident and migrant women workers developed strategies of labor activism quite similar to those of women working in urban centers. An investigation of industrial censuses, labor grievances, and state government reports indicates that on haciendas the only effective way to improve working conditions was through collective action. This circumstance is evidenced by the agrarian collectives created by workers from Hacienda Las Pilas (owned by the Zorilla family in Jaumave) and in a union organized by twenty campesinas from various haciendas near Xicotencatl (which included Haciendas El Conejo, Victoria, and Santa Isabel) that came to comprise two hundred women with access to a *cooperativa agrícola*.

Women worked in a variety of sectors considered "light" or "secondary" industries that focused on the production of piloncillo in small, medium-sized, and large *trapiches* (sugar mills) and *fincas* (countryside estates) that cultivated corn, beans, squash, and *ixtle de lechuguilla*. Particularly in south-central Tamaulipas, women worked in the cultivation of *ixtle*, a rough fiber extracted from a tough plant for use in the weaving of sacks, carpets, ropes, and other sturdy goods.[4] Ixtle production dates back to the precolonial period. The fiber was cultivated in the region of Miquihuana, Palmillas, Jaumave, Tula, and

Bustamante; the fiber extracted from the Jaumave plants ranked among the best in the world due to size and quality.[5] And, as indicated by numerous reports on the economic activity of the region, southern Tamaulipas was "not a cattle region; landowners [were] more interested in the exploitation of its ixtle."[6] Sugar mills predominated in present-day southern Nuevo León, where indigenous women, alongside men, worked long hours in the cultivation and refining of piloncillo during the colonial period.[7] Production continued in the region through the end of the Porfiriato and into the period of the Mexican Revolution.

Beginning at a very young age, girls worked alongside their parents, many of whom were native to the region and who had grown up in an agrarian environment. They spent their time working as domestic servants in the main quarters of the haciendas and smaller fincas.[8] Others worked as seamstresses, candy makers, midwives, washers, and pressers and operated small shops. Similarly, women rolled and packaged cigars, an occupation they would dominate up through the 1940s.

Since the mid-nineteenth century *industrias domésticas* (small-scale cottage industries) had supplied local residents in the region with a variety of goods. In local markets area residents enjoyed access to woven products such as *frazadas* (large blankets), *jergas* (sackcloth), and *sarapes* (small blankets) that women produced and sold.[9] These commodities were among the favorites in *ferias* (markets) in Matamoros, Victoria, Monterrey, and Saltillo. Other products to which norteños had access came from Texas, Coahuila, and Zacatecas. Textile production, cigar making, and the production of ixtle and piloncillo expanded by the late nineteenth and into the first decades of the twentieth century and soon represented the major industries in which women's work predominated. Clearly, as archival records from Tamaulipas and Nuevo León prove, women's wage work for both native and American (and other foreign) companies did not begin during the *maquila* period in the 1960s. As the historian Francie Chassen López points out, Mexican women had always worked.[10] In the northern borderlands in particular it was in the late nineteenth century when women's remunerated work began to expand. Their labor and their labor experiences formed part of the larger narrative on the region-wide shift to commercial agriculture, industrialization, and the transition from a relatively sparsely populated region to a borderland fully incorporated into the nation-state by the first decades of the twentieth century. As a result, women also became part of the agrarian proletariat.

The land privatization and enclosure process that intensified during the Porfiriato with the "*terreno baldío*" law dealt a final blow to village and pueblo autonomy but was presented to the public as a necessary step in the path toward

"A Hallway in the House of the Señora's Brother," Monterrey in *An American Girl in Mexico* by Elizabeth Viseré McGary (New York, 1904). (Courtesy Nettie Lee Benson Latin American Collection, University of Texas Libraries, the University of Texas at Austin)

modernity in Mexico. While there were large haciendas that had been formed during the colonial period and during the Benito Juárez administration from previously church-owned land (e.g., the Chocoy Hacienda in Tamaulipas), it was during the Díaz period that the great *latifundios* came to be. These estates became sites of intense cultural clashes between agrarian revolutionaries and those defending the interests of the estates. Southern Tamaulipas, south-central Nuevo León, and the lands along the Río Grande were among those greatly coveted and would become home to some of the largest haciendas and ranchos of the Northeast. Land would come to be organized as haciendas, ranchos, *rancherías,* or *poblados.*[11] The majority of laborers lived in poblados "that were not only found

TABLE 1. Partial list of haciendas and ranchos in Tamaulipas and Nuevo León, 1904–1910

	Haciendas	*Ranchos*	*Unclassified*
Tamaulipas	186	2,880	131
Nuevo León	508	1,436	3,327

Sources: Adapted from Toscano Hernández, *Haciendas ixtleras,* 11; Mora-Torres, *Making of the Mexican Border,* table 3.4; Mora García, *El General Alberto Carrera-Torres.*

in *haciendas* but in the vicinity."[12] *Aparceros,* or sharecroppers' homes, as historian María Zebadúa has observed, "consisted of two separate rooms: one for sleeping and one for cooking. . . . They were made of *barreta* [a type of clay], dirt and palms from the region." The hacienda main house was "a solid construction of brick . . . with various rooms . . . living area, dining room, open hallways, sugar mills where the processing of cane took place . . . [and] in some cases, the store which contained items that would be sold to or lent to peasants."[13]

Women's labor in haciendas and ranchos focused on the commercial production of ixtle, piloncillo, and cigars. Beginning at an early age, "niñas [girls] . . . worked on the smaller tasks that did not require so much precision." Particularly in southern Tamaulipas the "terrenos baldíos" law sped up the process of land concentration that had helped to fuel the expansion of existing haciendas or create new ones. Young girls could also find themselves on these haciendas in the "*limpieza de los terrenos* [clearing of land] . . . working alongside their parents."[14] In that area alone more than 30 haciendas and more than 151 ranches were in operation by the middle of the Porfiriato, and they employed hundreds of workers. Regional elites such as José R. Montesinos owned extensive properties, including the Hacienda San Pedro de los Saldaña in the town of Jaumave. Montesinos's hacienda comprised more than ten thousand hectares, and the Montemayor family owned "a chain of *haciendas.*" Calabazas was an ixtle-producing estate, while others were dedicated to a variety of agricultural products and to cattle grazing. The family later acquired an additional eight hundred hectares that included *terrenos agostadores* (pasture land) in two ranches: El Sauz and Salamanca. Nearby, Rudesindo Montemayor and Sons acquired Hacienda Calabazas and annexes that included El Ebanito and El Aguacate, "granted by the *Ley de Terrenos Baldíos* by the federal government." The estate and its annexed properties together totaled five thousand hectares. By the eve of the Revolution, as the historian Octavio Herrera Pérez has noted, Montemayor was one of fourteen individuals who "owned" Jaumave. Further, the governor of Tamaulipas named Montemayor to be commissioner of the *deslinde* (survey) and subdivision of Tula lands.[15]

By 1905, of the more than 700,000 hectares of "baldío" land in southern Tamaulipas, close to 400,000 hectares had been transferred to private hands.[16] Men such as Montemayor now formed part of an elite circle of *terratenientes* (landlords); his hacienda alone had 110 thatched-roof *jacales* to house permanent peon families. At Canuto Martínez's Hacienda de Santiaguillo and La Meca Vieja, also in Tula, there were 200 jacales for peon families in a property comprising more than 59,930 hectares, of which 3,510 hectares were considered lechuguilla lands.[17] In all of southern Tamaulipas, more than 6,500 peasants were reported as "engaged in *ixtle* production" in 1903—they worked in Tula, Jaumave, Miquihuana, Bustamante, Palmillas, and Ocampo.[18]

Salvador Zorilla, one of the regional elite, also took advantage of the "baldío" law and in 1894 "took appropriate action to acquire a *terreno baldío* in Jaumave . . . comprised of over 1,800 hectares."[19] As the historian Mario Alberto Toscano Hernández notes, in southern Tamaulipas, as in other parts of the region, "the process of the appropriation of public property was serving mainly the interest of *latifundistas* [landowners]."[20] What had attracted these men was the potential of the land for growing and processing lechuguilla. The lands were well suited to the fibrous plant whose cultivation and further extraction process was labor intensive and would require the labor of scores of norteño women and men.

Hacienda San Pedro de los Saldaña was among the leading haciendas in the production of ixtle de lechuguilla in southern Tamaulipas. As international markets demanded hard fibers for the production of ropes and related cordage-based goods, ixtle production increased and the output of San Pedro de los Saldaña reached some 8,500 kilos per week. In nearby estates, including El Ebano, multiple hectares had ixtle in cultivation, as well as more than 60,000 henequen plants.[21] Tamaulipas state representatives issued a report on agricultural production in 1891 that boasted of El Ebano as "the estate that has taken the lead in introducing new crops."[22] Similarly, at Las Pilas, owned by regional elite Bernardo Zorilla, ixtle, henequen, and zapupe were grown. At another Zorilla property, more than 3 million henequen and zapupe plants were grown, and at Hacienda La Puente, owned by Salvador Zorilla, more than 140,000 kilos of lechuguilla fiber were extracted in one year. The annual production in hard fibers at the aforementioned haciendas (all located in the town of Jaumave) was valued at more than 340,000 pesos. In nearby Tula, ixtle-producing haciendas had production valued at 175,000 pesos.[23] From 1891 through the end of the Revolution, the harvesting of ixtle alone "carried the municipality of Jaumave."[24] The hard fibers from Jaumave and Tula made their way via Tampico to places as distant as Le Havre, France.[25]

Working conditions at these ixtle-producing haciendas were among the harshest in the region and offered some of the lowest wages in the country. It was not until the early 1920s, after the Revolution, that the collective action of workers led to an increase in the value of each kilogram of ixtle to twenty centavos, which was a 10 percent increase. *Tallanderas* or *tallanderos,* as they were frequently called, also managed to get double pay when working "extra hours." They made great strides by forcing the Zorilla family to allow them to use hacienda lands for the grazing of their animals at no cost. After a long struggle that unfolded during the hearings of the central labor board, the Zorilla family was required to pay as per the board.[26] However, these victories were limited and came only after the Revolution.

At Hacienda Calabazas, proprietor Rudesindo Montemayor took the lead in investing in the latest technology in the extraction of ixtle. He acquired the Winfield *maquinas desfibradoras,* and at Hacienda Salamanca he ran steam-powered machinery for the extraction process. José Montesinos, from San Pedro del los Saldañas, also took notice and invested in the US-made Winfield fiber extractor, which increased production by more than three thousand kilograms of ixtle per day. While technology was introduced in the countryside and regional elites boasted of their modern and progressive haciendas, wages remained low; "salary and the rigidness and demands of the landowners remained."[27] The daily wage for a worker was from twenty-five to fifty centavos—the twenty-five-centavo wage was among the lowest in southern Tamaulipas; women were the recipients of these low wages.[28] In fact, as the historian Dawn Keremitsis explains, wages for campesinas during the Porfiriato "were half or two thirds [of the] wages men earned for approximately the same job."[29] The *auge ixtlero,* or ixtle boom, sparked migration to southern Tamaulipas, particularly from neighboring San Luis Potosí. According to eyewitness reports of the period, "a great multitude of families" resided in Tula and outlying areas, "and it is obvious that these families are poor."[30]

Peasant families in the southern end of the region lived in extreme poverty. Families lived in thatched-roof homes located on the work site on the outskirts of haciendas, which indicates that the majority of the labor force comprised both *peones permanentes* (permanent workers) and *trabajadores eventuales* (temporary workers). As the historian Mario Alberto Toscano Hernández has argued, among the temporary workers one could find small ranchers—*pequeños propietarios,* "who were displaced by the great *latifundios.*"[31] The distribution of water was also unequal and usually favored the larger growers, as the meticulous research of Toscano Hernández, Veronika Sieglin, and José Antonio Olvera Sandoval on water access has demonstrated.[32]

Working conditions for *peones acasillados,* or indebted peons, resembled those of slaves. The wages were among the lowest in the nation and led to "extreme poverty." Campesinos from southern Tamaulipas in the Xicotencatl area named their organization "El Despertar del Esclavo," meaning the awakening of the slave, after working as farm hands for years.[33] Given the descriptions of abuse offered in detail by norteño workers—both female and male—in their mutual-aid societies' by-laws, in the official registrations of unions after the Revolution, and in written petitions, conditions for northern Mexican workers were harsher than previously argued. As the case of two hundred campesinas who organized in 1925 illustrates, "given the years of slavery . . . we seek moral and intellectual betterment."[34] A rhetoric of justice, freedom, and autonomy developed in the years prior to the Revolution.

That more than 200 campesinas organized to create a union also points to how government collection of data during the period under examination often was gender biased and did not accurately represent the number of female workers. If we examine labor statistics for the northern district of Tamaulipas from 1906 through 1911, there were 12,272 men classified as *jornaleros* or peons, whereas only thirteen women were placed in that category.[35] We know that Nuevo León reported 30,000 jornaleros for the entire state in 1910.[36] However, an examination of archived documents that at first glance have no relation to issues of labor reveal how women who worked as domestic servants also labored as peons and jornaleras. Documentation on cases of "*injurias, falta de respeto a la moral*" (abuse or slander and lack of respect), as well as related subarchives containing materials on civil matters, prove crucial to the task of recovering the history of female laborers. The grievance submitted by the norteño Esiquio Martínez in 1898 against Cesareo Ramírez García is a case in point. Esiquio submitted a complaint to Monterrey authorities accusing Cesareo of disrespecting his daughter, Guadalupe. All three worked as jornaleros in an orchard belonging to Don Eugenio Gómez in Monterrey. The accusation itself is significant because it reveals the vulnerability of women agricultural workers who labored alongside men and who often had no supervision or protection. Esiquio proceeded to submit his grievance after Cesareo slapped Guadalupe when she attempted to free herself as he sexually assaulted her. Further, Cesareo called her a prostitute after realizing he would not have his way with her; the name calling, according to Esiquio, "was more hurtful" than the slap itself. Calling his daughter a prostitute was a direct attack on his reputation as a father and as a man. Yet, the accusation also sheds light on how frequently domestic servants also labored as jornaleras in the fields, orchards, or hacienda factories—not just in cleaning, cooking, washing, and overseeing children in the main house. Landowners cut costs by assigning multiple tasks to women. Guadalupe was a "minor" and, "besides offering her services as a domestic servant," collected fruit from the orchard trees. The case was never resolved, and the record is limited as to whether or not Guadalupe and her father continued working in the same orchard.[37]

Just as these cases dealing with sexual assaults or *abusos de confianza* (violations of trust) shed light on labor relations, labor grievances filed with the Junta Central de Conciliación y Arbitraje also help to recover the history of female laborers. Women provided rich details of their labor experiences while working in the fields as *peones de campo*.[38] Evidence from labor disputes demonstrates their contribution to the expansion of commercial agriculture. While it is difficult to provide precise numbers, these cases indicate that women's labor participation was much higher than reported in government statistics. A look at several major haciendas in the region points to the roles of women in the expansion of commercial agriculture.

In southern Tamaulipas, for example, the Haciendas Rascón and Chamal stood out as remarkable examples of the changes in the socioeconomic and cultural landscape engendered by the expansion of large commercial estates focused on agriculture, as well as the role of US capital in their growth. Hacienda Rascón, owned by an American, Cora Townsend, and covering 1.45 million acres, exemplifies the extent of modern technology in agricultural estates. Her hacienda was equipped with a hydroelectric plant, advanced irrigation equipment, warehouses, and several sugar mills operating with American technology. Rascón was ample evidence of the extensive foreign investment in the region and the elaborate capitalist social network that characterized such ventures. The Townsend family, George Lee, and the Minor family of New Orleans invested in the Rascón property along the Tamaulipas–San Luis Potosí border. The Minor family was co-owner of Hibernia Bank of New Orleans; the other owner of Hibernia was none other than James Stillman, the chairman of the board of National City Bank.[39]

With the "terrenos baldíos" law, as well as government concessions and tax incentives, Americans such as the Townsends and the Woolmans invested in rural and urban properties, raking in huge profits. Dixie Reid of Mississippi and her brother, James R. Clayton of Navarro County, Texas, acquired a property in southern Tamaulipas known as El Caracol. It included eight haciendas and forty-five ranchos and encompassed more than 7,000 acres that Clayton and John M. Reid managed. El Caracol contained "fertile lands," and its proximity to the Río Purificación and the Mexican National Railway station near Padilla raised the value of the property substantially. Nearby, the American Land and Cattle Company and H. H. Reeder owned more than 189,000 acres that made up Hacienda San Juan and Hacienda El Chamal.[40]

Hacienda Chamal was among a handful of major haciendas near Ocampo, about fifty miles south of the Tamaulipas capital, Ciudad Victoria. Chamal was founded with an investment of more than sixty thousand pesos by the Blalock Mexico Colony, a colonization project made up of American settlers from Texas, Oklahoma, and various midwestern states.[41] The proposal for Chamal had received the endorsement of Governor Prieto, and in 1903 George E. Blalock, from Barnsville, Georgia, along with more than thirty US families, founded Chamal Colony.[42] As reported by Sr. Dávila, a notary public and close friend of Prieto, the "boundaries of Chamal include the space enclosed by the three sierras or mountain ranges[,] including Tamalabe, Cucharras and Guatemala," which were offsets of the Sierra Madre Oriental. Dávila ensured that competing local land surveying companies such as Colonizadora de la Sierra de Guatemala did not "cross its [Chamal's] boundaries, as it plans to do," and he thus enforced the boundaries of Chamal. Chamal comprised more than 230,000 acres of Tamaulipas land. By the eve of the Mexican Revolution, more than five thousand American citizens lived in that state.[43] In the southern part of the state, US companies, including the Cruz Plantation Company, American Land and Cattle Company, Celeste Irrigation Company, Mexican Land Company, Mexico Realty Company, and Bernal Orchard Company, acquired land and established colonies and commercial estates.[44]

Even in Nuevo León, where the number of Mexican-owned businesses surpassed the number of American-owned properties, officials took a proactive stance in creating and maintaining an environment conducive to attracting foreign investors. Gov. Bernardo Reyes became close friends and business partners with a handful of Americans anxious to invest in the region. Jesse F. Holt, president of the International Land and Investment Company of Oklahoma and one of several hundred Americans in Nuevo León, owned properties totaling more than sixty thousand hectares. Holt also owned the Hacienda Santa Ana de Florida, near the towns of Burgos, Tamaulipas, and China, Nuevo León. The hacienda operated with various technological improvements, including a dam over the Río Conchos, and became one of the most profitable estates in the region.[45] In southern Nuevo León, near Montemorelos, George W. Hanna (a former US consul), C. W. Andres, and Anna Wredenhoff purchased Hacienda La Eugenia in 1906. "One of the most prosperous and attractive *haciendas* . . . one of the showplaces of that region," Hacienda La Eugenia included a modern irrigation system and represented large investments in land development.[46] The estate included farm land and more than fourteen thousand orange trees and was equipped with two railroad stations, which allowed La Eugenia to participate in regional and international trade.[47]

A real problem with regard to the monopolization of lands existed, particularly over fertile lands. Most of the lands were categorized as *tierras temporales,* given the lack of capital for irrigation technology.[48] However, those with sufficient capital, such as American investors and large landholders, could survive and realize profits. Juan Fernández of Las Rusias in northern Tamaulipas had the financial resources needed to build extensive irrigation systems. Jesse Holt of the International Land and Investment Company channeled water from the Río Conchos to his Hacienda Santa Ana de Florida, located along the Burgos-China boundary. The estate became one of the most profitable properties along

"Patiently awaiting customers," Monterrey in *An American Girl in Mexico* by Elizabeth Viseré McGary (New York, 1904). (Courtesy Nettie Lee Benson Latin American Collection, University of Texas Libraries, the University of Texas at Austin)

the Tamaulipas–Nuevo León border. Holt's estate extended beyond the 60,000-acre hacienda proper; his holdings totaled 148,500 acres.[49] While these American-owned estates were smaller than the largest hacienda in the state of Nuevo León, Soledad Hacienda (256,123 hectares), owned by a Mexican, American-owned properties had easier access to capital, which meant modern irrigation systems and other resources that facilitated crop production. In the Northeast, by far the largest haciendas were found in Tamaulipas; only the estates in Coahuila, particularly those owned by the Terrazas family, were comparable in size.[50]

Besides having an economic presence in the Northeast, Americans brought with them cultural and racial ideas of superiority. Encounters with foreigners and worker-supervisor confrontations exposed racial and class-based attitudes toward Mexicans. Interactions in haciendas became sites of intense cultural encounters between American owners and Mexican domestic servants, the majority of them women.[51] American women such as Mrs. Hester Woolman and Elizabeth Visère McGary brought with them their ideas about Mexicans, whom they called "brown people."[52] A look at the interactions between American and Mexican women sheds light on how ideas of class and race, held by both American and Mexican women, led to tense moments. Elizabeth Visère McGary resided on a large hacienda in the growing urban center of Monterrey.[53] American women in Monterrey, similar to the American women who accompanied their husbands to oil-rich Tampico, held racial and gendered ideologies of Mexican women whom they oversaw in their homes and as agricultural workers

TABLE 2. Partial list of occupations for women by district (Tamaulipas), 1906–1911

	Laundry	*Sewing and pressing*	*Candy making*	*Hat making*	*Agricultural estate management*	*Agricultural work*	*Retail trade*	*Business ownership*	*Tenants*
North	120	176	1	4	1	10	11	55	88
Central	225	122	0	5	0	17	4	18	50
South	293	173	1	0	2	2	2	32	54
Fourth	44	286	0	0	0	3	5	7	3
Total	682	757	2	9	3	32	22	112	195
								Total population of Tamaulipas:	249,641

Source: "Anuario 1910–1911," caja s.n., Fondo: Anuarios Estadísticos del Estado de Tamaulipas, AGET.

on their estates. McGary commonly referred to Mexicans she encountered as "brown people," creating and sustaining an unequal relationship that helped to fuel the growing nationalism in the years preceding the revolution.

The attitudes expressed by the wealthy Cora Townsend, from the sugar complex Hacienda Rascón, exemplified the general disregard for working-class Mexicans, despite their active role in making Rascón a profitable hacienda. After her husband, José Rascón, died in 1896, Townsend took over estate operations. Assisted only by a handful of American foremen, she oversaw fourteen thousand Mexicans. The Rascón estate also exemplified the gross wage discrepancies that existed on the commercial estates in the region. American foremen earned five dollars a day, while Mexican male laborers earned less than fifty centavos a day.[54] In extracting fiber from the ixtle plants, male workers could earn up to fifty centavos a day for one *arroba* (twenty-five-pound load); on average, male workers could work up to three arrobas per week.[55] Women earned 20 to 30 percent less; their wages often went directly to the *tienda de raya,* or hacienda store, to help clear debts.[56] Wages were usually further reduced to pay for religious services or medical care for unexpected health problems.[57]

Rural Mexican women factory owners found it difficult to compete with better capitalized corporations, particularly those owned by foreigners who could offer higher wages. In southern Nuevo León in the town of Doctor Arroyo, women owners of *fábricas de tallado de ixtle de lechuguilla* experienced first-hand the realities of competing with larger foreign corporations. The Companía Anglo-Mexicana had established itself in the region and could entice workers with wages that were 15 to 20 percent higher. In Doctor Arroyo, Companía

Anglo-Mexicana employed more than 265 men. In comparison, the norteñas María Rueda de Reynoso, María Dolores Rincón, and María Medrano all owned smaller factories engaged in the processing of ixtle, and their employee base was 3, 10, and 60 men, respectively. Of the women factory owners, María Medrano had the largest operation; in 1903 her profits were 5,200 pesos—one-third of the 15,696 pesos that Companía Anglo-Mexicana earned. Medrano paid her male workers twenty-five centavos a day while Anglo-Mexicana paid six centavos more to its 265-member male labor force. The presence of Anglo-Mexicana was felt throughout the Northeast. In nearby Galeana it established two lechuguilla fiber–processing factories in 1902. In one of its establishments, Anglo-Mexicana employed 30 males and 100 females. In one year it produced more than 64,046 pounds of ixtle valued at more than 5,000 pesos. Anglo-Mexicana paid female workers the same wages paid to males: thirty-one centavos a day.[58]

There were a handful of Mexican women who offered higher wages, either due to their connections to other regional elites or access to family capital. Galeana native María Eulalia Garza owned and operated an ixtle factory, and she employed fewer female workers than the nearby Companía Anglo-Mexicana. She employed fifty-three workers, but she paid her female workers six centavos more than the thirty-one centavos Anglo-Mexicana offered its female workers.[59] In southern Tamaulipas, mainly Tula, there were thirteen ixtle factories reported in 1905 with 1,150 workers who made ropes and fishing nets.[60]

Women such as María Eulalia Garza, who were from the *clase acomodada,* or affluent class, oversaw the work of campesinas on a daily basis and generally did not employ foremen. In Tula, Tamaulipas, among the elite and landed oligarchy were Isabel G. de Grillo and Rosenda Viuda de Otero. The historian Octavio Herrera Pérez writes that such women "formed an elite described by contemporaries as exquisite and in touch with the interior of the country." These regional elite women formed part of the upper crust of norteño society and had access to recent inventions, entertained guests with songs played on their home pianos, and "enjoyed the latest French fashion."[61] Regional elites also received catalogs offering the latest furniture fashions, garden fountains, and other sorts of "modern" amenities.[62] Isabel de Grillo seized every opportunity to boast that President Díaz's wife, Carmen Romero Rubio, had been born in Tula (Grillo's hometown) in 1864.[63] Indeed a member of the landed oligarchy, Carmen married President Díaz in 1881 when he was fifty-one years old and she was sixteen.[64] Given their status and smaller labor force, these women were able to compete with foreign enterprises capable of offering higher wages.

In textile factories, located primarily in Monterrey and its vicinity, women were responsible for "cleaning and carding the cotton, twisting the yarn, winding

TABLE 3. Ixtle production in southern Tamaulipas (Fourth District) during the Porfiriato

	Annual production (kilos)	*Value (pesos)*
1901	2,284,000	183,000
1902	2,575,000	515,000
1904	1,600,000	240,000
1905	32,400	186,745

Source: Mora García, *El General Alberto Carrera Torres,* 89.

it onto spools and removing them when filled . . . [and they] operated weaving machines."[65] Women also worked for hat-making factories producing *fieltro* and *paja* (felt and straw) hats; Los Hermanos Maiz was a factory that produced more than thirty thousand hats in 1903. Earning a peso a day (wages much higher than those earned by tallanderas), both women and men earned the same wages in most textile factories, while women comprised a third of the textile workforce in Monterrey. Their *compañeras* in nearby perfume- and candle-making establishments, however, earned much less: thirty-three centavos a day. Their male counterparts, engaged in similar kinds of work making wax candles and perfumes, earned eighty centavos a day.[66]

As previously noted, wages in ixtle factories were among the most depressed in the region and were even lower for women in most cases. The most extreme case found during the research for this book was in the town of Aramberri, Nuevo León, in the small Solis Hermanos ixtle factory, which had eighteen employees. The six women who labored as tallanderas in the factory, performing the same extraction work as their male coworkers, earned a miserable eighteen centavos a day, as compared to the thirty-seven centavos the men earned.[67] In the same town the Companía Anglo-Mexicana paid its one hundred female workers only three centavos more than Solis Hermanos did, and the company paid its males at the same level as Solis Hermanos. In cigar factories, however, wages tended to be higher, not only in the Northeast but throughout the country.

In the Northeast, most of the cigar factories were in Nuevo León. Ninety percent of the tobacco came from Nayarit and Veracruz, while the remaining 10 percent was grown in the state. A third of the cigars rolled and packaged in the tabacaleras of Nuevo León were consumed in northern Mexico, with the majority exported to central and southern Mexico.[68] As early as 1890 La Reina del Norte tobacco factory operated with some fifty workers. By 1904 the Black Horse Tobacco Company had been established, followed by El Liberal and other, smaller factories. The majority of these smaller production centers were found in Linares, Montemorelos, and Monterrey.[69] La Esmeralda, Compañía Cigarrera de Linares, Fábrica de Hojas La Quintana, and Fábrica La Violeta were among the tobacco factories employing women in Nuevo León. On the eve of the Revolution, the value of materials produced in two factories alone in the countryside town of Montemorelos surpassed eight thousand pesos per month. Production

TABLE 4. Selected cigar factories operating in Nuevo León from the Porfiriato to 1940

Factory name	*Location*
Black Horse Tobacco Company	Monterrey
Cigarrera de Cipriano Flores Ayala	Monterrey
Cigarrera de Francisco Cabrera	Montemorelos
Cigarrera de Ismael García	Linares
Cigarrera de Lázaro Torres	Montemorelos
Cigarrera de Linares	Linares
Cigarrera de Wenceslao Gómez	Linares
Cigarrera de Wenceslao Gómez	Montemorelos
Cigarros de Hoja de León Salas	Galeana
Cigarros de Hoja de Placido Cedillo	Galeana
Cigarrera La Moderna	Monterrey
Dionicio Ramírez Rico	Monterrey
El Liberal	Monterrey
La Bohemia	n.d.*
La Esmeralda	Linares
La India	n.d.
La Norteña	n.d.
La Quintana	Linares
La Reina del Norte	Monterrey
La Violeta	Linares
Luciano Galindo y Cía	Monterrey

Source: Compiled from data collected from 1918 to 1940 by the Junta Local de Conciliación y Arbitraje, AGENL; and from "Cuadro de Estadísticas de la Secretaría de Fomento, Colonización y Fomento, Cuadro Industrial," caja 17 (1903), Fondo: Secretaría General de Gobierno, Serie: Estadísticas, Asunto: Monterrey (y otros municipios), AGENL.
* No data available.

value could reach twenty thousand pesos a month.[70] In other light industries such as textiles, also dominated by female labor, the annual value of goods produced surpassed fifteen million pesos.[71] Women also comprised 30 percent of the Cervecería Cuauhtémoc labor force (consisting of more than a thousand workers) and played a key role in the success of Cuauhtémoc, which became the leading modern brewery of Latin America.[72] The growth of these light industries provided basic consumer goods for a rising population—middle-class consumers of cigars and beer on both sides of the Río Grande.

Female labor dominated the tobacco industry from the colonial period through the Porfiriato. Due to the overwhelming number of female laborers, the industry sought to "preserve [women's] dignity as virtuous wives and mothers."[73] During the last decades of the nineteenth century, women comprised three-quarters of the cigarette workers in Mexico. Given the fact that the industry was not regulated by guilds, tobacco factory owners heavily recruited women, a practice that continued well into the first decades of the twentieth century.[74] Earlier industrial censuses point to the presence of women in small tobacco product factories. Labor census records from 1900 report more than 400 *cigarreras* in Nuevo León. Approximately 192 cigar rollers were reported for Monterrey and 123 for Linares—the two cities in the state with the greatest number of tabacaleras.[75]

By 1906 Nuevo León industrial censuses were reporting more than 700 cigar workers (also known as *torcedoras*), of which 586 were women, or more than three-fourths of the cigar-making labor force.[76] In the two decades after the Revolution, some 15 percent of the Monterrey workforce was female according to state census records. However, the figure was probably higher given that industrial censuses failed to include those who made cigars or did other paid work at home.[77]

In the town of Galeana, in small to medium-sized cigar factories, female and male workers earned higher wages. In Placido Cedillo's small cigar shop, male workers earned thirty-seven centavos a day, while in León Salas's business, women workers earned the same amount. Fábrica de Cigarros de Wenceslao Gómez, founded in Linares in 1879, employed close to 140 women, who earned thirty centavos a day, while the small labor force of 15 men each received fifty centavos a day. However, the 3 women working for Luciano Barrera in the same town also received fifty centavos for their daily labor. Wenceslao Gómez opened another factory in Montemorelos in 1901, and it came to produce more than 104,000 boxes of cigars a year with 23 workers, 20 of whom were women. The average work completed each week consisted of nearly 15 boxes or *moletes* containing sixty cigars each. Gómez paid women in Montemorelos slightly more, thirty-seven centavos a day; however, these wages were still lower than those of males, who received fifty centavos a day.[78]

Wages for women in general agricultural or jornalero/peon sectors, ixtle factories, and in related industries considered "light," including textile factories, were on average 15 percent lower. The exception, in most cases, was cigar production. Women earned on average 10 percent more than men and dominated this sector. In some cases, wages could be 20 to 25 percent higher than those of *jarnaleros*. This was the case in the central part of Nuevo León.[79] In neighboring Tamaulipas, however, the number of cigarreras was low as compared to Nuevo León, where the largest concentration of cigarreras could be found. During the Porfiriato only thirty cigarreras were reported for all four districts in Tamaulipas.[80]

In Mexico City, women typically earned about fifty centavos to one peso a day.[81] In nearby Chihuahua, the forty women cigar rollers in El Tigre Negro earned about seventy-five centavos a day in 1904, but compared to the wages earned by the thirty male workers at the same factory, women earned 25 percent less.[82]

Work was based on a sexual division of labor. In the piloncillo industry, for example, men worked the cane fields, planting seeds, cutting the cane, and extracting the liquid that would then be processed and turned into *melado.* Men generally operated the mills, which ranged from more rudimentary ones to modern grinding machines. Women then worked pouring the syrup, or melado, into *moldes* or cone-shaped pans. After some twenty minutes, the brown sugar was ready to be removed from the pans and packaged in the traditional conical shape.[83]

On the ixtle haciendas, men worked cutting the tough plant from its roots and then cutting the long stems; the stems were allowed to dry for several days and then work resumed. Both men and women extracted the fiber by hand—the *tallado* part of the process. Men then were engaged in the transportation of the fibers. As seen in the *danza del ixtle,* a cultural dance that represents the sexual division of labor in ixtle production, the women carried the rolled-up fiber attached at the waist and the men then proceeded to unfold it and create a variety of products.[84]

Agricultoras and *Propietarias de Fábricas*

Mexican women, a good number of them widows, operated small shops employing both men and women. In 1903 in Abasalo, Nuevo León, 2 *fábricas de piloncillo* had female owners: Marta Villarreal Viuda de Ozuna and Petra Villarreal. Both *propietarias* oversaw an all-male labor force. In Cadereyta Jiménez, of the 230 piloncillo factories, 9 were owned by women, and all nine owners

TABLE 5. *Piloncillo* and corn production in southern Nuevo León, 1905–1906, 1916

Town	*Corn (tons)*		*Piloncillo (tons)*	
	1905–1906	*1916*	*1905–1906*	*1916*
Allende	—	23.2	—	185
Cadereyta	2,350	240.4	2,600	430
General Terán	—	175.2	—	1,050
Linares	3,960	148	3,960	220
Montemorelos	3,110	167.5	2,350	530

Source: Sieglin, "Agua, acumulación de capital, y burguesía," 20, table I.

employed an all-male labor force, paying them from thirty to fifty centavos a day. Two of these nine owners, Rita Galindo and Manuela Cantú Viuda de De León, owned factories capitalized with more than 10,000 pesos. Galindo's factory was valued at 17, 940 pesos, and De León's two factories were valued at 11,040 and 13,800 pesos, respectively. In the nearby town of Terán, there were 101 piloncillo factories, all founded between 1880 and 1899, and women owned 6 of them. The most lucrative factories produced more than 4,000 pounds of sugar with a small employee base of five male workers who earned fifty centavos a day. Terán resembled the town of Guadalupe, which had 89 piloncillo factories, 8 of which were owned by women. These female-owned factories generally featured a small labor force averaging four males earning from thirty-seven to fifty centavos per day.[85] In Santiago, of the 162 piloncillo establishments, 8 were owned by women. Altagracia Z. de Tobar's factory, founded in 1898, produced up to 27,600 pounds of sugar and employed five male workers.[86]

A closer look at the state *censo industrial* detailing the various industries in the region, their ownership, and the labor force sheds light on women's roles in the expanding regional economy vis-à-vis male workers. We know, for example, that in the *municipio* of Villaldama the widow Josefa G. Villarreal owned a small piloncillo factory valued at more than a thousand pesos. Starting business in 1885, Josefa employed fifteen campesinos and paid them fifty centavos a day. Her factory annually produced more than ten thousand kilograms of sugar.[87] Women who were married, widowed, or single did not operate factories only in the countryside. In the growing urban center of Monterrey, women owned businesses ranging from bars to bakeries and employed a mixed-sex labor force.[88]

The narrative of industrial development and commercial agriculture has typically been couched in terms of men hiring women. While 10 percent of factory owners were female, the fact that some fifty piloncillo factories were owned by women who hired male workers reveals a different picture of regional development and labor relations.

The growth tied to urban and industrialized Monterrey and Tampico caused shifts in migration and general demographic patterns. Factory work still offered workers an alternative, and norteños migrated within the region in search of new economic opportunities. Others came from afar to join norteña campesinas in the trek to urban centers, as in the case of Ana María, a native of Río Grande, Zacatecas. The twenty-two-year-old migrant had trouble securing employment in a factory and recalled, "I came to work, to find life, and I found it working in homes, with the help of my parents." Ana María found paid work as a domestic in the urban zones of Monterrey.[89] Like Ana María, many women labored in private homes, washing and pressing "*ropa ajena*" (other people's clothing) and earning a couple of pesos per week. Girls as young as eleven and twelve "washed and pressed other people's clothes," often with their mothers' guidance.[90] Evidently, migration to urban centers did not translate into factory employment for all. Women continued to be listed as paid domestics in the census records of the region. In fact, domestic work remained the largest occupation for women in the northern borderlands during the first half of the twentieth century.[91] In Tamaulipas, there were 739 female "*criados o sirvientes*" (servants) in all of the four districts, and 75,968 women were reported as dedicated to "*quehaceres de la casa,*" or household chores, out of a total state population of close to 250,000 persons.[92] However, the 1900 census indicated that there were more women employed in factories than as domestic servants.[93]

Women, like their male counterparts, migrated to growing urban centers or crossed into the United States, where greater economic opportunities could be secured. Indeed, as Veronika Sieglin points out, "it was imperative that women and children work," and thus migration was unavoidable.[94] Even up to the postrevolutionary period "at least one member of the family had to migrate to urban centers or the United States."[95] There were cases of women who migrated, leaving family members behind. Such was the case of Juana Vásquez, who left Monterrey and headed toward Laredo, Texas, "in search of better fortune."[96] Juana had been working for Pérez Maldonado as a domestic servant at his Monterrey estate, and when she left for the border town of Laredo, she decided to leave her young daughter in the care of her *patrón.* She could not return to Monterrey, given that she did not have enough money, so several years passed. When she did return, Pérez Maldonado refused to return the child, arguing that Juana was a "bad mother." The situation forced Juana to, "with great shame, file a complaint against Pérez Maldonado." Relying on a local public scribe because she was illiterate, Juana submitted her petition to the Monterrey authorities, claiming that "now that I have returned, [Pérez Maldonado] has grown fond of my daughter and he does not want to return her."[97] After several months of legal deliberations, Juana lost the case. Maldonado, a practicing lawyer with access to resources that Juana lacked, easily won the case. Juana never saw her daughter again. Peasant women and their families did not make enough money to hire prominent lawyers and often relied on "poor people's lawyers" appointed by the municipality or the state. Despite their proactiveness in resolving these types of cases, they frequently lost. In Juana's case, the price of migrating to seek employment was her daughter.

Racial Encounters between "*Gringas*" and *Mexicanas*

Haciendas became sites of cultural clashes and misunderstandings. Encounters between *gringas* and *mexicanas* revealed not only the frustrations felt by Mexicans over the extent of American investment in the region but also the cultural dimensions of the accumulation of capital in American hands. When Hester A. Woolman traveled to Mexico to conduct business near the San Luis Potosí–Tamaulipas boundary during the 1890s, his wife accompanied him. Mrs. Woolman quickly moved to establish her own business, focused on "modernizing the sewing trade," near the Hacienda Rascón.[98] She soon met with a local Englishman who advertised himself as a "modern tailor" and helped Woolman establish her business. As this business expanded, Woolman sought to hire local women. One of Woolman's Mexican female servants informed her of two sisters from the area who were in need of work. Agreeing to a verbal work contract, the Mexican sisters María Gómez and Altagracia Gómez began working for Woolman. Introducing the "scientific dress-cutting system used in the United States," Woolman taught María and Altagracia "modern" techniques of sewing. Woolman's business continued to grow, and according to the American instructor, she "controlled the patent rights in Mexico."[99] In exchange for learning this "modern method" of sewing, the sisters agreed to work for Woolman for twenty-five centavos per eight-hour shift. After several months without pay and disagreements between the sisters and Woolman, the local dispute became a regional and eventually a transnational affair when the sisters chose to protest against Woolman's labor practices.

When Woolman refused to pay María and Altagracia, they contacted local authorities, hired a "poor people's lawyer," and presented their claim regarding an unpaid sum of sixty-three pesos, seventy-five centavos. Woolman also moved quickly, contacting the US consuls in Tampico and San Luis Potosí and pleading with them, arguing that all she wished to do was "through scientific methods of sewing and dress-cutting transmit this new knowledge to other women in small towns or *haciendas.*"[100] News of the incident reached Washington, and, as was customary, the consuls' obligations were to protect the rights of Americans. Woolman, however, would have little luck.

When the sisters accused Woolman of failing to pay their wages, the dressmaker replied that she paid them what they earned minus the cost of goods provided to them during their tenure as *costureras.* Woolman had purchased clothes for the women "so that they'd be presentable when teaching" and had also "provided carfare to the local *haciendas.*" After traveling to nearby towns, including Ciudad del Maíz and Guadalcazar in San Luis Potosí, Altagracia and María decided to stop working for Woolman until they received their back wages. The affair became tense as the women exchanged strong words. According to Woolman's testimony, "María and [her] mother came in and called me some name they have for Americans, *gringa,* [and] they say that all the Americans come here to rob the Mexicans."[101] In a confrontation between María and Altagracia and Woolman, with the sisters' lawyer present, María yelled to Woolman that "the Americans come here to take advantage of Mexicans."[102] Woolman failed to win her case against the sisters. The presence of her husband, Hester Woolman, who traveled frequently to check on his investments, might have helped his wife and prevented the Mexican sisters from winning their case. The presence of an American male in cases involving workers, especially Mexican women, could significantly influence results in such cases. More importantly, María and Altagracia's protest against Woolman revealed the underlying racial tensions and prejudices between Mexicans and Americans. We know Woolman purchased sewing machines from the Singer Manufacturing Company, which had established "numerous branches" in Tamaulipas and had an agreement to pay the state government 360 pesos a year "for a contract fee." Representatives of "modern" companies like Singer catered to local women and engaged in door-to-door sales, with representatives visiting towns and villages. Even the journalist-turned-revolutionary Catarino Garza worked for Singer, introducing the modern sewing machine to many homes on both sides of the border during the 1890s.[103]

Prejudices and racialized ideas about both Americans and Mexicans were articulated and expressed on a daily basis. Just as María's frustrations culminated in her labeling Woolman a *gringa,* Americans, too, applied their own negative labels to Mexicans. While valuing Mexicans' "hard work," Americans' disdain for "such strangeness" became apparent and informed day-to-day relations.[104]

However, although both groups formulated racial assumptions about each other and articulated them, the relationship between Mexicans and Americans was an unequal one. The nature of their interactions derived from the socioeconomic differentiation and from the idea that American investment was part of the greater effort to civilize Mexicans.

Given the nature of the social, cultural, and economic climate of the period, the use of labels such as *gringa* by workers like María Gómez is not surprising. Cultural interactions unfolded on a daily basis in the cities and countryside.[105] And, as the historian Myrna Santiago has argued, foreign women who accompanied their husband-investors to oil-rich Tampico and northern Veracruz "were key, if unacknowledged, players in promoting and maintaining gender, race, and class ideologies and structures at home and abroad."[106]

A glance at the labor force and living conditions on commercial haciendas sheds light on the context in which such cultural interactions occurred. The Hacienda Guadalupe in the municipality of Sabinas Hidalgo, Nuevo León, for example, was representative of the numerous large and modern estates employing a large Mexican workforce under the supervision of a handful of Americans. Owned by the Morton family, this hacienda was equipped with a steam boiler and steam engine and had a large number of livestock. The Mortons employed more than forty Mexican laborers, who resided in one-room quarters located at a distance from the sixteen-room *casa grande,* or main house. Mexicans labored on the immense estate and purchased basic goods in the hacienda store. Not surprisingly, the hacienda—fully equipped with horses, several large barns, more than one hundred avocado and peach trees, and modern machinery—would become one of the targets of norteños during the Revolution.[107]

Interethnic or interracial marriages, which functioned as a type of strategic negotiation between middle-class or upper-class Mexicans and Americans, were common in the region and represented the kind of alliances that previous elites had sought, as in the case of the Treviño and Ord families. Regional elite Juan H. Fernández and Andrea F. Bayless, an American, married and jointly owned an extensive tract of land covering 1.2 million acres in northeastern Tamaulipas, in Soto la Marina and Aldama. The property represented the growth of large private estates during the late nineteenth century. Equipped with an advanced pumping plant large enough to irrigate approximately 650 acres at a time, the Fernández hacienda channeled water from the Río Grande through an extensive system of canals. The couple's export-oriented estate ranked among the top producers of cotton, corn, rice, and sugarcane.[108] Fernández's marriage to Bayless produced three daughters. After Fernández's death, his wife and daughters inherited the hacienda, which consisted of more than 280 ranches. By 1910 the property had a value of 307,000 pesos.[109] Similarly, in central Tamaulipas, near Padilla, the Milmo family of Nuevo León and the Reeders, an American family, created a lasting alliance through marriage. Sara Milmo, a member of the Monterrey elite, married George Reeder, and together they owned the corn- and sugar-producing Hacienda San Juan and the Hacienda San Patricio, a corn- and bean-producing estate comprising more than forty ranches.[110]

As single foreign men invested in different sectors of the region or gained employment in the oil fields, railroads, or smelters, they mingled and interacted with Mexican women. Americans such as J. M. Reckless of Philadelphia and Thomas Foster and Fred King from Salisbury, North Carolina, traveled to Mexico in search of employment and soon married Mexican women. Reckless resided in Monterrey, while Foster and King lived in Matamoros, where they worked for the Ferrocarriles Nacionales.[111] Others relocated to Tampico to work in the shipping and oil industry. Another American, B. F. Moats, left his native Ohio and moved to Tampico, where he found employment with the Ferrocarriles Nacionales and later the Waters Pierce Oil Company. He soon courted Mexican women.[112]

Likewise, elite Mexican men courted and eventually married American women. Mexican elites were considered "many shades whiter than the peon," as the American Elizabeth McGary put it. When McGary moved to Monterrey, she was courted by elite Mexicans.[113] Despite language obstacles, Mexican men and foreign women managed to formalize courtships and marry. With little contact during the courtship—usually only exchanges of letters and evening walks (under constant supervision)—couples married knowing little about each other. For interethnic/interracial couples, racial and cultural differences presented new challenges. As McGary wrote in her memoir, "after the civil ceremony has consummated the marriage, they leave, to learn whether or not they love each other . . . alas, that so often it should be a rude awakening—a falling short of expectations, for neither knows a thing of the other's thoughts and ways."[114]

Racial attitudes about "brown people" as McGary often referred to Mexicans, colored everyday interactions between foreigners and Mexicans in both the countryside and urban centers. Among the organized railroad workers such attitudes informed interactions between the masses of Mexicans laying tracks and a handful of foreigners who supervised them. The Order of Railway Conductors and the Brotherhood of Locomotive Firemen often excluded Mexican workers, even though these groups were operating in Mexico. Racial and ethnic ideologies informed decisions to hire or fire workers. One railroad worker complained that "American conductors . . . always enjoyed impunity from top officials[,] and when Mexican conductors stole a pittance they were dismissed from their jobs in shameful ways."[115] Oil workers faced similar conditions. American and British oil workers resided in "American quarters" and earned more than twice the wages paid to Mexicans. The so-called Mexican quarters resembled tenements in urban ghettos due to overcrowding and numerous sanitary violations. The separate living arrangements resembled the everyday segregation experienced at the work sites. Mexicans and some foreign workers, including Chinese workers, labored in the *chapapoteras,* where oil oozed from the ground, or worked in the lower paid, more dangerous kinds of jobs associated with the oil industry.[116]

Americans did not leave their cultural baggage at home. They brought with them the racial and ethnic assumptions about Mexicans that were prevalent at the time and that shaped everyday actions, thoughts, and business decisions. Those prejudices, combined with social Darwinist ideas held by norteño elites, placed working-class residents in a vulnerable position. Years of exploitation at the hands of native elites and regional leaders paralleled the socioeconomic differences between Mexicans and foreign workers and contributed to the violence imposed on foreigners during the Revolution.

By the late Porfiriato, Americans and other foreigners controlled the vast majority of the lands in Tamaulipas, especially between Soto la Marina and Tampico. Despite their demographic minority status, the foreigners' per capita income surpassed not only the wages of hundreds of norteños combined but even those of elite regional Mexican landholders.

A case involving an American named Howard Taylor Oliver illustrates the way in which American businessmen exercised their cultural and economic belief systems with regard to the native population. A Yale graduate whose expertise was in mining, Oliver headed to Mexico after being prompted by literature boasting that "Americans were welcomed." He began to work for an American-owned mining company in Pachuca, Hidalgo. In 1911 he moved to Tampico, where he began working as assistant division engineer for the Mexican National Railways and supervising more than three thousand Mexican laborers. Oliver experienced the rising violence against foreigners, particularly during the struggle over the Tampico oil fields. As the fight for oil raged on, Mexicans called for a "Mexico for the Mexicans" and succeeded in forcing "all American engineers, conductors, and employees," including Oliver, out of the region.[117]

While Oliver gained valuable work experience in Pachuca, he developed cultural assumptions about the "natives" that he carried with him to his new job in Tampico. In Pachuca he had helped "put some 75 unemployed Mexicans to work at higher than prevailing wages." Oliver also boasted of how he "made them bathe, [and] put shoes on their feet," all for "better[ing] their living conditions and contribut[ing] to the welfare of the community." For the native workers, "better[ment]" and "progress" represented discrimination, marginalization, and foreign supervision in their own land.[118]

BETWEEN 1880 AND 1910 WOMEN'S remunerated work expanded in sectors that had traditionally been occupied by women since the colonial period, and their work included the production of ixtle, tobacco products, and piloncillo. While it is difficult to come up with a precise figure in terms of the number of women workers, evidence indicates that industrial development and the making of the borderlands did not exclude women. Organizing efforts of "*campesinas agrícolas*," or peasant women engaged in agriculture and the creation of agricultural cooperatives in the rural Northeast, point to the large number of economically active female peasants.[119] Women's labor proved crucial to the making of a borderlands that by the end of the Porfiriato had become highly commercialized and capitalized through US investment. The modernization of the borderlands was a contradiction: while campesinas earned some of the lowest wages in the nation, some of the highest wages could be secured in the urban factories of Monterrey. In sectors where commercial haciendas expanded as a result of the "terrenos baldío" law and closer linkages with American capital and international markets, "local labor was insufficient."[120] Women's labor, generally less remunerative than that of males, filled that gap, allowing for the expansion of ixtle- and piloncillo-producing haciendas and other estates dedicated to increasing commercial output.

On these estates, work was just as dangerous as in the factories in large urban centers such as Monterrey. In *trapiche* work in the modern sugarcane mills, workers, particularly those with little experience, often got hurt or died as a result of accidents. It was not until after certain labor codes were passed that families received some type of compensation.[121]

The historiographical record on the transition to modernization, industrialization, and commercial agriculture in the Northeast has largely ignored the labor of women. Women made up half of the population of the states of Tamaulipas and Nuevo León, and, given the historic shortage of laborers, there was a real urgency to hire women. As Veronika Sieglin has argued, "the insufficient number of laborers . . . and extreme poverty . . . [made necessary] the integration of women and children" into the wage labor force.[122] The migration of men from neighboring states such as San Luis Potosí would not sufficiently ease labor shortages. The demand for workers helped place women in wage labor and integrated them more rapidly into commercial agriculture. Working conditions were harsh, and their wages were far lower than those of their male counterparts—in some cases 30 percent less. The research on rural women's work presented here contradicts the long-held view that work was better paid in the North. This was not the case for tallanderas or piloncilleras. While cigarreras in the North did fare better on average, tended to earn wages comparable to those of their counterparts in the interior of the country, and received pay comparable to that of cigarreras in the United States, jornaleras at large haciendas did not. As the next chapter shows, migration to higher-paying Texas farms and ranches was a constant threat and a concern to both absentee and resident latifundistas. The threat of immigration (and migration within the region) exacerbated the conditions for workers as haciendas turned to harsher labor control mechanisms, which included physical abuse. Nonetheless, norteño women and their families would rely on the old cultural practice of the petition for aid in the form of intervention from local, state, and national authorities guided by the principle of reciprocity and community. They also turned to collective organizing and formed a variety of mutual-aid societies to address their basic needs.

Chapter Three

"We cannot suffer any longer from the *patrón*'s bad treatment"

Everyday Forms of Peasant Negotiation

> We are obliged to suffer all kinds of abuses and bad treatment. Instead of being compassionate because of our miserable situation this man has the habit of physically abusing those who serve him as the many cases that have been brought against him demonstrate. [These cases] should be on file in the town. Governor, I ask you to please consider my plea.
>
> MANUEL AGUILAR TO THE GOVERNOR OF NUEVO LEÓN, 1889

> We do not doubt that you are a protector of the *clase obrera* which suffers greatly. We appreciate your protection . . . you are aware of the benefits that this society will extend to the protector class.
>
> SOCIEDAD DE OBREROS DE LINARES TO GOV. LÁZARO GARZA AYALA, 1888

AS THE GOVERNORS OF TAMAULIPAS and Nuevo León—Alejandro Prieto and Bernardo Reyes—delivered eloquent speeches to their constituents about the need to modernize the region by clearing land and building roads and railways, residents of the two states sought to negotiate everyday labor conditions that emerged as this vision of progress materialized. Peasants such as Manuel Aguilar, from Apodaca, Nuevo León, felt pressure from resident landowners who sought to retain labor and prevent workers from crossing the border into Texas or from moving to nearby haciendas and ranchos where the pay was better. The alliances among political leaders like Prieto and Reyes, regional elites, and American investors had created a pro-investment climate in the borderlands. This type of economic climate led to what elites termed *progreso,* embodied in the factory, permanent wage labor, the commercial estate, and the enclosed farm. This progress, however, carried with it a distinct meaning for the *norteños* who would come to provide the labor to make such progress possible. Yet, they would also come to directly engage the state to address changes brought about by this vision of progress. As regional and political elites' vision of progress clashed with the everyday realities of life for the peasantry and small *rancheros,* the transformation of the region would become a highly contested one. By 1910 the Northeast would become the site of numerous bloody confrontations.

In the 1880s, scores of Mexicans from nearby states and from the interior of the country were heading north in search of work. The growth of the *población flotante,* or transient population, in search of employment opportunities coupled with the resident population created demands on industries geared toward consumer goods.[1] The mass production of clothing, food, beverages (namely beer), and glass became the predominant "light" industries associated with women's labor and industrialization by the late nineteenth century. Addressing the needs of the growing population, one of the "most modern" glass factories and the "first modern brewery" in Latin America were founded in Monterrey. While the introduction of heavy industry revitalized Monterrey through the expansion of smelters and the exploitation of oil fields in the Tampico vicinity, the countryside suffered depopulation through outmigration. As the majority of the population in the countryside remained in small villages of fewer than two thousand inhabitants, the countryside-to-city migration pattern began in the 1880s and continued well into the twentieth century.[2]

The proximity of the region to the United States had historically played a key role in labor relations given the higher wages in agricultural sectors in Texas and in railroad projects as distant as the US Midwest. As one *campesina* from Monterrey put it when asked about her cousin's whereabouts, she reported, "He was going to work for a couple of days here [Monterrey] to earn enough to then be able to cross into the United States."[3] Regional and foreign landowners (both resident and absentee) had to contend with the threat of peasants' migration to urban centers or to the United States. As a response, *hacendados* used strategies of labor control (typically involving debt peonage and physical abuse) to retain their laborers. Peasants witnessed firsthand the realities of a labor system that operated and was directly shaped by historical processes tied to the establishment of the geopolitical border. Landowners had struggled to secure a steady labor force since the early nineteenth century as haciendas expanded during the transition to commercial agriculture and as industrial development required a more permanent labor force. The creation of a national market, the linking of the United States with Mexico via the railroads, and the capital relations between the nations made it easier to attract laborers to urban centers that offered higher wages but especially difficult to maintain laborers in the countryside, where wages had historically been depressed.[4]

While the arrival of the railroads, the growth of breweries and glass and textile factories, and the emerging petroleum industry shaped the socioeconomic landscape of the Mexican Northeast, the large haciendas and ranchos in the region stood as stark contradictions to urbanization and factory wage labor. Residents and transients alike would come to work on increasingly commercialized estates and also form part of the industrialization efforts of regional elites and state representatives. However, industrialization developed differently in the Northeast. Large haciendas and ranchos, principally those owned by Americans, did become increasingly commercially oriented and increasingly "modern" by 1910. Technological advancements were put to use in the citrus region, in the cotton-growing areas, on some milk and egg farms (*granjas*), and on vegetable and fruit estates.[5] A handful of haciendas and ranches employed more extensive technology and produced goods for the regional, national, and international market. The Haciendas San Vicente, San José de Las Rusias, Rascón, and Sauteña (the latter three owned by Americans) produced large quantities of corn, rice, cotton, and sugarcane and were already reaching out to external markets.[6] Hacienda San Juan de la Generala and Hacienda La Mesa de Hidalgo, both in the municipality of Padilla, were sugar-producing estates. In the same municipality, Hacienda El Caracol, owned by James R. Clayton and his sister, Dixie R. Reid, comprised more than seventy-four hundred acres in its farm and stock ranch.[7] By 1910 the managers of these large estates were experimenting with "the most modern cultivation methods using steam and water turbines."[8] Great portions of the southern Nuevo León countryside, particularly in Montemorelos, acquired a reputation for introducing technological advancements. Once again the American investor Joseph A. Robertson, with the cooperation of Montemorelos elites, would emerge as a leader in technological innovation in the countryside. He experimented with grafting and harvested the first crop of oranges in the region using that technique.[9]

At the Hacienda La Clementina in southern Tamaulipas, owned by the US Bernal Orchard Company, peasants were exposed to new labor relations as they had increased contact with foreign supervisors and foremen.[10] Also in southern Tamaulipas, the sugar complex owned by Augustus Curby employed hundreds of Mexican peasants earning no more than fifty centavos a day. Only a handful of workers were taught to use imported machinery, under the close supervision of American foremen.[11]

Peasants in the countryside found themselves laboring on commercially oriented agricultural estates, and they not only felt the effects of technology but were also subjected to modern ideas of labor. On haciendas such as Rascón, a 1.4-million-acre, American-owned agricultural estate in the southern part of

Tamaulipas, fourteen thousand Mexican workers witnessed the introduction of imported modern milling equipment and elaborate power plants, as well as the presence of American men and women as their immediate supervisors.[12] For many of these laborers, progress and modernity in the region meant longer work-days, low wages, and supervision by foreigners. By the end of the first decade of the twentieth century more than 5 million acres of northeastern land, principally in Tamaulipas, were owned by Americans.[13] The fact that Americans owned "the largest and best conditioned bearing orchard[s]" (in Tamaulipas) points to the gradual economic takeover of the Northeast by Americans. By 1910 more than 80 percent of land in the Northeast was owned by Americans. This research supports the findings of the historians John Mason Hart and Friedrich Katz and suggests that American investments were greater in the Northeast than previously documented.[14]

While peasants had worked on a seasonal basis by selling their labor to commercial estates during harvest season and working their own plots during the off-season, by the early 1900s wage labor had become the norm. As free laborers, peasants earned wages and often rations of corn or other basic goods as well. Norteño resident and transient workers could be categorized as *aparceros* (sharecroppers, who also hired workers), *jornaleros acasillados* (indebted peons), *jornaleros no acasillados* (peons not in debt to a hacienda or ranch), *trabajadores permanentes* (permanent workers), *asalariados temporales* (seasonal workers), or *aparceros minifundistas* (small landowners-sharecroppers), with categories often overlapping.[15] Peasant sharecroppers were also frequently indebted to the estate after falling behind on payments for the use of land, for advances, and for food, medical supplies, or other resources obtained on credit. As the historian Friedrich Katz has explained, "in the case of the North, there is every indication that low population density led to a scarcity of labor which made the *hacendados* utilize all means at their disposal to force laborers to remain on their *haciendas*."[16]

For *peones acasillados* it was extremely difficult to abandon their jobs due to the large debts they had incurred over the years or for fear of reprisals. As their handwritten petitions to state authorities or petitions submitted via public scribes illustrate, their wages were often too low to allow them to repay debts and thus be able to leave their jobs and work sites. Wages for male peons rarely surpassed fifty centavos a day in 1900, while female laborers generally employed in domestic service at the haciendas or as workers in the ixtle and piloncillo haciendas earned only about eighteen to forty centavos.[17]

Besides dealing with harsh working conditions, norteños also found it increasingly difficult to subsist on their own plots of land given the rapid consumption of land by large corporations. As previously explained, regional elites often supported these large companies despite the hardship such support placed on their own *vecinos.* For example, residents from the border region extending from San Fernando to Matamoros were accustomed to using the salt from the various *salinas,* or salt deposits. Governor Prieto was an investor in a salt-mining outfit, the Compañía Salinas Obregón, and his *compadre,* Timoteo Castañeda, an elite from Matamoros, had the title *comisionado especial para defender la propiedad de las Salinas.* Castañeda thus was in charge of protecting the property known as Salinas, the salt, the investments made in the company, and the investors. Prieto wrote to Castañeda and expressed his discontent over the man's failure to stop the "large bulk of salt taken by locals without permission."[18] A year later, in 1904, as the railroad made its way from the Corpus Christi and Robstown area to the border to Brownsville, Castañeda urged Prieto that, while his term as governor had expired, he had the power to intervene because he had the backing of regional elites who respected him as a well-trained engineer and businessman. Castañeda urged him to "take possession of the Salinas and of the salt" because, given that the railroad now crossed the property, "this would result in huge profits for the company and would raise its value." Not only would the land be worth more, argued Castañeda, but salt could easily be exported for profit to other countries and to points farther south in Mexico.[19]

As the borderlands became primed for investment, *enganchadores,* or labor recruiters representing native and foreign companies, played a role in attracting workers and increasing migration to the area. The case of thirteen-year-old Isauro Alfaro Otero illustrates the way in which these labor contractors persuaded workers to move to the region. In 1904 Isauro decided to work with his father, Evaristo, who worked as a *carrero* (muleteer) transporting metal ores from the Santa Ana mines to the *fundiciones,* or smelting centers, of Cedral, San Luis Potosí. Father and son left their family in Potrero and moved to Matehuala to work in transportation services for the contractor Pedro Pedraza. For several years, both worked for Pedraza, with "*rudas jornadas habituales,*" or long workdays, for wages that were below regional standards. After working long day shifts, Isauro prepared the *carruajes,* or cars, for the long haul between Cerritos in northern San Luis Potosí, Matehuala, and Tula in southern Tamaulipas.[20]

The rest of the Alfaro family stayed behind in Potrero, and while Isauro and his father's income helped the family survive, migration was tough on all of them. Weeks and even months could go by without family members seeing each other. Women who stayed behind often had to extend their work hours, seek new employment, or take on an extra job. They often assumed the double role of father and mother. Once again this father and son team from Potrero would migrate in 1906 as they heard labor recruiters along the San Luis

Potosí–Tamaulipas boundary announce "better paid work" in the port of Tampico. Now fifteen years old, Isauro joined his father, and when they arrived in the city, they proceeded to contact an American whom enganchadores had singled out as the main contractor. The Alfaros went to work unloading coal at the docks of Tampico for Edward M. Rowley. Two years later, Isauro would find work at the Muelle Fiscal de Tampico, the main docks where workers unloaded ships at the port.[21]

Isauro observed the influential presence of large, foreign-controlled oil and shipping companies such as Rowley's, and "this reality opened [Isauro's] eyes . . . and he attempted to organize workers so that, together, they could devise a plan to improve their moral and economic status."[22] He set his plans aside, quit working for Rowley, and, for the next three years, worked for the Ferrocarril Central Mexicano shops in Tampico.[23]

Poor working conditions prompted people like Isauro and their families to become organized and even radicalized. Isauro encountered foreigners who influenced his developing bent toward labor activism. He met Samuel Albino Kelly, an Irish Mexican who worked as a foreman for the Rowley Company. Samuel Albino's father, Samuel R. Kelly, had met and married a Mexican woman, Josefina Cano. The couple lived in Burgos, Tamaulipas, and then had Samuel Albino, who as a young adult traveled extensively in Europe and gained exposure to pro-worker ideas circulating there, mainly "*mutualismo* and *sindicalismo*." These ideas inspired Isauro, and, together with Kelly, he saw "in these doctrines a seed of hope for his fellow distressed Mexicans."[24] As the Rowley Company celebrated a contract with Ferrocarriles Mexicanos for the stowing of cargo in 1910, Kelly, along with norteños Lorenzo Picazo, Melitón González, Luciano Cervantes, and the young Isauro laid the foundation for what would become one of the largest cooperative unions in Mexico.

The early meetings between Kelly, Isauro, and other Mexican dockworkers led to the creation of the Gremio Unido de Alijadores (GUA) in 1911.[25] The port workers argued that "our goal is to find improvement in our work . . . [thus] we formed a mutualist society."[26] In his numerous writings on the Tampico working class, the historian Carlos González Salas has argued that because the Díaz regime prohibited any kind of worker organization, permitting only mutual-aid societies, Kelly and Alfaro probably "used the title of *gremio* [guild] while in actuality they had organized the stevedores into a union." Under the guise of a mutualist society, the organization assumed the radical characteristics of the syndicalist groups that later appeared in the country, and the dockworkers' collective efforts would have a lasting impact on not only norteño society but the entire country.[27] Quickly, the GUA set forth its demands, which included higher wages, the elimination of labor recruiters, direct dialogue with contractors, shorter workdays, and paid holidays. A month after the *gremio* outlined those basic goals, it employed nonviolent means to push for better conditions: the group went on strike against Casa Rowley, forcing it to meet their demands.[28]

Rowley's business in Tampico suffered a setback in 1921 when the Gremio Unido de Alijadores pressured Ferrocarriles Nacionales to cancel its contract with Rowley. However, before the cancellation of the concession, the dockworkers walked off the job in July 1911, demanding recognition of their union. In 1921 the organized workers took over the dock contracts, marking the first time that a union contracted its own work with a major corporation.[29] Rowley attempted to evade national embarrassment by reporting that the company had abandoned its contract with Ferrocarriles Mexicanos due to financial losses. Rowley's monopoly on commercial activity (unloading coal for the Ward Line) at the docks of Tampico and Doña Cecilia, and its relationship with Ferrocarriles Mexicanos grew weak with the GUA victory.[30]

Even while some family members remained at home while fathers and sons migrated, they too faced the risks associated with organizing, which was perceived as radical at that time. Before the success of the GUA, dockworkers from the town of Doña Cecilia who had joined the group faced threats of unemployment.[31] Dockworkers organized precisely to extend protection to their families, as they explained to José Etienne, a member of the elite in Tampico: we "joined [the GUA] so that our families would not go without food if we are sick."[32] The struggle of the workers to gain recognition and transform their demands into reality was a long one, but the commercial growth of Tampico, second only to that of Veracruz, facilitated widespread worker mobilization.

Like Isauro Alfaro, a young peasant named Petra Reyna, also from San Luis Potosí, made the decision to migrate in search of better opportunities. On the eve of the Mexican Revolution, Petra left her native San Luis Potosí and headed toward Monterrey. Like other migrants, Petra became part of a new urban society that included many former residents of San Luis Potosí when she joined the labor force at a hacienda on the outskirts of Monterrey. She continued to perform tasks associated with ranch life; she "woke every day to grind the corn in the *metate* . . . and took the cows out of the pens."[33] She remained in Monterrey and later married an older man. The couple lived in the San Luisito barrio, named after its large population of San Luis Potosí migrants. Their neighbors came from such San Luis Potosí towns as Charcas, Venado, and Matehuala. Petra's barrio provided Monterrey factories with a steady supply of laborers. By 1910 Monterrey's population was seventy-nine thousand—a significant increase from the fourteen thousand residents in 1877.[34] Migrants in the resident populations of

TABLE 6. Population growth of Tamaulipas and Nuevo León, 1910–1940

	1910	*1921*	*1930*	*1940*
Tamaulipas	249,641	286,904	344,039	458,832
Nuevo León	365,150	336,412	417,491	541,147

Source: Visión histórica de la frontera norte, book 5, 176.

Monterrey, Tampico, Matamoros, and Reynosa were predominantly from the north-central part of Mexico, as well as from the Nuevo León, Tamaulipas, and San Luis Potosí countryside. The majority of the migrants identified themselves as campesinos, while a small percentage of them claimed to be artisans or workers with some industrial experience.[35]

The mix of migrants and countryside peasants came to constitute the bulk of the norteño population by 1910. Their culture was rooted in long traditions of defense against "*indios bárbaros,*" of economic autonomy, liberal political ideology, and, importantly, a mutual reciprocity dating back to the precolonial period. Of particular importance was the use of the written word to express demands that affected all vecinos and emphasized community autonomy. Indeed, petitioning was not restricted to the northern part of the country, being quite common across Mexico. As Arturo Warman writes of the eastern Morelos peasantry, "in the old colonial documents, they start their declarations with this sentence: '*Y venimos a contradecir:* And we come to object.'" While petitions yielded few results, "peasants have always been present to object, to denounce injustice, and to defend their right to cultivate the land and retain its fruits."[36]

The lived experience of Manuel Aguilar is a case in point. Despite his illiteracy, Manuel, an elderly peasant from Apodaca in southern Nuevo León, visited the public scribe in his town and presented a complaint against his *patrón* regarding abusive treatment at the hacienda where he worked. The scribe wrote as Manuel recited his complaint and his plea for help from the authorities. Manuel explained, "Since some time ago, my family and I have worked for José María Garza Elizondo. . . . We are molested, mistreated, and physically abused on a daily basis." He tried to find an explanation for his employer's actions: "Perhaps it is that we owe money . . . that we are obliged to suffer all kinds of abuses and bad treatment." However, he continued, "instead of being compassionate because of our miserable situation this man has the habit of physically abusing those who serve him." The petition also made reference to "the many cases that have been brought against him." It is unclear if Manuel or the public scribe knew about the other complaints, but the petition points to physical abuse as a widespread problem. He closed the petition by speaking directly to the governor: "I ask of you to please consider my plea."[37]

Manuel Aguilar's case points to the practice of officially petitioning (both verbally and in writing) local, state, and national government representatives. It was a practice that derived from a long tradition of mutual reciprocity and actively engaging the state because there was an expectation of respect and reciprocity. As the historian Susie Porter has argued, "[in] these pleas, men and women often provided an assessment of their position in Mexican society and economy."[38] Peasants opted to voice their concerns to negotiate their situations and generate some form of structural change. Such demands for protection and intervention revealed the cultural resiliency of norteños and peasants' perception of state authorities as members of the community with responsibility to it. This view implied that heads of state had a responsibility for the well-being of the citizenry, and it points to the way in which tradition—principally the ideas of *cooperativismo* and mutual reciprocity—helped residents cope with change or, as some put it, "*modernidad.*"[39]

Petitions were popular at sites where exploitative conditions abounded, including Tamaulipas, particularly in the southern part of the state, where large ixtle-producing haciendas were numerous. In the Tula area, "on a daily basis more than 2,000 souls collected ixtle, extracted the fiber, and transported . . . [it]." Ursula Tapia, who as a young girl worked as a *tallandera,* and her family suffered physical abuse at a hacienda in southern Tamaulipas. In an interview years later she recalled how, "for whatever reason[,] they whipped us. . . . Yes, the abuse was too much."[40] The mostly permanent and indebted labor force of women and men worked from sunrise to sundown in the labor-intensive extraction of fiber from the ixtle and lechuguilla plants. *Tallado* work did not pay well, and often campesinos had to augment their income working as temporary laborers on nearby ranchos and haciendas.

The working conditions on Juan Castaños's estates illustrate the extent of exploitation and worker discontent, as presented in petitions and, eventually, in uprisings. In Miquihuana, Tamaulipas, Castaños owned the Haciendas La Peña and La Perdida, which were corn-, bean-, and lechuguilla-producing estates. In Ocampo he owned El Tigre Hacienda, which produced cattle, rice, corn, and sugarcane. Castaños was a member of the regional elite and a shareholder of the Banco de Tamaulipas. Workers complained about Castaños's "exploitation of servants" and the abusive labor relations rampant on his estates, which would later play a major role in the uprising of the Carrera Torres family in that region.[41] The peasants seized the city hall of Miquihuana in 1908, prompting the mayor, Adolfo Alcocer, to send an urgent telegram to President Díaz: "'more than 100 men . . .

threaten authorities and are armed . . . there is panic." The uprising revealed that the owner of Hacienda La Perdida, Juan Castaños, "who committed illegal acts against the peasants," was the main target. The peasants were arrested and jailed for one month, while their leader spent an extra seven months behind bars. Evidence indicates that the schoolteacher in Miquihuana (home to the more than one hundred peasants who rebelled against the hacendado)—Alberto Carrera Torres—retired from his obligations in 1909 and began to work as a lawyer in nearby Tula. By then, he had become known as the "defender of the poor."[42]

Even though, as Friedrich Katz has argued, by 1917 debt peonage had been abolished because in 1915 "*servicio personal*" was outlawed, thus preventing workers from selling their person to pay off debts, workers were still subjected to exploitative conditions. As Veronika Sieglin explains, this change placed indebted workers in a vulnerable position, given that most ended up mortgaging their means of subsistence as payment.[43] For those who were literally stuck in the cycle of debt, they began to sell their "means of production" in exchange for basic goods from on-site hacienda stores; among the items sold were plows, animals used to haul goods, and crops (for sharecroppers who were indebted).[44]

Sharecroppers, including some women, received pay plus their portion of the crops, which "they then sold to *comerciantes* who extended them credit . . . those were from the *pueblo* . . . but [who] paid very low."[45] Just like their male counterparts, women too worked on "*lo suyo*" (their own), spending a day or two on their own plots. While there were sharecroppers who hired their own day laborers to help them harvest their crops, by the eve of the Revolution the number of sharecroppers had declined, given the difficulty in competing with the larger growers. By the 1920s, however, the number of sharecroppers had declined in places like southern Nuevo León, and rent was set at more than 30 percent of the crop.[46]

Records on the conditions of workers from Tamaulipas and Nuevo León contradict the long-held view that the Mexican North was more egalitarian, a place for worker autonomy, and a place where higher wages could be secured. While there were moments of cross-class cooperation, as in the case of the Carrera Torres uprising in southern Tamaulipas and during the Emilio Portes Gil era of labor unionism, evidence supports the assertion that there were divisions and marginalization based on class. While wages, on average, were higher in the North in industrialized sectors, the cases reported by workers themselves or through public scribes reveal that norteños in the countryside found themselves in much more abusive and poorly paid worksites.

A peasant's decision to leave the estate could threaten the safety of the entire family. Pedro Salas, a peasant working for Eugenio Ortiz's Hacienda La Soledad in Doctor Arroyo, located in southern Nuevo León, wrote to the governor of the state describing his situation and how his attempt to flee the hacienda jeopardized his wife and children's safety: "My family has been abducted and I want the authorities of Dr. Arroyo to know so that they can help me. . . . My dear friend, I fear for my life after this complaint because I am sure it will be avenged, and it will not only affect me, but my entire family."[47]

Pedro Salas argued that the hacendado Eugenio Ortíz "owned" his two sons. He also explained how his *patrón* threatened to detain his sons until the family debt was paid off.[48] While the archival record does not tell us whether or not Pedro's situation improved, it does shed light on the strategies used to retain labor. Estate management dealt with the daily occurrence of outmigration from the countryside to urban centers or to Texas and other US border states. Hundreds of men and women, single or with their families, left the countryside. Like Pedro Salas, Esteban Garza and his family, peasants from the same municipality, decided to leave since his "wages barely covered the essentials at fifty centavos a day." We know that, unlike Pedro, Esteban was successful in his flight. Esteban's father was a campesino and his mother was "*dedicada al hogar*" (dedicated to the home) and ended up in a one-room house with their twelve children. Shortly after arriving in Monterrey in search of work; Esteban found employment in a railroad company and later joined the leading brewery owned by the Garza Sada family, Cervecería Cuauhtémoc.[49]

Workers continued presenting grievances and asking state authorities to intervene and provide assistance. From 1891 through 1896 the peasant Andres Rodríguez labored on Antonio Tamez's hacienda in Allende, near the citrus region of Montemorelos. When Andres completed his fifth year of work, he decided to ask for a raise. Tamez received his request and, instead of negotiating with his worker, terminated Andres's contract and fired him. With no job and a family to sustain, Andres proceeded to petition the governor, asking for some kind of intervention. His plea revealed the hardships that many rural workers experienced. Andres had sold his "*persona para trabajar*" in 1891 in exchange for weekly rations of corn and a monthly salary.[50] When Andres complained to authorities about his dismissal, they arrested him for a debt he owed, according to the hacienda records; an advance payment made to Andres before the beginning of his contract had not been paid off despite his five years of employment. This strategy had enabled Tamez to keep Andres and other disgruntled workers. After the release of Andres from the town jail, he was forced to work fifteen days out of the month to pay off his debt. Andres's petition illustrates his desperate situation. Through a public scribe, the Allende peasant pleaded with the governor: "I petition the Supreme Government as a son would petition a father, asking for protection and guarantees for me and my family. Sir [Governor,] help me clear my debt, they are obligating me to pay the balance. . . . I ask for no violence against me, I do not want to be punished in any way. . . . If they were to take my job away my daughters will go hungry. . . . *Ciudadano Gobernador* these complaints come from an honest and hard working man."[51]

Unfortunately for Andres, the governor's office rejected his petition and suggested that he petition the judicial authorities of Allende. By 1900 Andres's case had been returned to the state archives. While we do not know what happened to Andres, his case reveals not only his experience working under debt peonage but also, and more importantly, his proactive stance, especially when it involved the well-being of his daughters. Petitioning the governor, just as a son would a father, Andres expressed his loyalty and acceptance of authority, using the language of benevolence and of subservience, and hoped his situation could be rectified by the "*gobierno superior.*"[52] This rhetoric of benevolence and deference employed by Andres was used quite frequently by working-class people when asking for intervention in labor conflicts or petitioning for general aid.[53]

In some cases, peasants left haciendas for temporary work at other haciendas or ranchos in nearby areas. By the 1880s landowners from the citrus region of Montemorelos were hiring seasonal workers for three-month periods.[54] Given that, once collected, fruit could not be stored but had to be sent immediately to its destination, orchard owners extended "*trabajo eventual,*" or temporary contracts, to large numbers of workers. In most orchards, workers were provided ladders and, in a few cases, "scissors and gloves," yet, for the most part, workers used their bare hands. Only a few of the workers were hired before "collecting time" to tend the fruit trees. Both female and male workers migrated from rural estate to rural estate adapting to various crop cycles.[55] Their labor helped to make the citrus sector in the Northeast the second largest in agricultural production by 1896. Between 1890 and 1910 the bulk of the citrus, mainly oranges, was being exported in wooden crates to the United States via the new railroads.[56]

Another case underscores the often desperate situation in which workers found themselves during the late Porfiriato, as well as their attempts to negotiate and improve their situations. In mid-September 1892 Teodora Cepeda of Monterrey contacted a public scribe and submitted her petition to the governor. Four years had passed since her husband, Pedro Serrano, had agreed to a work contract offered by the hacendado Abraham García Calderón for "*los trabajos de labranza*" (plowing). But Teodora argued that García Calderón had not "formally liquidated [Pedro's] debt" and "had not given him some form of certificate or proof allowing him to leave the *hacienda*" despite his four-year tenure as a worker. Teodora decided to petition the governor: "I find myself in this situation so that is why I come to you, that is why I come to the *Supremo Gobierno,* begging you to help us contact a poor people's lawyer so that my husband's rights can be acknowledged by competent authorities. My family is faced with a difficult situation suffering from extreme poverty and that is why we have not been able to file a lawsuit against Sr. Lic. García Calderón."[57]

Two days later, the governor's office proceeded to contact an "*abogado de pobres* to help the petitioner with her situation."[58] Both Teodora Cepeda and Manuel Aguilar perceived the governor as an ally to whom they could voice their demands as they sought to leave the hacienda in search of a better life. Through the local scribe, Teodora made use of her right to plead to no other than the "supreme government" and its leader, the governor. Furthermore, Teodora's petition points to not only the intimate relationship between work and family but also how gender shaped such petitions. She noted, "With my husband's permission, I write because he cannot suffer any longer from the bad treatment of his boss." Her closing stated, "I come to petition the *gobierno supremo*."[59] That Teodora's petition referenced permission granted by her husband sheds light on expected behavior for men and women. If the scribe added that clause, it might have been to make the authorities aware that Teodora had gained permission from her husband before proceeding with her claim, which asked for aid on behalf of the male patriarch of the family. If Teodora made the decision herself to refer to the permission she obtained, it might have been to strengthen her position or increase her chances of receiving a favorable response. However, that Teodora, as a campesino's wife, could have some leverage negotiating her husband's future was quite powerful.

Teodora's petition points to how workers' livelihoods were directly tied to their families' livelihoods. While people from working-class backgrounds had access to other means to intercept and influence state-elite sponsored projects, including violence, avoidance, and resistance, as noted by the historian James Scott, petitioning was a strategy commonly used by norteños.[60] While state intervention consisted of helping peasants contact a poor people's lawyer in some 15 percent of the cases presented, the petitions are evidence of how physical abuse was rampant and tied to debt peonage. Ironically, as the borderlands were shaped into a "productive," "modern," commercially oriented space, the method used to achieve that vision was backward and exploitative.

Collective Petitioning and Creating Mutual-Aid Societies

As described above, residents and workers sought to petition authorities individually, but they also did so collectively. In the spring of 1888 a group of workers congregated in Monterrey with "a desire to mutually help one another."[61] These *obreros*—Pedro Cavazos, Ysac Uranga, Francisco Ramos, and Rafael Rocha—joined forces to establish an organization dedicated to the "improvement of the material and moral conditions of the workers."[62] They then proceeded to notify the northern branch of the Gran Círculo de Obreros (GCO), in Monterrey, about their new organization: Sociedad Unión Regiomontana de Monterrey. After contacting the Círculo, they prepared a letter describing the goals of their organization and sent it to the all-female Sociedad Mutalista de Señoras y Señoritas. The Unión Regiomontana was grounded in the ideals of mutual aid, *cooperativismo,* and a collective approach to solving issues related to work and family. "Equality, justice, and work" became their motto.[63]

That the men of the Unión Regiomontana informed the Sociedad Mutualista de Señoras y Señoritas points to the progressive nature of the organization. The Sociedad Mutualista had broken new ground by creating one of the first all-female organizations with a motto of "justice, equality, and progress." Sociedad Mutualista remained committed to the improvement of workers' conditions. In 1885 women from Monterrey, including María B. Martínez, Francisca M. de Avila, and María Dolores Treviño, created that collective for the "good of all women." Similar to the practice of asking for *amparo* via written petitions, Sociedad Mutualista members expected a response from local authorities based on the idea of mutual reciprocity. Women in *mutualistas* adopted similar strategies, emphasizing their political loyalty by choosing a high government official to serve as a *socio honorario,* or honorary member, of their organization. In a politically savvy move, given the antiworker atmosphere of the period, the Sociedad Mutualista secretary, María B. Martínez, wrote to Governor Reyes of Nuevo León, asking him to serve as the honorary member of the group. In her letter María explained that "this society, celebrating its [one] year anniversary in January 1886, asks the governor of the state of Nuevo León, General Bernardo Reyes . . . for his *amparo* and important protection for the growth, progress, and success of this society."[64]

Francisca M. de Avila, the president of the Sociedad Mutualista, along with María Martínez and a general member, María Dolores Treviño, were pleased with the governor's positive response. Reyes represented the conservative faction in Monterrey, and maintaining a good relationship with him could prove useful to the group.[65] Mutual-aid organizations such as the Sociedad Mutualista provided women the opportunity to engage in collective activities and demonstrate leadership abilities. The women promoted their agendas, carved out an actual physical space for themselves, and helped to broaden political participation in a city with a strong conservative faction.[66] By 1901 there were more than fourteen all-male and five all-female mutual-aid societies, many of which functioned as quasi-labor unions. The Gran Círculo de Obreros remained the strongest all-male organization, with more than eight hundred members.[67]

Playing the politics of servitude, deference, and loyalty, mutual-aid societies elected honorary members as the ultimate expression of gratitude. While it is likely that many of these mutualist and labor-centered societies did not think highly of their *socio honorario,* who was almost always the governor of the state, they elected him as part of their strategy to advance their agendas. Members could not only call upon their honorary member for political support but also submit petitions asking for financial aid in emergency situations or complain about abusive *patrones.*

Despite the proactive stance taken by women to protect their labor rights as certain sectors in the region underwent rapid industrialization, deeply rooted gender ideologies and expectations continued to shape the larger conversation about women and paid work. While the presence of women in industrial work expanded society's perception of the industrial worker, many of the same prejudices against women that had existed long before the industrial revolution in Mexico continued to prevail. When María Olivares de Arriaga of the Sociedad Hijas de Hidalgo, an all-female mutual-aid society, volunteered to take part in an independence celebration in Monterrey, she was chosen to represent "industry" in the parade. However, María was chosen because a committee member, Lauro Aguirre, felt that María's "perfect curves that are so admired by many" and "the way she carries herself" represented industry in a perfect way. He added that "vigor, pride, the heart of nations, are the source of infinite wealth."[68] While some valued qualities of physical beauty over work abilities, others expressed concern about the threat that women's work in unsafe environments posed. A government report in 1911 on the labor situation revealed the concerns about women's roles in the path to modernization. It warned the citizens that "child labor and the excessive work of women in industry . . . often disregarded . . . is detrimental to our country's well-being."[69]

While attitudes about women's labor changed during the nineteenth century and had a direct impact on middle-class women (predominantly married women), this shift in attitudes had less effect on working-class women. Liberal politicians argued against wives' participation in "productive labor" because women were seen as "guardians of private life in the home."[70] However, working-class women, both married and single, often had no choice other than to financially contribute to the household. Historically, women had been active in the production of goods at home, or in the streets as vendors and washers, or in small-scale industries. The shift to widespread wage labor created a greater demand for laborers, and given women's historic participation in a variety of industries in northern Mexico, women would also come to form part of the growing wage labor force.[71]

Women's mutual-aid societies during the Porfiriato were complex and hierarchical. A handful of documents found in the Nuevo León state archive points to the existence of the Sociedad Hermana Obrera de Linares, a union of women workers from Linares, eighty miles southeast of Monterrey. From 1892 through 1896 women belonging to the Sociedad Hermana met regularly and practiced what was essentially a popular form of liberalism employing a strategy of loyal citizenry. The group notified the governor's office of every scheduled meeting and election.[72] During its five years of existence (there was no record of the organization after 1896) the organization elected four different presidents: Paula Flores de Rodríguez, Antonia Barreda de Flores, Cristina Jano de Rivas, and Josefa Villarreal de Cárdenas. The Sociedad Hermana included a president, vice president, secretary, treasurer, accountant, collector, president of the commission for public health, and four representatives of the commission for public health. A collective group such as the Sociedad Hermana with eleven elected officials seems to correspond well to a town with approximately ninety-seven hundred women in 1880 and in which more than five hundred women worked as cigarreras, "public washers," and domestic servants at haciendas and ranchos and in urban homes. Sociedad Hermana represented its own system of female hierarchy. The various positions held by women pointed to one way in which they crossed into the public political sphere. The power of office in an all-female organization provided women a space in which to articulate their own agendas and take on positions of leadership. At the same time, belonging to a mutual-aid society with specific political and social goals meant having a communal and familiar space where women could openly discuss issues and provide support in times of strife.[73]

The motto of the Sociedad Hermana Obrera de Linares was "God, union, and fraternity," and it thus echoed the goals of numerous mutualistas throughout the Mexican borderlands. The male counterpart of the group, the Sociedad de Obreros de Linares, founded in the early 1880s, stressed "union, morality, and fraternity." These mutualistas used the language of popular liberalism to accomplish their greater goals and also attempted to manipulate authorities by expressing their loyalty as worthy citizens and emphasizing the plight of the worker. Doing so was quite risky at the time, given Governor Reyes's close relationship with President Díaz and his support for using physical force to quell any threats to the peace and order of the region. When petitioning the governor of Nuevo León, the Sociedad de Obreros pointed to a sort of natural right to submit such requests or petitions for help. In 1888 the Linares workers wrote to the governor, "We do not doubt that you are a protector of the *clase obrera* which suffers greatly. We appreciate your protection . . . you are aware of the benefits that this society will extend to the protector class . . . we are grateful and appreciative. Union, morality, and fraternity."[74]

In some cases, the organization received support in the form of donations or help in building workers' libraries. Among the accomplishments of the Linares mutualista was the raising of funds to complete the construction of the Hospital Civil in that town.[75]

Throughout the region, organized workers sought the support of the highest ranked community member—the governor. Regional and local branches of the national workers' association Gran Círculo de Obreros remained active in petitioning the governor for members' needs. Branches in the towns of Mier and Camargo functioned as support centers for the incipient industrial working class in the region. Mutualistas also petitioned heads of state to raise funds for their respective branches. Together with the Sociedad de Obreros de Ciudad Juárez, workers wrote to Governor Reyes asking for funds to purchase books on "recreation and instruction" for its members. Claiming that "the poor condition of the organization [has] prevented them from reaching success," they asked the governor to cooperate with them. Praising the governor's "humanitarian" qualities, members also asked for funds to purchase books to create a library for workers.[76]

The written form of negotiation employed by workers and the use of collective action resembled the efforts of workers across the border in the United States. Mexican Americans and recent emigrants from Mexico formed associations and chose group names such as the Sociedad Unión México-Texana in Brownsville, across the border from Matamoros. Upriver in San Diego, Texas, ethnic Mexicans came together and formed the Sociedad Mutualista Hijos de Hidalgo.[77]

The majority of these early mutual-aid societies reserved their limited funds for emergency situations. Workers belonging to mutual-aid organizations such as Sociedad Cooperativa "El Porvenir de la Unión" in Monterrey earmarked funds for "loans for individuals and for legal purposes." "Several poor workers" from Monterrey pitched in modest sums of cash on a monthly basis, creating a *caja de ahorro,* or communal bank. The practice of creating these community chests dated back to the precolonial period and was commonly used by indigenous peoples. Vicente Cavazos, the president of the Sociedad Cooperativa "El Porvenir," explained that having access to resources in emergency situations could make a real difference for workers. While the communal bank was a small financial resource, it benefited the workers and their families by providing loans in times of strife. The practice of creating these communal banks continued well into the twentieth century.[78]

As late as 1925 cajas de ahorro were being recorded and registered in the state. In 1925 peasant women connected to the Unión de Obreras "Fraternidad Femenil" from southern Tamaulipas founded a communal bank, as evidenced in the formal registration of their union in the capital of Tamaulipas.[79] While historians have pointed out that mutual-aid societies adopted a less radical approach than the later *sindicatos,* or unions, the act of organizing or joining a mutual-aid society certainly had its share of risks; members could be jailed if accused of illegal organizing.[80] We know that many of these mutualistas were the basis for sindicatos even before these organizations were allowed to operate.

Workers from Ciudad Victoria strengthened relationships with one another as they put the ideals of cooperativism to work. Together, the workers founded the Alianza Obrera Progresista in 1901. Alianza Obrera recruited workers from nearby factories and the burgeoning commercial haciendas. A good number of workers came from the ixtle-producing haciendas near Jaumave and Victoria.[81] The president of Alianza Obrera, Jesús Peña, created a *botica;* under the supervision of a local teacher, Emeterio B. Gómez, the Botica Alianza provided medical care for members. Concerned for members' health and the limited funds of the organization, Peña sent requests for aid to several regional politicians, including Reynosa mayor Jesús Tarrega. Using the rhetoric of progress and *cooperativismo,* Peña reminded Tarrega of his role as a "good Tamaulipeco" and a "progress enthusiast . . . we know that you are concerned for the working class." Peña wrote that "regardless of the amount, your help will be greatly appreciated . . . and you will become part of our organization's social history."[82] Alianza became one of the first mutualistas to establish both a community pharmacy and a library for its members.[83] Two other organizations followed the example set by Alianza. The Sociedad Obrera Progresista de Ciudad Victoria "Unión, Progreso, y Tolerancia," founded in the early 1900s under the leadership of Antonio Fernández and Anacleto Portales, and the Sociedad Benito Juárez de Auxilios Mutuos in Soliseño, Tamaulipas, adopted similar strategies to attract Mexican workers from various industries.[84]

NORTEÑOS SUCH AS PETRA REYNA and Isauro Alfaro Otero had embarked on journeys to urbanized areas in search of better economic opportunities, just as hundreds of other Mexicans did at the turn of the twentieth century. News of work opportunities in the northeastern region of the country circulated throughout the Mexican countryside thanks to enganchadores and an entrenched social network among residents. The considerable growth of a floating population forced authorities to address numerous issues associated with the growth of commercial agriculture and the expansion of urban centers.[85] The growth of Monterrey was principally due to its massive smelters, brewery/glass industries, and associated industrial development, while the Gulf of Mexico ports, including Tuxpam, Veracruz, and Tampico, witnessed a demographic shift due to oil production and associated industries such as dock work and shipping activity.[86] In the midst of profound transformations, pre-industrial cultural practices such as holding community representatives accountable for the well-being of the community, the practice of the *petición* for work or family-related issues, and collective organizing survived and thrived in some sectors. However, structural change would have to come through more direct struggle.

Throughout the countryside, vecinos claimed ownership of lands they had been working since "time immemorial," and by the 1880s they were engaging in uprisings. In the summer of 1889 a group of Linares residents who called themselves *comuneros* and counted the mayor, Jesús María Benítez, among the members scuffled with hacendados from La Parrita and the vicinity. La Parrita was a village of close to four hundred people. The comuneros argued that the lands they worked had belonged to them "since twenty years ago" and directed their complaints to the landowner, Juan Antonio González.[87] The early revolutionary rhetoric, depressed wages, and gradual decline of landownership among small and mid-sized rancheros would also influence uprisings across the international line. Along the Río Grande, in Starr County, Texas, the *tejano* journalist Catarino Garza launched a revolution against Díaz using Rio Grande City and other Texas border towns as his base of operations. While the uprising failed to unseat Díaz, the rebellion gained popularity and added impetus to the greater struggle for worker autonomy and to discontent with escalating levels of poverty and land loss on both sides of the border.[88]

During the 1880s the governor's office in Tamaulipas received multiple telegrams on the "alarming situation" in some of the southern municipalities in the state. Authorities from Tula and Jaumave sent telegrams reporting "groups of armed vecinos."[89] Dismal working conditions throughout the country signaled the eve of one of the most massive and widespread revolutions of the twentieth century. One government official observed, "Certain factors affecting the workers [in industrial establishments] concern us. In the mines, the wages are higher, but the harsh work that continuously deteriorates workers' health cannot be repaired by work limits nor by a healthier diet. Similar to the mines is the textile factory. Conditions have improved but we still face the problem of the company stores. . . . Workers' energies are often exhausted in the long shifts, and since most of the wages are based on piecework, the worker commits himself or herself to tasks that are often beyond his or her limits."[90]

In Alejandro Prieto's final report to congress during the late 1890s, he urged the politicians to support the translation of Maria Robinson Wright's novel, *México actual.* Prieto argued that Wright's novel should be translated "so that it could be circulated throughout Europe and America . . . the advantage of this would result in great benefit to our nation . . . the world needs to know about the availability of labor and the various industries." He ordered that at least two hundred copies be printed.[91] Prieto, like other regional elites, was on a nonstop path toward modernizing Tamaulipas and the entire nation. Yet, for Prieto and other regional elites, modernization translated into transforming the predominantly ranchero and campesino population into permanent wage laborers to assist in this transition.

The transfer of large tracts of land from Mexicans to Americans continued to take place throughout the region. The historian José Antonio Olvera Sandoval notes that a basic examination of the *libros del registro público,* or register of deeds, in the town of Montemorelos in southern Nuevo León for 1889–91 reveals eight land transfers of "*fincas rústicas,*" or rural estates, from local agriculturalists to foreigners. Of the eight transfers of property (note that while the number is low, the amount of property was significant), one involved a woman, Carmen Becerra, who sold to Luciano López, a US citizen from Floresville, Texas, in Wilson County. The sale was for eight hundred pesos.[92] Even those small landowners or *pequeños agricultores* (and even sharecroppers with small tracts of land) in southern Nuevo León who were not losing their land to Americans or other foreigners still lost all or part of their land because they used it as collateral to secure credit. This practice appeared to be a greater cause for loss of land than droughts because most of the land in the hands of small farmers and sharecroppers tended to be *tierra temporal,* or dryland acreage.[93]

The situation in Tamaulipas was similar. The expansion of the large estates that had begun in the 1870s continued well into the early 1900s. The Tamaulipas state historian Octavio Herrera Pérez has explained the formation of the agrarian elite: only a handful of families owned the majority of land in the southern region of the state. The (Rudesindo) Montemayor, (Canuto) Martínez, (Blas) Uvalle, (Amador) Cervantes (also mayor of Palmillas), (Rufino) Lavín, (Marcos) Báez, (Dionisio) Montelongo, and (Pomposo) Alvarez families together owned more than 70,500 hectares; Martínez was the largest *latifundista* in that region, with nearly 60,000 hectares.[94]

It was not long before government reports revealed that "conflicts between capital and labor . . . have already begun," and they increased in "manufacturing and [were] frequent and dangerous."[95] In June 1904, as Díaz celebrated his sixth term as president, the "convulsion" that shook the far northern borderlands began to manifest itself in the factories, expansive haciendas, oil fields, and smelters. Mexicans demanded safer working environments, called for an end to debt peonage and physical abuse on the haciendas, and insisted foreigners leave the country. Armed men whom authorities labeled "*bandoleros*" attacked a ranchería along the Gulf Coast near Soto la Marina in 1905; the "four or five men" would continue their attacks in nearby San Luis Potosí.[96]

Between 1900 and 1910 corn had doubled in price, reaching four centavos per kilogram, and bean prices grew threefold, to five centavos per kilogram; prices did not stabilize until 1919.[97] Given the low rural wages (rarely exceeding one peso per day) and average industrial wages of one peso daily, the price hike "create[ed] an atmosphere of social instability and agitation among the workers."[98] Land enclosure, widespread wage labor, state preference for foreigners over Mexicans, and far-reaching changes at the community level all culminated in a massive uprising. Norteños from Nuevo León became attracted to the revolutionary rhetoric of men such as Adolfo Duclós Salinas, the author of *México pacificado, Emigrados políticos,* and *Héroe y caudillo.* Exiled in Saint Louis, Missouri, Salinas collaborated with the Mexican anarchist brothers Ricardo and Enrique Flores Magón, who were already gaining ground in Tamaulipas and enlisting men and women in their Partido Liberal Mexicano (PLM). The PLM represented the counternarrative to the vision of a modern borderlands held by local and regional elites. Theirs would call for a worker-controlled society, and for promoting this goal, many PLM members and supporters spent years in US and Mexican prisons. The revolutionary, pro-worker ideas of the Magón brothers and other revolutionaries, embodied in their sociopolitical nationalist organization, soon attracted residents of the Northeast, including Higinio Tanguma, a worker from the Hacienda de Santa María (the former Manuel González property) in Tamaulipas who came to represent one of the norteño branches of the PLM.[99] Tanguma as well as other local residents, including women, would heed the call for revolution.

Chapter Four

(En)Gendering Revolution in the Borderlands

Revolucionarias, *Combatants, and Supporters in the Northeast*

> We are poor because a handful of wealthy ones have everything in their possession. They own the land, they own the mines, they own the forests, they own the homes, they own the water, they own the railroads, they own the machinery, and they control the power of labor.
>
> "EL MOVIMIENTO AVANZA," 1911

> Because of the Revolution, my property was destroyed . . . the *agraristas* destroyed all of my belongings, furniture, and work tools . . . leaving only the bare land.
>
> LUIS DIBILDOX TO THE GOVERNOR OF NUEVO LEÓN, 1925

THE NUMEROUS HANDWRITTEN petitions submitted by *campesinos* themselves or through public scribes and protesting abusive conditions did not yield much success. With fewer than 15 percent of requests for intervention, financial aid, or help securing employment receiving a favorable response, residents would turn to more direct and violent action to address their mounting discontent.[1] As massive walkouts took place in urban Monterrey, local uprisings occurred throughout the countryside. The Revolution in the Northeast was a direct response to growing socioeconomic disparities, mainly in the countryside: physical abuse at haciendas, depressed wages (particularly in the southern region), and the increasing concentration of land in American hands. For thousands of *norteños* the road to revolution created a moment of hope for real structural change, yet it also brought the very real experience of war. For factory workers it meant an end to steady wages and was thus no cause for celebration; for those working on the commercial haciendas, disruption of work awaited them as well. Uprisings along the northern borderlands had begun to take place as early as the 1880s, and there were soon repercussions throughout northern Mexico.

As the historian José Antonio Olvera Sandoval has argued, the Revolution against Porfirio Díaz by the wealthy Francisco I. Madero of Coahuila created a flurry of local uprisings against the aged dictator. By "1912 and especially in 1913[,] when the first revolutionary battles occurred in these *norteño* lands . . . the roads traveled by General Bernardo Reyes . . . used to transport goods and merchandise, now carry men who despise *porfirismo's* anti-worker policies and await a new beginning for the rural and urban proletariat."[2] "Maderista" clubs quickly emerged, and sympathizers joined the struggle. Madero's abrupt death at the hands of Díaz's general, Victoriano Huerta, however, shocked and angered Mexicans who saw in Madero hope and a new beginning for their country.[3] Early in 1913 one of the followers of the murdered Madero, Venustiano Carranza, also from Coahuila, refused to recognize General Huerta as leader of Mexico after Huerta's military coup in February 1913, and he emerged as the new revolutionary leader. His followers, who called themselves Carrancistas, avenged the death of Madero in a series of battles and engaged federal troops who continued following Huerta's orders. The Carrera Torres brothers carried out a grassroots-based campaign in southern Tamaulipas, while José Agustín Castro, Lucio Blanco, and Luis Caballero operated throughout the central and northern part of the state. In Nuevo León Maderistas now supported Carranza, and norteño leaders such as Antonio I. Villarreal and Pablo González Garza emerged as regional strongmen. There, the struggle would be against Huertista government forces and Reyistas, supporters of Bernardo Reyes. Carranza's men soon controlled the region from Lampazos to Doctor Arroyo and from Matamoros to Ciudad Victoria. Carranza appointed sympathizers to lead the struggle in their respective regions and proceeded to name Pablo González Garza as "Jefe del Ejército del Noreste" to direct military operations in Tamaulipas, Nuevo León, and Coahuila. Francisco Villa, who had emerged as a key supporter of Madero and now worked with Carranza to avenge Madero's death, oversaw operations in Chihuahua.[4]

During the hot summer of 1911 angry protesters took to the streets of Monterrey. Catarino Fernández and Cándido A. Vallejo led the Club Liberal Anti-Reyista "2 de Abril de 1903" against Gov. Bernardo Reyes, who, like Prieto, supported the modernization of the borderlands. The men proceeded to hold the anti-*porfirismo* demonstrations and denounced the Reyes administration in the Alameda Porfirio Díaz, one of the public squares of Monterrey. As the club members marched, the city police arrested and charged them with violation of the penal code under Article 855 of the Constitution of 1857. Fernández insisted that he had not broken the law, claiming his arrest was political abuse. The governor approved marches only if they were in support of his political agenda, and anyone marching without approval was charged with "disrupting the public peace." Telegrams flooded

Nuevo León politician Leobardo Chapa's office congratulating him on "the peace that reigned during last Sunday's demonstrations."[5] While Fernández and Vallejo complained to the Ministro de Gobernación in Mexico City about the "violent treatment" they received at the hands of the Monterrey police, Chapa assured authorities that he had treated the detainees well and insisted that "they received all considerations."[6] Even though the men were soon released from detention, public protests continued. Approximately fifty individuals belonging to the Club Liberal Anti-Reyista congregated in the Alameda Porfirio Díaz and marched toward the center of Monterrey through Calle Cuauhtémoc and up Calle Washington. Accompanied by music playing in the background, the protesters shouted "¡Francisco Madero!" and headed toward Calles Juárez and Matamoros, ending their march in the Plaza Zaragoza. The march commemorated the peaceful protests of April 2, 1903 (hence the name of the club) against Bernardo Reyes. What had been organized as a peaceful demonstration, however, resulted in the deaths of three men and the wounding of several participants.[7]

These public demonstrations against pro-Reyes factions formed part of a larger response to a political atmosphere of increasing anti-worker rhetoric and repression. Political injustices committed against residents, as seen in the case of the anti-Reyes demonstrators, only provoked disgruntled workers to join the call for revolution. Meanwhile, through repressive tactics, Reyes sought to occupy the office of governor for the fourth time.

Reyes's power was challenged, and as revolutionary factions emerged, women from the region—of all backgrounds, from the ranchero class, to small landowners, campesinas, and factory workers—joined the struggle.[8] For example, the Galeana native Julia Nava de Ruisánchez expressed her dissatisfaction and frustrations with Reyistas and supporters of the now-exiled Díaz. Together with Dolores Jiménez y Muro, José María Bonilla, and Antonio Gutiérrez, Julia organized a series of anti-reelection demonstrations. She also helped organize the Club Femenil Antireeleccionista "Hijas de Cuauhtémoc." Julia and the Hijas de Cuauhtémoc actively sought to alter the political and social development of their country and the region. With the support of the Hijas de Cuauhtémoc, Julia defended *maderismo* and condemned Gen. Victoriano Huerta in public gatherings. Shortly thereafter, government authorities apprehended and jailed her. The time spent in jail did not keep Julia from supporting the Revolution. When she was released, she continued working with other like-minded women and men and resumed both protesting against Huerta and calling unrelentingly for a worker-led society.[9]

In the Matamoros-Brownsville corridor, the *Brownsville Herald* reported in March 1913 that "five women under the orders of [Gen. Lucio] Blanco . . . took an active part in combat on their horses and shooting their pistols," citing key witnesses from nearby San Benito, Texas.[10] The newspaper also reported that several women under the command of María González fought alongside fifty mounted rancheros in Matamoros. It is unclear if González assisted the Matamoros garrison under the control of Esteban Ramos, a Huertista major, or if she sided with Blanco and fellow Carrancistas.[11] While the precise number of *soldaderas* is unknown, archival evidence points to the involvement of female soldiers at different levels and with different factions. María Guadalupe Barrera, a thirty-year-old campesina from Linares, Nuevo León, fought alongside Isidro Paz, the father of Guadalupe Paz de Hernández. During the Revolution, María went with Isidro Paz to Monterrey and lived there in 1915. Their relationship would not last long due to problems between María and her stepdaughter, since Guadalupe disliked the idea that María and her father had been lovers since the beginning of the war. María Guadalupe traveled with Isidro, participating in various military campaigns alongside other women.[12]

María González and *soldaderas,* Matamoros, 1913.

When not participating in the Revolution as soldaderas, women provided key assistance by serving as nurses, caring for the wounded and aiding other *compañeras,* or acting as spies, sometimes smuggling weapons across state and international borders. Some joined La Cruz Blanca, a transnational organization founded by Leonor Villegas de Magnón to assist Carrancista soldiers.[13] Other Mexican women took advantage of the revolutionary climate to advance their own agendas promoting social and gender equity and labor issues. This revolutionary idealism was expressed in the actions and articles of female journalists, writers, and activists in political parties such as the Partido Liberal Mexicano (PLM).[14] With cross-class support that included women, the PLM had made gains as early as 1906; PLM members were involved in the major strikes across the country, including those in Río Blanco and Cananea, and they participated in numerous strikes initiated by railroad workers in 1908.[15]

In the late nineteenth century and first years of the twentieth, activists who opposed Díaz had met to launch a revolution to remove him from power. Organizing the PLM branch in San Luis Potosí were Camilo Arriaga, an affluent norteño, and Ricardo and Enrique Flores Magón, the intellectual siblings who would come to represent the anarchist branch of the Revolution. The PLM traversed national boundaries, garnering female support from both sides of the border. As the historian Emma Pérez has argued, "the discourse of the revolution knew no boundaries. Language, words, *corridos,* and concepts crossed back and forth along the Mexico-U.S. border."[16] By fully participating in the PLM and other radical groups, women proved critical in carrying the message of the Revolution and acting on it. While much attention has been paid to the wave of immigration sparked by the Revolution, not until recently have scholars addressed the revolutionary work performed by women transnationals, who frequently criticized both nation-states. Sara Estela Ramírez and Andrea and Teresa Villarreal, two sisters from Nuevo León, were women who represented the radical wing of the Revolution and played a crucial role in spreading revolutionary ideology. Ramírez, born in Coahuila, immigrated to Texas and eventually settled in Laredo at the age of seventeen. She was a poet and activist who wrote on behalf of Mexican women. Her writings, in the form of articles, poems, and other works, were published in *La Crónica* and *El Démocrata Fronterizo.* Andrea and Teresa Villarreal addressed issues affecting the transnational community while writing for newspapers, including *El Obrero* and *La Mujer Moderna.*[17] They wrote about "the need to educate the proletariat along the U.S.-Mexico border."[18] Still, other women of more affluent backgrounds, including those who sought to create and sustain a "Mexico de afuera," made Texas their home.[19]

Women writers who adhered to the PLM used a gendered rhetoric to promote women's labor rights. Isidra T. de Cárdenas, for example, founded *La Voz de la Mujer* in El Paso to advance a pro-women, pro-PLM agenda. *La Voz de la Mujer* and *El Obrero,* founded in 1909 in San Antonio by Teresa Villarreal, were publications that represented ethnic Mexican women's decision to act on "the need to disrupt the social formation."[20] *La Voz de la Mujer* employed the concept of the family, and, as one editorial in that newspaper stated, "women are an integral part of the great human family; therefore, it is their duty and right to demand and struggle for the dignification of their country."[21]

Women from Tamaulipas, Nuevo León, and Texas would come to support the PLM as uprisings were plotted in the region. They would form part of "Zone Three," which comprised the northern border states and was considered the "best organized" of the five-zone PLM organization, given the radical activity on the north side of the border.[22] After a series of attacks planned for 1906 failed, in July 1910 PLM member Higinio Tanguma, a worker from the Hacienda de Santa María (formerly owned by Manuel González but by 1910 the property of the wealthy and influential Bartolo Rodríguez), finally led a group of PLM supporters who called for the taking of the offices of the hacienda and the burning of all records. Tanguma gathered thirty-six peons and ranch hands and proceeded to burn down the building containing all of the records. Riding their horses and wearing their large sombreros, Tanguma and the men waved a handmade red silk flag embroidered with "¡Viva Tierra y Libertad!"[23] Echoing the words of Villa and the southern Mexican revolutionary Emiliano Zapata, Tanguma and the workers' actions symbolized widespread discontent over working conditions, and their raid was a direct attack on debt peonage.

After Tanguma's successful attack on Hacienda de Santa María, he found himself in the Rio Grande Valley in late 1910 and early 1911, securing recruits. Using the rhetoric of the Revolution and its principal goals of land reform, worker autonomy, and the right to a dignified way of life, he quickly garnered support on the Texas side of the border. Matamoros authorities received word that armed Mexicans in Brownsville and from all across the Rio Grande Valley

TABLE 7. Population of Tamaulipas and Nuevo León by gender, 1910

	Male	*Female*
Tamaulipas	126,888	122,752
Nuevo León	183,353	181,897

Source: Visión histórica de la frontera norte, 133.

were busy recruiting; Tanguma led some four hundred Mexicans and possibly Mexican Americans, and together they prepared to cross into Mexico. Tanguma had garnered recruits from Cameron, Hidalgo, and Nueces Counties. The planned assault failed. Tanguma was detained in Brownsville on February 17, 1911. Sometime between late February and the summer, Tanguma was released.[24]

Supporting Madero but with clear Magonista rhetoric, Tanguma, along with Blas Vázquez and Zacarías Flores, summed up the frustrations of locals in an issue of the PLM newsletter published in 1911. These PLM norteños outlined the basic problems existing in their country in a proclamation in *La Bandera Roja en Tamaulipas.*[25] The PLM became one of the most outspoken advocates of the working class in Mexico and in the United States and one of the most vocal supporters of women's labor rights. Tanguma, Vázquez, and Flores claimed to be "workers who are willing to join in the fight to redeem those belonging to our class, the poor."[26] Women, according to the PLM, were part of that same exploited "class . . . , the poor."[27]

One of the main concerns of the PLM, and particularly of Ricardo Flores Magón, was implementing a minimum wage for women. In the textile mills of Mexico, women earned two-thirds to three-fourths of males' wages and even less as compared to men in heavier industries, particularly steel and oil. Even in the factories of Monterrey that paid better wages, women still earned less than men. As early as 1906, the Flores Magón brothers had noted the depressed wages of women, calling for a minimum national daily wage of forty centavos.[28] The activism of these Mexican brothers and their supporters in the United States also incorporated the same rhetoric to address conditions for women on the Texas side of the border.[29] Sara Estela Ramírez, a PLM supporter herself and a major player in the organization, used the leadership experience she gained in advancing the revolutionary principles of the PLM and general socioeconomic improvement in Mexico and applied those principles to the Texas situation, particularly to improve the labor conditions of fellow working Mexicans.[30]

Indeed, the Revolution provided a unique opportunity to address labor conditions in Texas. Scores of peons and rancheros and small landowners who had supported the revolutionary rhetoric left the area, choosing to cross into Texas. However, they maintained communication with relatives and friends in the Northeast. PLM supporters active in Tamaulipas and workers who had heard about the PLM agenda crossed the river, carrying with them ideas about socioeconomic justice. The ideology of the PLM underscored a Mexican nationalism that was anti-American and called for worker autonomy, which directly challenged industrial capitalism and commercial agriculture. It questioned the low wages in the expanding commercial agricultural enterprises led by Anglo and affluent Mexican growers not only in Tamaulipas and Nuevo León but also in the fertile Rio Grande Valley just across the border.[31]

Norteños heeded the call for revolution and proceeded to attack private property belonging to regional elites and foreigners. K. H. Merren, the superintendent of the Mexican Realty Company and owner of the citrus-producing Hacienda La Victoria near Xicotencatl, witnessed violence against foreigners, some of whom were his business partners. A supporter of American capital, Merren complained to local authorities about the numerous attacks on Americans by Mexican citizens. Merren claimed that "all Americans were ordered out of Mexico in 1913" and argued that rebels from "all factions" took valuable materials and tools from his hacienda and nearby estates. Revolutionaries took what they could and destroyed what had been an estate comprising approximately two hundred acres with twenty thousand citrus fruit trees, as well as numerous acres of henequen. Carrancistas under Gen. Agustín Castro attacked the hacienda in 1913, other military contingents attacked it during 1914, and César López de Lara's supporters attacked once again in 1915. Merren represented the pro-American segment of growers in the region and would continue submitting complaints pertaining to assaults and property destruction for the next three years.[32]

Sharing the same fate as Hacienda La Victoria, the Hacienda San José de las Rusias "became the scene of serious agrarian troubles."[33] Through purchases and leases, American investors, represented by H. C. Swanson and E. T. Rowson, had gained access to a huge tract of land in northern Tamaulipas—4.5 million acres. Through a collaborative agreement, regional elites Iñigo Noriega, Félix Díaz, former president Manuel González of Matamoros, and his son, Manuel González Jr., came to control the commercial estate.[34] During the early years of the Revolution, Mexicans from surrounding areas in Tamaulipas claimed rights to the hacienda and accompanying ranch lands, arguing that the properties belonged to Mexicans, not foreigners. Similarly, by 1915 Mexicans were headed toward the "prized orchards" of the American-owned Blalock Colony, which comprised nearly 1.25 million acres. The Mexicans stole fruit while others camped on the property. American colonists, including Pleasant E. Crabtree, Charles B. Pettus, and Seymour Taylor, had no choice but to abandon the farms. Due to the numerous attacks, the majority of the residents abandoned the estate, reclaiming it only in the 1930s.[35]

That same ideology of worker autonomy, land reform, and the right to a dignified way of life appealed to Mexican immigrants residing and working in Texas during the Revolution. As working and living conditions for people of Mexican descent in Texas worsened, the revolutionary cause made a lot of sense to them. From 1911 through 1917 scores of PLM-affiliated local branches emerged.

A total of fifty-two branches, and possibly more, were organized throughout Texas (see appendix 1). A handful of these PLM-affiliated groups had been organized by women or included women. In 1913 ethnic Mexican women founded Grupo Regeneración "Prismas Anarquistas" in Burkett, Texas. The group was founded by Alida Martínez, who in her public speech to commemorate the inauguration of Prismas Anarquistas, reminded her compañeras that "what brings us together, our goal, is to come together as a group so that our demands may be heard. . . . While we are weak women, we also have rights to life, especially when it is us that sustain the human race." The discussion on labor rights was shaped by a specific rhetoric emphasizing women's role as the reproducers of community, underscoring their maternal role. Martínez closed by reminding the women that "we have the unavoidable obligation to defend this right and to die for it if possible."[36] Similar groups emerged in the state; in Morin, Texas, for example, Grupo Femenino "Aspiraciones Libres" was founded in 1912, with goals similar to those of the Prismas Anarquistas.[37]

Mexican women on both sides of the border worked to promote their ideas to the public. One organization that comprised a great number of women dedicated to advancing the goals of the Revolution in the area of labor, education, and medical assistance was the Brigada Cruz Azul.[38] One Cruz Azul member, Sra. Vallado de González, spoke of "*abnegación, caridad y patriotismo,* virtues held close to women's bosom."[39] In fact, "abnegation, charity, and patriotism" formed the main tenets of the Cruz Azul. The organization and its numerous branches throughout the region had a large female membership. The Cruz Azul became one of the leading organizations to use the unique opportunity that the Mexican Revolution and its aftermath offered to women. It also blurred gender lines, if only temporarily, combining women's and men's charitable works for the common good. As Ephraim Frisch, rabbi of Temple Bethel in San Antonio, put it, "[the Cruz Azul] is engaged in a noble labor of bringing relief to the stricken and of uniting men and women into the common bonds of humanitarian sentiment and service."[40] By the end of the Revolution the organization had branches extending to southern Texas, in cities such as San Juan.[41]

Speaking on behalf of all working Mexican women and moving beyond women's roles as mothers, Laredo native Jovita Idar, an activist, educator, journalist, and supporter of the Cruz Azul, vehemently advocated gender equity. She wrote, "If men and women are to be made better spiritually, better morally, and if they are to enjoy a better social life and greater opportunities for education, self-expression, and self-development, then they must live under conditions that make for the enjoyment and realization of these things."[42] To be sure, Idar exemplified the ardent activism expressed by female labor and social leaders on both

Jovita Idar. (Courtesy University of Texas at San Antonio Libraries Special Collections)

sides of the border. Idar is well known for her leadership and participation in the Primer Congreso Mexicanista, the first cultural conference organized by ethnic Mexicans to address issues affecting the Mexican community. As the scholar José Limón has pointed out, "Texas-Mexican women and their particular social problems received the attention of the congreso."[43] Educator Soledad Flores de Peña expressed her concern about Mexican women when she argued, "It is necessary to understand each and every one of our responsibilities. . . . I believe that in order to achieve this[,] the best means is to educate women, instruct her, and at the same time respect and support her."[44] Women also contributed to a broader discussion that was not necessarily viewed in gendered terms; they protested against social, political, and economic discrimination. In fact, Idar, like her African American counterpart, Ida Wells Barnett, vehemently opposed the lynching of Mexicans throughout the Southwest. She also took it upon herself to write in opposition to Pres. Woodrow Wilson's decision to send troops to the border during the height of the Mexican Revolution; when the Texas Rangers attempted to close her family's newspaper, she stood up to the agents, refusing to allow them to enter the premises.[45]

Idar also presided over La Liga Femenil Mexicanista, a pioneering organization dedicated to the advancement of Mexican women's rights. Founded in October 1911, the organization crossed national boundaries by also operating in the Tamaulipas town of Nuevo Laredo. Besides assisting in the area of promoting women's education and children's bilingual education, the organization extended aid to immigrant families. Regarding the latter, Idar focused on the working conditions of immigrants but zeroed in on working women. Her activist writings advocated "equality with respect to men's work in order for women to integrate themselves into society and demand political rights."[46] Her article, "Debemos Trabajar" (We should work), which appeared in *La Crónica* on November 23, 1911, expressed Idar's ideal of the modern working woman. According to Idar, women should strive to exit the domestic sphere and work. She wrote that "the obrera recognizes her rights, proudly raises her head and joins the struggle, the time of her degradation is over, she is no longer a slave sold for some coins, she is no longer a servant, but the equal of a man."[47] The Revolution had carved out an opening for women to vocalize issues of gender equity that certainly could have appeared as radical during peacetime. For Idar, the Revolution did not create or lead to her activism; the Revolution strengthened her female consciousness. She had witnessed not only the deplorable conditions in which her fellow Mexicans and Mexican Americans found themselves but also the problem of women's second-class status. The revolutionary rhetoric of worker autonomy, labor rights, and women's rights further heightened Idar's activist outlook.

The kind of revolution that had taken shape in Mexico and whose ideas had been carried across the border influenced women to claim labor rights. At the same time, it had helped to promote the cause of women's issues in general. Mexican immigrant women and *tejanas,* through their writings and activism, exemplified what Emma Peréz called "a kind of renaissance [for women]."[48] Idar wrote in a letter that "I am not content with what my modest cooperative work has accomplished for the present revolution [referring to her service to the Cruz Azul]. . . . When noble and loyal friends of the revolution appeared at my door with the mutilated and bloody bodies of our soldiers, my heart jumped, and since that moment, my life was transformed."[49] Idar's position as an educated writer from the progressive and well-established Idar family of Laredo allowed her to claim a privileged space in a transnational community and speak out on behalf of working-class women and their families. Idar wrote extensively for the family newspaper *La Crónica* (Laredo), as well as for *El Eco de Corpus Christi* and *La Luz* (San Benito). She also founded *Evolución* in 1916, which ran until 1920, and co-edited *El Heraldo Cristiano,* published by the Rio Grande

Methodist Church Conference.[50] As an activist, educator, and journalist, Idar addressed issues concerning working-class women who labored as cotton pickers, *lavanderas* in commercial laundries, domestic workers, and in other occupations, spreading a transnational message of labor activism. Indeed, her writings, often under the pseudonym "Astrea," cut across national and gender boundaries, addressing gender equity and other issues affecting the Mexican community on both sides of the border.[51]

It should be noted that Idar's contributions were highly radical as compared to those of other women from the region. Not all women experienced the Revolution in the same way. For Esther González Salinas of Matamoros, the revolutionary rhetoric prevalent at that time produced different results. Salinas had spent her life as an educator at schools for girls in Matamoros, Reynosa, and Villa Hidalgo, Tamaulipas. When the civil war broke out, she headed to Texas, where she continued to work as an educator. Within a short period of time, Salinas, who had been living in San Diego, Texas, founded a Spanish-speaking school, which she named "México." She later opened up a similar school in Kingsville. After the Revolution, she returned to Matamoros, where she lived and taught for the rest of her life.[52] The threat of violence and war caused by the Revolution led to an increase in immigration, and for González Salinas, like many others, it had provided an opportunity to continue her work as an educator on the north side of the border.

Conditions north of the Río Grande resembled those in Nuevo León. Residents in that state complained about the lack of political freedom and took their frustrations to the streets, facing jail time, hefty fines, and even death. The suppression of alternative political ideas, the gross violations of human rights, including the use of whips on hacienda workers, and racial tensions at haciendas and factories, as well as limited political rights for women, only fed the mounting social unrest. Throughout Mexico the social and political discontent grew. In the southern part of the country Zapatistas led by the muleskinner and *ejidatario*-farmer Emiliano Zapata fought against old Spanish and mestizo hacendados and sugar capitalists. Others, including the muleskinner Pascual Orozco, supported *maderismo* and later Carranza and rallied a mass of norteños.[53]

By 1913 the Revolution was felt in almost every corner of the Northeast. In La Fama, a textile factory financed by Charles Stillman and Joseph Morell and later managed by Florentino Cantú, "the situation with the *obreros* was bad." Cantú telegraphed the labor department in Mexico City that the textile workers were "driving him mad" and 3 "unruly *obreros*" out of a labor force of 120 demanded higher wages and were threatening to strike. The strike at the nearby La Leóna textile factory concerned Cantú and spurred him to seek help.[54] Hacendados throughout the region and factory owners also complained to the labor department about the threats and demands made by their workers.[55] Workers from the Hacienda La Peña in Miquihuana rebelled and complained about the "work pressures and bad pay." At the nearby Hacienda San Carlos domestic servants submitted complaints regarding "bad treatment." Workers from Ferrocarriles Nacionales in Tampico organized a strike due to unpaid wages, and by the summer the Gremio Unido de Alijadores of Tampico (GUA), organized in 1911, had rebelled against American contractor Edward Rowley, who threatened to dissolve their organization.[56]

The GUA "had now become part of the revolution."[57] GUA members had been influenced by the Casa del Obrero Mundial members whose Tampico branch was among the most radical and well-organized recruiting centers in the country. Similarly, the International Workers of the World had organized one of the strongest international labor organizations, and it appealed to a segment of the working class. However, nationalism among members of the Mexican working class, particularly in foreign-controlled sectors, placed limitations on such international-based organizing.[58]

In 1918 workers were still walking off jobs, demanding better working conditions. At Compañía La Industrial in Monterrey, the owner confidently reported to the labor department that the situation "could not get out of control" since only thirty workers had walked off their jobs. The owner's accountant, A. García Rodríguez, claimed that "it was absurd that workers asked for a peso for the weaving of a *pieza de manta* [cloth-based product], as some agitators made them believe they deserved."[59] The workers resented the fact that La Industrial, one of ten businesses in the state of Nuevo León with more than one hundred workers and with a capital outlay of more than 400,000 pesos, refused to increase their wages. When the strike ended, the owner demanded that the workers return to work, but they refused. The owner then proceeded to order the workers move out of their company-owned houses, but they reported that they "would leave only if they were kicked out."[60] Soon thereafter, several obreros returned to their jobs, giving the owner a pretext to declare victory. The others found employment at Garza Sada, the local Cervecería Cuauhtémoc brewery, and at a smelter, the Gran Fundición de Fierro y Acero. Those who went to work in the brewery and the smelter soon met other radicalized workers. As they entered the factory, they encountered workers who had been involved in work stoppages and had advocated worker control of the factories. In the Gran Fundición de Fierro y Acero three strikes took place between 1918 and 1922.[61]

Strikes became widespread as the layoffs and slow industrial production continued and because substandard conditions prevailed in industrial establishments.

Labor department reports detailed the deplorable working conditions throughout the country and in the North, despite higher wages offered in some industrial establishments to retain a population that historically viewed the United States as an escape valve. One labor report in the fall of 1911 described the appalling working conditions: "there is lack of hygiene in many factories and shops and safety work regulations regarding the workers' health are nonexistent." The report also indicated that "friction and tension between . . . bosses and workers . . . is less intimate [i.e., became more formal in nature and structure]."[62] Lastly, the report referenced the abundance of labor recruiters who "take advantage of workers who fall prey to their abuses; they [*enganchadores*] exploit the ingenuousness and ignorance of a people who is simple and in great [economic] need."[63]

In the countryside, train service was disrupted. Revolutionaries stopped trains and co-opted them for use as troop transportation and for moving supplies to various locations. They often targeted rancherías and haciendas as places to secure provisions or to serve as their bases of operations.[64] El Porvenir, a cattle, horse, and fruit operation about eighteen miles from Reynosa, became a target of Carrancista general Lucio Blanco. As Blanco and Col. Cesareo Castro moved their four-hundred-man army to Reynosa, the majority of the inhabitants of the town fled to the city of Hidalgo, Texas, while others headed east toward Matamoros. The general and his troops camped near the Hacienda El Porvenir after their victory in the Battle of Reynosa against Huertistas in August 1913. The owner of the ranch, Antonio Piña, an American citizen, had crossed the river into Hidalgo County during Blanco's attack. Through a variety of messengers, Blanco demanded money from Piña "to sustain Carranza's revolution" and threatened to confiscate the property. Piña denied him the money, and several days later, on August 11, Blanco confiscated the ranch.[65]

Blanco, Castro, and their men moved several miles east to Río Bravo. Men, women, and children from Río Bravo and nearby rancherías crossed into Texas as Carrancistas proceeded to take the small town. The major commercial estate in the area, La Sauteña Compañía Agrícola, would become Blanco's target. Following Blanco's orders, Carrancistas kidnapped Juan Alamía, a thirty-four-year-old employee of the Sauteña estate, shot him twice in the head, and then hanged him from a water tower. The Sauteña, located along the banks of the Río Grande, comprised one million acres of land, stretching from the Río Grande to the Río San Fernando and west toward the boundary between Nuevo León and Tamaulipas.[66]

By the end of August the general had moved his troops to the cotton- and corn-producing Hacienda Los Borregos, another American-controlled estate, on the outskirts of Matamoros. Los Borregos had belonged to the president's nephew, Félix Díaz, and had capital investments from the Texas Company of Mexico. Without consulting Carranza, Blanco proceeded to distribute the Borregos lands among local campesinos, thus carrying out one of the principal goals of the Revolution. Calling his soldiers "*representantes del proletariado,*" or representatives of the proletariat, Blanco gave land to eleven peons who worked on the hacienda.[67] The general's actions, however, caused Carranza to relocate him to western Mexico given that, by 1913, Carranza was collaborating with American capitalists in the region, including the Texas Company of Mexico, represented by Joseph Cullinan, Richard E. Brooks, Edwin Jessop Marshall, and Will Hogg.[68] That same year, Alberto Carrera Torres promulgated his Ley Agraria, which served as a blueprint for the Ley del 6 enero de 1915.[69]

Attacks on foreign properties continued well into the Revolution period. In the spring of 1919 ten men armed with pistols and rifles headed toward the refinery grounds of Edward Doheny and Weetman Pearson's Mexican Petroleum Company in the early hours of the morning. The men broke windows, threatened the workers, took twenty-five dollars in cash, and burned several offices. The workers notified company headquarters the following day, describing the assailants as "dressed in khaki pants and wearing *tejano* hats."[70] With few alternatives, several foreign oil companies turned to Mexican citizens willing to protect them in exchange for a hefty dollar amount.

Tired of the continuous depravations by rebels and government troops alike, Doheny and Pearson created a pact with local strongmen who knew the region and could recruit locals to work for them. The most notorious agreement was between El Aguila and Manuel Peláez, a Huasteco. Born in Temapache near Tuxpan, Veracruz, Peláez and his family owned the Haciendas Potrero del Llano and Tierra Amarilla, both rich in petroleum. Peláez grew up in a ranchero family dedicated to the raising of cattle. Acquiring the title of "El Cacique de la Huasteca," Peláez made a fortune receiving payments from companies, including El Aguila, to use on his family's land for oil explorations. However, in 1916 Peláez agreed to cooperate and protect the interests of El Aguila and other foreign oil companies with his *guardias blancas* (white guards), as Peláez's men became known. Pearson and Doheny each agreed to pay Peláez a sum of five thousand dollars per month. Peláez did not receive money only from them, however. The Pennsylvania Mexican Fuel Company agreed to pay him three thousand dollars.[71] The US media "always treated Peláez well," and he was seen as "a strong defender of the allies vis-à-vis the *germanofilia* of President Venustiano Carranza."[72] Controlled by Peláez and Félix Díaz, the nephew of the now exiled dictator, the Huasteca region and its oil were important resources during World War I and as such contributed to the internal problems in Mexico.[73]

Unlike Mexican families who rented and eventually sold their lands at low prices to petroleum companies, Peláez sought to obtain the highest returns, and he played his cards well. In a 1957 interview with the historian Gabriel Menéndez, Peláez recounted how he advised Eufrosina Flores, a Mexican woman, to negotiate a higher rent for her lands in oil-rich Cerro Azul in Veracruz. When Doheny asked Eufrosina's husband, Hilario Jacinto, to cosign the lease, which gave his company virtually full rights over the lands, Jacinto sought legal advice and later claimed that Doheny's men had threatened him. Jacinto transferred the subsoil rights to his sister. But Doheny's luck did not run out. Before the lawsuit could be filed (it was never filed) Jacinto met an untimely death; a Mexican man stabbed Jacinto while he enjoyed a beer at a local bar. Rumors about Doheny's involvement in Jacinto's murder circulated in the region.[74]

With the financial backing of William Salomon of Salomon Brothers of New York, Edward Doheny organized the Huasteca Petroleum Company in 1906 as a subsidiary of his Mexican Petroleum firm. By the last years of the Revolution, Doheny's properties totaled more than six hundred thousand acres, encompassing southern Tamaulipas and northern Veracruz. Eufrosina Flores's lands soon became part of Doheny's oil fields. Fearing for her life, the widow had sold her Cerro Azul property to Doheny for 500,000 pesos. Before she sold the properties, and sometime after her husband's death, Eufrosina had received a marriage proposal from a Huasteca Petroleum *trabajador de confianza* (trustworthy employee) along with a bid for Cerro Azul. Peláez advised Eufrosina not to sell at that price. The instability along the Tamaulipas-Veracruz border and fear, however, forced Eufrosina to sell her property and abandon her native Huasteca lands forever.[75]

Eufrosina's story also sheds light on the variety of ways in which gender frequently intersected and interfered with business matters. Eufrosina's position as a widow gave her the power to negotiate with companies as daunting and lucrative as Huasteca Petroleum. Unlike many Huasteco and mestizo men native to the region, Eufrosina, described as an Indian, managed to negotiate the terms of her land sale. Her position as a wealthy Indian (probably Huasteco) allowed Eufrosina to rent parts of her land while living on it as well. For other natives the choices were limited. Indigenous and poor mestizo communities witnessed how frequent, uncontrollable oil gushers damaged their fields and rivers and observed firsthand how quickly their environment was being destroyed. Labor recruiters working for the oil companies often forced indigenous and mestizo men to leave the fields, thus converting farmers into reluctant industrial workers. Company labor brokers went to great lengths to acquire and retain a steady workforce, not shying away from physically forcing individuals to perform the labor. Even so, many of the new workers consciously or unconsciously disrupted oil production as they abandoned their jobs when harvest time arrived; they were effectively part-time industrial workers and part-time agriculturalists. But for those with economically superior positions such as Eufrosina, the social reality was different.

On the one hand, Eufrosina could dispose of her property as she pleased, without having to defer to her husband or a male guardian, yet that same source of power placed her in a position of vulnerability. Appearing perhaps defenseless and without the protection of a man in Edward Doheny's view—so much that one of his employees attempted to court her and then persuade her to sell—Eufrosina nonetheless stood her ground against the oil company.

However, the power of oil would win the day over Eufrosina and other inhabitants but at a high cost. Oil companies had no choice but to acknowledge the complaints and demands of the labor force. For Peláez, the story had a different outcome. Peláez would earn a higher profit. Soon, the cacique began hiring hundreds of local Mexicans, predominantly mestizos and Huastecos. Most of them labored at the various *pozos,* or oil wells, now controlled by Doheny. Peláez's familiarity with the locals and new migrants aided him in his fight against Carranza's troops for control of the oil fields; he had assumed the role of an *enganchador* for several oil companies and was supervising at one point up to five thousand workers who had recently arrived, "attracted by new jobs and high[er] wages." Peláez supervised new arrivals and residents with what one water vendor working for an oil company called "Indians with large white pants and big hats [*indios calzonudos con tamaños sombrerotes*]."[76] Peláez was well connected and played the role of a transnational power broker who was frequently sought by US investors in need of protection. In 1919 he traveled to New Orleans to "obtain resources to protect the oil region," and he also held "important meetings with notable American politicians."[77] Peláez's transformation from ranchero to powerful transnational oil labor broker and defender of foreign interests placed him at the forefront of not only the Revolution in the Northeast but also the larger international struggle for oil and power.

On other occasions, American investors themselves served as the first line of defense for their properties. Before being expelled from Tamaulipas, William Mangum Hanson from Hacienda El Conejo served as secretary and general manager of the Tamesi Petroleum and Asphalt Company and of Standard Petroleum Company. During the Madero and later Carranza fight against Huertistas, his hacienda served as a base for operations that included protecting the property, spying on Mexican affairs, and reporting to officials in Texas and Washington, D.C. A transnational agent of sorts, Hanson not only promoted American

Lucio Blanco at the *Hacienda Los Borregos* (August 1913).

investments in the region but also provided detailed reports on troop movements and was key in shaping racial attitudes about Mexicans. Hanson and other investors believed that Mexicans welcomed American oil companies and Anglo growers; they believed they were doing Mexican laborers a favor.[78]

American companies hired thugs to protect themselves and other foreigners in the oil business, and this strategy worked for a short period of time. Meanwhile, in the more isolated commercial haciendas, foreigners were not as lucky. Americans living on these estates faced frequent attacks from Mexican citizens expressing their discontent over foreign control of properties. During 1917 and 1918 James R. Clayton, owner of the Hacienda El Caracol in Padilla, reported numerous rebel attacks on his property. These men, wrote Clayton, "from time to time . . . ordered property and farm products delivered to them" and often "took the same without permission . . . without paying for the same in any manner."[79]

Companies also hired noted military officials for protection. E. P. Nafarrate, who during 1915 and 1916 served as commander of the Constitutionalist forces in the Northeast, by 1922 was reportedly working for the Texas Company of Mexico.

He shared updates on new oil explorations with his friend Teódulo Ramírez, who had fought for Carranza in Matamoros, Palmillas, Tula, and in Nuevo León and had played a crucial role in keeping the pro-Villa Carrera Torres brothers at bay. He wrote, "Companies are now drilling new holes in the region, including the Texas Company, for whom I work."[80] With or without protection, companies faced attacks by Mexicans.[81]

Antonio Piña, whose property had been confiscated by Lucio Blanco, and other growers and large-scale ranchers living between Reynosa and present-day Río Bravo complained that "*caballadas de la gente de tropa* [soldiers' horses] frequently invaded their crops and lands."[82] Local authorities were intimidated by the large number of complaints and revolutionaries, given that their only source of protection was a small contingent of *policías rurales.*[83]

Like Piña, Bartolo Rodríguez, a regional elite and supporter of American interests in Tamaulipas, also complained about attacks on property and incursions by revolutionaries. When Madero was newly elected, Rodríguez wrote to him in early 1912 and explained,

> *This critical situation forces all good citizens to contribute their services in whichever form possible. . . . The state [Tamaulipas] has entered a period of great agitation not due to politics . . . but due to banditry, because they [bandoleros] only murder and steal as it has just happened in the Hacienda de Acuña and neighboring estates. I come to you asking for arms and ammunition, at least 300 rifles and the necessary ammunition for the defense of our lands and* gente conocida. *We are responsible for our actions . . . we who subscribe to you form this league as hacendados* de mayor capital y mejor prestigio *[league of landowners with significant wealth and great prestige] in the Southern District of Tamaulipas.*[84]

In a second letter, Rodríguez informed Madero that he and his fellow hacendados had petitioned him directly, instead of Gov. Joaquín Arguelles, given the "very critical situation." Rodríguez also reminded Madero that among the old haciendas "were those very powerful American companies such as Conejo Land Co. and Caleta Land Co." The Tampico cattle rancher continued in a threatening tone, writing "that the [American] companies had invested more than two million pesos in agriculture and we do not want any attacks on them."[85] Rodríguez's plea regarding not only his properties but foreign companies' properties exemplified the cooperation between regional elites and Americans that had begun during the Prieto and Reyes administrations and by 1911 was deeply entrenched in norteño society.

W. M. Hanson of the Conejo Hacienda was representative of the successful American investor-*políticos* who had been prominent in the region since the early years of the Porfiriato. By 1898 Hanson was already residing along the border in Laredo and was working as a US marshal for the Western District of Texas. By 1906 he had crossed the border to manage the thirty-thousand-acre Hacienda El Conejo, near Xicotencatl, some eighty miles northwest of Tampico. With tens of thousands of citrus trees on his hacienda, "Hanson became one of the most important citrus growers in the country." He also served as president of the Buena Vista Land and Irrigation Company, which oversaw operations of the eight-thousand-acre Hacienda San Procopio. He owned the three-thousand-acre, citrus-producing Hacienda Guadalupe. During the Revolution, Hanson, fearing for his life and property, quickly moved against Maderistas by working as a secret agent paid by the Mexican government. His Conejo Hacienda was the base for antirevolutionary forces under his command. When Victoriano Huerta took the reins of the government in early 1913, Hanson breathed a bit easier.[86] The fury of the Revolution would spare neither these American investors nor the native regional elites who supported them.[87] By 1914 the Conejo estate had been largely destroyed in the bloody confrontations between Huertistas and Carrancistas. Hanson attempted to get compensation from the Carranza government, but his espionage activities for the Díaz and Huerta governments were soon discovered and pro-Carranza forces under Luis Caballero apprehended him. Hanson was spared execution thanks to the intervention of Mexican allies such as K. H. Merren of Hacienda La Victoria and the American consul. He left Tamaulipas for Texas in 1914 and worked for a railroad company; from north of the Río Grande, he continued to provide materials to antirevolutionary forces under Félix Díaz.[88]

Similarly, in southern Tamaulipas Vicente Cedillo and Alberto Carrera Torres, along with their "Voluntarios de Tamaulipas," fought Huertista troops over control of the region, particularly Tula, Guadalcazar, and Ciudad del Maíz. Carrera Torres, a rural teacher turned revolutionary, emerged as a pro-Madero rebel and later Villa supporter who ably gathered recruited mid-sized rancheros and campesinos. He became "Jefe del Ejército Libertador de Tamaulipas" in the Tula area. Carrera Torres had been influenced by PLM ideology. His elementary professor, Manuel Villasana Ortíz, who worked for *El Tulteco,* a progressive newspaper in Tula, influenced the young Carrera Torres. PLM junta proclamations endorsed by the Flores Magón brothers while in the United States were reprinted in *El Tulteco* and detailed the politically motivated arrests of journalists. Carrera Torres had grown up in rural southern Tamaulipas, where record-low wages were reported among the ixtle *tallanderas* and *tallanderos.* The break between Villista supporters and Carrancistas, however, would create divisions in the Northeast, with most Villista supporters being in the southern region. Carrera Torres would remain a hard-core Villista until the end. The citizens of Tula and Bustamante, who by 1913 had grown accustomed to the frequency of the fighting, remained loyal to Carrera Torres.[89] For the cross-class alliance of small rancheros, like the Carrera Torres family, with peons, the affair between the two factions became part of their daily lives. Tula resident Ursula Tapia became involved in the conflict by traveling with her insurgent brothers and father, who supported the Carrera Torres family. Ursula explained the reason for the uprising in her own words years after the Revolution ended: "I knew about the lands. I always heard people talk about that. My father dreamt of a little piece of land."[90]

Ursula and her family epitomized the experiences and struggles of many norteño families who took part in the Revolution. More importantly, their experiences point to the very intimate relationship between war and family. Ursula, her father, and her brothers became fighters in their community. The Tapia family regularly escaped to the mountains of the Huasteca, "where the government could not reach [them.]" According to Ursula, the government troops, whom she called *pelones,* avoided the mountains because they were "unwilling to risk their lives." The small population of both indigenous Huastecos, who had lived in the mountainous eastern region of San Luis Potosí, parts of Hidalgo and Veracruz, and southern Tamaulipas since 200 BC, and mestizos endured several years of civil war and often sought refuge in the mountains.[91] Many families left the region to seek refuge in San Luis Potosí and southern Nuevo León or headed toward the center of the state of Tamaulipas, which brought them closer to Texas.[92] Others, like the Tapia family, reinvented themselves, often acting as military contingents when pressured by the very real presence of violence and the consequent threat of death. While popular images of the Revolution, such as those by photographers Agustín Victor Casasola and Robert Runyon, capture the images of families traveling in railcars with troops, the presence and participation of families went beyond simply "riding along."[93] For many families the Revolution became entrenched in their daily lives. Ursula explained that she "was not even thirteen yet and walked through the brush . . . already confronting the government."[94] Further, Ursula's experience reveals certain gender assumptions that intensified with the coming of the war. Her father and brothers wanted to "protect her," yet her active participation in the conflict contrasted with the men's desire to provide "protection." If male family members were expected to "protect" a female member during peacetime, expectations of doing so during the war grew enormously. Ursula was the only woman in her family and was, without a doubt, an extension of her family's honor; thus her "protection" became crucial. The Revolution had provided a new context in which gendered notions of survival and protection acquired new meaning, even as women took up arms and provided the same kind of protection to men. Given the likelihood of sexual assaults, protecting Ursula was of utmost importance to the family.[95]

A similar need for protection, as well as a desire to join the Revolution, drove Alberto Carrera Torres's mother, Juana, to join her sons and her husband, Candelario Carrera Muñoz, as they fought first the Huertistas and then the Carrancistas. As a member of the small ranchero class, she had owned and run a store at the Atarjeas ranch in Bustamante.[96] As the anthropologist Casey Walsh has explained, rancheros would lose land and decline as a class by the first years of the twentieth century. Land concentration and enclosure coupled with the emergence of commercial agriculture in the United States had diminished rancheros' position in the Northeast, and their numbers in the region had decreased due to emigration. Thus, the Carrera Torres family had felt the pressure of socioeconomic change, particularly from the expanding ixtle haciendas in southern Tamaulipas.[97] Such pressures ensured that the Revolution would continue to receive ranchero support. The Carrera Torres matriarch herself engaged in espionage activity, took up arms and fought, provided medical assistance alongside other women, and provided meals to soldiers, thus making it possible for them to continue fighting.[98] Juana, like Ursula Tapia, was representative of not only the major roles entire families played in the Revolution but also the diverse social backgrounds of the revolutionaries and their supporters.

There were also those women, married or single, who chose to remain at home during the Revolution. When possible, soldiers wrote to their wives, and often months passed without soldiers hearing from their families. Teódulo Ramírez, a Carrancista officer, wrote to his wife, Refugia, who remained near the border in Laredo, and told her he was sending a fellow soldier to escort her safely to Matamoros, where he was recuperating: "My dear and never forgotten wife, in this letter I say hello to you and my unforgettable children. . . . I would like to introduce you to Captain Garza[;] he is my confidant, and he will look for you to bring you and my children to me now that it is peaceful and I am tending to a wound. Please talk to him as if it were me . . . your husband who anxiously awaits to see you."[99]

Protecting women family members like Refugia Venabides de Ramírez and Ursula Tapia had become a primary concern for male family members. Yet, for ordinary citizens who lacked access to family members and thus had no protection, the larger community functioned as an extended family. For Paula Serna, community protection meant the difference between life and death. Serna, a teacher in a rural school at a ranchería near Hidalgo, welcomed the "protection" provided by the rancherías' vecinos. From 1911 to 1913 and from 1920 to 1924 neighbors from the ranch area protected Paula when there were military incursions. Assuming a patriarchal role, vecinos claimed the status of "*jefes de familias*" (heads of household) to "support and provide sustenance."[100] One unusual form of protection came in 1915, when Gen. Emiliano P. Nafarrate, overseeing the División del Noreste, informed Tamaulipas residents that those who "lived in cities, *villas,* or *rancherías* were prohibited from carrying arms without proper documentation" from his office. In another protective move, the general issued a call the following year for the widows and orphans of Constitutionalists who had died in battle to submit requests for pensions. He also declared the availability of public assistance to disabled veterans who had given their service to the Constitutionalist cause.[101]

Not all teachers had protection during the fighting, as Paula Serna did. Many school buildings suffered heavy damage and were left without supplies, and as a result teachers abandoned the area. Community members struggled to protect the schools and did the best they could. Petitions from various ranches flooded the offices of local town leaders, as was the case when vecinos from Rancho Soliseño petitioned the Matamoros cabildo to rebuild their schools. Cabildo members found it difficult to secure teachers willing to move to the area, particularly to serve isolated schools for ranch children; it would take the efforts of the entire community to rebuild the school. For the Soliseño community, it was not until 1921 that it finally found a replacement teacher.[102]

Conditions in the region gradually improved. Women and men who had remained in the Northeast during the bloody encounters managed to resume their everyday activities. Tampico resident Guadalupe Juárez requested permission from municipal authorities to rent a small space in the Plaza Méndez to "establish a *puesto* [stall] to sell food." She obtained the required permit and proceeded to go about her daily life, selling a variety of meals in the main square.[103] Many Mexican women who had migrated to Tampico during the oil boom and remained there during the Revolution had to take on any available jobs that provided cash for rent and basic needs. They worked in laundry service, at hotels, and as domestics in the homes of the foreign elite homes; some engaged in legal and extralegal prostitution.[104] Residents began to reconstruct their communities after the destruction. Still others joined loved ones or began new lives in different places, as was the case of Guadalupe Barrera, the soldadera who had fought with Isidro Paz and then moved to Monterrey with him. Others, such as Jovita Idar, continued to write of their revolutionary experiences and demand that women's issues be adequately addressed.

The Revolution had unleashed the frustrations felt by thousands of workers whose main complaints concerned physical abuse, depressed wages, women's labor issues, worker autonomy, and privileges extended to foreigners. The Revolution also provided a space where women expressed their support for the struggle and widened the discourse on worker control to include women's labor issues. As Idar succinctly put it, "the *obrera* recognizes her rights" and would fight to exercise them. As the remaining chapters explain, women from the region on both sides of the border used a variety of strategies to demand labor rights; they would come to couch their political and social agendas within the context of their productive roles as mothers, wives, and daughters. However, as women from both ends of the geopolitical boundary made gains, their labor activism was co-opted and subjugated by a new government that, while it acknowledged women's place and contributions to wage labor, did so with a gendered lens that defined their new role as being compañeras (to their men), the key to the modern nation-state, and the reproducers of community. The success would be a limited one; by the late 1930s, women's labor activism had largely formed part of a government-controlled and supervised labor movement, subjected to labor union patriarchs. Despite attempts to define women's roles in labor and in society more generally, women's activism continued to shape the development of the nation-state and its borders.

Chapter Five

Women's Labor and Activism in the Greater Mexican Borderlands, 1910–1930

When noble and loyal friends of the revolution appeared at my door with the mutilated and bloody bodies of our soldiers, my heart jumped, and since that moment, my life was transformed.

JOVITA IDAR, LAREDO, TEXAS, CA. 1910

Acordamos organizarnos en unión de obreras biendo [*sic*] los años de esclavitud que hasta esta han pasado sobre la clase oprimida. [We organize as a union of workers acknowledging years of slavery to which the working class has been subjected.]

"ESTATUTOS DE LA UNIÓN DE OBRERAS 'FRATERNIDAD FEMENIL,'"
XICOTENCATL, TAMAULIPAS, 1925

IN THE TUMULTUOUS ENVIRONMENT of late nineteenth- and early twentieth-century Mexico, women heard the rhetoric of revolution and adopted it in order to improve working conditions—on both sides of the border. Because of extensive ties between northeastern Mexico and South Texas, the experiences of women residents and transients at this crossroads are better understood within a transnational framework. Women migrated back and forth, maintained ties with family "back home," and shared a common labor experience.[1] More real on a map than in people's everyday lives, the border did not stop the flow of ideas and certainly did not stop cultural exchange. The porous nature of the border in the decades before the 1930s, when the US government began a massive campaign of deportation targeting Mexicans, meant there was a revolving door for laborers from both nation-states. Laborers, mutual-aid societies, and labor organizations—comprising both male and female workers—maintained close ties with one another and, whenever possible, supported each other's agendas. They did so because, to a great extent, they were fighting for the same kinds of things: livable wages, the right to organize and strike, safe working environments, and the right to a dignified way of life. Women also fought for these guarantees, yet they advanced a specific female worker or *obrera* agenda focusing on women's rights in general.[2]

One of the central debates in the historiography of Mexican women is whether or not the Mexican Revolution was in fact "revolutionary" for women. Scholars have focused in particular on whether or not the Revolution shaped labor and gender relations and, if so, how it worked to alter traditional patterns. While feminist historians and historians of women's history tend to agree that the Revolution created opportunities for women to fight alongside males and to express their views concerning women's rights in journals, magazines, and newspapers, opinions on whether or not the Revolution altered gender relations vary.[3] Given the transnational influence of the Revolution, we can pose the same question about Mexican American women or Mexican immigrant women residing on the northern bank of the Río Grande. What exactly did the Revolution mean for working women in this extended borderlands region? What kinds of work did working-class women perform and what was the legacy of the Revolution in the greater Mexican borderlands? The Revolution provided a unique opportunity for women to voice demands, which were often articulated within a revolutionary framework. However, the Revolution did not alter gender relations significantly; gender inequities continued in the workplace and beyond.

Women's Labor during the Revolution

Some women left their mark on the Revolution by contributing to newspapers and journals, teaching, taking up arms, or assisting in the acquisition of weapons in their cross-border activities, while others helped to build the borderlands by working in factories, agriculture, and a variety of other occupations. As women fled across the border to get away from the war in Mexico, they found themselves selling their labor and working in predominantly low-paying jobs, much like their *tejana* counterparts. Working-class Mexican women's labor in the region was concentrated in specific "light" industries or on commercial agricultural estates. Their tasks were frequently paid by the piece and were thus low-paid jobs meant for the unskilled. As was the case in the Tamaulipas and Nuevo León countryside, the greater South Texas border region, including the rural Rio Grande Valley towns of Robstown and Alice, as well as the farms in the more central part of the state, was where thousands of *mexicanas* worked. While a small segment of the female population found jobs laboring in commercial laundries, making cigars, or working in factories, the majority of women toiled in agriculture. Like their male counterparts, they formed part of the "seasonal and migratory workforce for the commercial agriculture that developed in the state in the late nineteenth and early twentieth centuries."[4] Women, working alongside men, contributed to the development of entire cities. Deep in South Texas, on the seven-thousand-acre San Juan Plantation, women picked cotton and worked the sugarcane, alfalfa, and onions in the early twentieth century; the plantation, owned by John Closner, would later become part of the city of San Juan.[5] Farther north, in San Antonio and El Paso, just as in the urban and industrialized center of Monterrey, Mexican women factory workers tended to hold higher-paying jobs.

The Revolution forced many Mexicans to flee the country for safety. A wave of immigrants from all social classes crossed the border to find refuge and work in Texas. The Palomo Acosta sisters, Sabina and Juanita, formed part of this immigrant generation. Sabina arrived in Texas at the tender age of four, and Juanita was born several years after the end of the civil war. From a *campesino* family background, the sisters grew up with this tradition and labored in the spinach and onion farms of South and Central Texas. In 1910 one whole family might have been able to earn up to five dollars a day for picking cotton in counties where the pay was somewhat higher, such as Collin County. Several years later, after the war, each working family member could earn three dollars a day laboring on a Texas farm.[6] Like the Palomo Acosta family, Esteban and Piedad Tijerina Cantú fled Mexico during the Revolution. In 1912, the Cantú family left rural General Bravo, Nuevo León, and became seasonal migrant workers. They traveled to Refugio, Texas, to work the fields, and eventually they were able to purchase land of their own in San Juan, Texas, "where they raised crops such as carrots and cotton."[7]

In the years leading up to the Revolution, an estimated 15 percent of Mexican immigrant women earned wages in the border region of South Texas. Some 17 percent of Mexican women in the El Paso area were earning wages by 1920.[8] However, it is quite possible that the actual numbers are higher, given the uncertain nature of labor statistics because of low reporting, transient workers, and related factors. In the Rio Grande Valley, the majority of the workers were of Mexican descent and wages were relatively low for occupations held by women. In towns such as Laredo and Brownsville jobs available to women included teaching and clerical work. By 1910 ethnic Mexican women had begun to move to larger and more urbanized cities, including San Antonio, Houston, and Dallas. As the historian Emilio Zamora explains, "improved job opportunities [in these urban centers] encouraged the movement of Mexicana workers into industrial occupations."[9] In larger urban areas such as San Antonio, women worked in pecan-shelling and cigar-making establishments, as well as in candy and hat-making shops. In El Paso, large numbers of women worked in commercial laundries and garment factories.[10] Other women, such as Marcelino Solis and Leonor López Alonzo, and their families left Mexico during the Revolution and set up their own small shops. The Solis family opened up a shoe shop, and the Alonsos opened a barbershop. Nearly one hundred years after the Revolution, both businesses were still operating in San Juan and still family owned. In both urban and rural centers, ethnic Mexican women also performed the important job of *partera,* or midwife. Anselma Garza Sloss of San Juan was one of several midwives who served numerous *tejano* and Mexican immigrant families.[11]

Women employed in the hotel and restaurant, manufacturing, and laundry industries earned substandard wages. Mexican women working in hotels and restaurants in the El Paso area, for example, earned an average weekly income of a little less than nine dollars. Those in manufacturing jobs earned close to eight dollars a week. On average, women employed in laundries earned between four and six dollars, fifty-six cents, a week.[12] Many of the *mexicanas* who worked in commercial laundries were heads of households or contributed significantly to the family income. As one laundry worker put it, "I find it difficult to live on my wages, which I turn into the family budget."[13] As the Mexican labor activist Clemente N. Idar said of the wages being paid to female laundry workers, "[they do not permit women] to live decent and respectable lives as American citizens."[14]

As early as 1918, women workers joined the numerous American Federation of Labor (AFL)–affiliated unions in the "*planchaduría y limpia-ropa*" (clothes ironing and laundry) sector. However, apprentices and women were placed in separate categories related to their union membership. While all union members were required to pay one dollar as an initiation fee, male workers paid a monthly fee of eighty-five cents while apprentices and women paid only fifty cents. A fee reduction of twenty-five cents for obreras translated into extra income for the nuclear or extended family. Nonetheless, while the Revolution certainly shaped the rhetoric of labor activism in that gender equity and *compañerismo* (fellowship) were hailed as priorities, the reality was that much of the rhetoric did not alter women's status. The gender discourse grounded in nineteenth-century conceptions of morality, abnegation, and ideas of domesticity and femininity persisted after the Revolution and continued to shape labor relations and helped to maintain women's separate status as reflected in the lower wages they received. They continued to be barred from numerous traditional male unions and continued to assume the double burden of work both at home and outside the home.[15]

Female and male cotton pickers who had escaped debt peonage in Tamaulipas, Nuevo León, and Coahuila encountered similar labor practices when they went to work in Texas. Referring to Mexican agricultural workers, Clemente N. Idar wrote to B. F. Patterson, a pro-labor judge in San Antonio, and explained that they "are treated brutally, abused, and robbed."[16] Female farm workers faced similar treatment and unfavorable labor conditions. Women, alongside their children, siblings, husbands, and fathers, toiled for long hours under the hot Texas sun and encountered harsh labor practices. In Central Texas between Gonzales and San Marcos, at farms in Luling, Fentress, and Martindale, organized farm laborers reported that "hundreds of complaints are made at all times of the year against the cruel treatment they ordinarily get from the land-owners with whom they raise cotton crops."[17] One farm worker became ill, and he and his family "were left in a public road and all the work they had performed in the farm was lost with the exception of the miserable groceries they had been receiving."[18] Not surprisingly, as early as 1911 a PLM branch, "Grupo Regeneración de Agricultores," was organized in the Fentress area.[19]

Working conditions for female migrant workers were among the worst in the region. One farmworker, Miguel Pavia, candidly described the situation for Mexican male and female agricultural workers. He wrote that, "with respect to the . . . agricultural workers' wages, it varies and *esta al antojo del terrateniente* [is at the whim of the landlord] . . . the most they'll pay when they are in real need is $1.50 per day." He continued, "To sum it up, the Mexican farm workers in this area [Central Texas] are like slaves, waged workers and [we are] in the same system as Mexico's *hacendario* [*sic*]."[20] What Mexican immigrants with predominantly campesino backgrounds encountered was a brutal labor system that, while providing higher wages, featured the standard harsh labor practices rampant on haciendas and ranchos throughout northern Mexico. What working-class Mexicans had protested before and during the Revolution were precisely these kinds of labor practices.[21] Indeed, the abolition of debt peonage had ranked high on the list of grievances outlined by revolutionaries.

Engaging in labor activism went beyond simply writing about it. As the farmworker Pavia indicated, "it was not easy to organize." He confessed that "the majority of Mexicans were afraid to organize. . . . However, I have been working hard to promote the worker[s]' cause. . . . I hold meetings every Sunday . . . and I have several individuals who have joined the union."[22] Organizing mutual-aid societies and/or unions had its challenges, particularly for women, who continued to struggle for recognition of their contributions to labor.

Living conditions for Mexican migrant families were substandard, to say the least. If Mexican families were not housed in "empty farm buildings during harvest," they could find themselves "sleep[ing] and cook[ing] on the open road, waiting for seasonal work."[23] Women and their families followed the crops.

During August, Mexicans worked on the cotton harvest in Corpus Christi, Robstown, and other small towns, while another group headed toward the Houston area. Growers from Austin and the vicinity then hired the cotton pickers. By September the workers were headed to other parts of the state.[24] These cotton-picking women in extended families were for the most part transients, often crossing into New Mexico to work until February, when they headed south again, often to the Rio Grande Valley.[25] To make ends meet, Mexican women also tended home gardens and preserved foods. These measures were options mostly for those who remained in their farm homes for long periods of time as compared to women who were itinerant workers.[26]

While data are limited, early studies on Mexican agricultural labor reveal that for the most part the wages of women who were part of a family were distributed to the head of the household, usually a male. For example, in a study of more than two hundred Mexican women in Central Texas, more than half labored in the fields alongside their families. A much smaller percentage "performed field work for hire. . . . Only three women besides the widows received the income from their labor; one of the three was married and the other two, single. . . . In the case of the other married women the husband received all income."[27] For those women who received their wages directly, they amounted to approximately one dollar a day for up to ten hours of work. As has been argued by historians of labor, agricultural work, categorized and defined as unskilled, probably ranked among the worst paid.[28]

Labor contracts drawn up between farmworkers and landowners, or *terratenientes* (as Mexican immigrants called them), frequently named only migrant males and the landowner. However, part of the agreement of payment, housing, and related issues involved women. In 1925 a public announcement about information crucial to Mexican laborers reminded *aparceros* and *medieros* residing in Texas that they "all should have a written contract," particularly by late in the year, since it was in November and December that most contracts were renewed. These workers had to ensure that the landowners specified if the agreement included "*troncos de caballo* [harnesses], field tools, housing, water, and firewood."[29] The announcement specifically stated that "no married man should accept a contract lacking prepayment of at least $30.00 per month."[30] The fact that married male workers were encouraged to seek this prepayment testifies to the critical role of the women in the family for the survival of the workers and support of the household. As the historian Zaragosa Vargas has explained, women and children contributed to all facets of agriculture work.[31] Female farm workers essentially worked double shifts—in the fields and in the shared makeshift homes, where they did the cleaning, washing, mending, and cooking for the entire family. Women continued to perform the double shift after the Revolution and up to the present day. As the *corrido* "Bellos Recuerdos" reminds us, the women workers of the family laboring in the region around El Chapeño, Robstown, and Corpus Christi provided the meals on site: "right at noon, my mother called us, come my children let us eat; under the big truck, we all had refried beans, potatoes, and coffee."[32] While they prepared meals and worked in the fields themselves, the majority of women did not receive wages directly. Frequently, payment to the patriarch (grandfather, father, husband, or the eldest son) included women workers' wages. The 1925 public announcement further explained how the thirty-dollar prepayment should be divided: "$20.00 for provisions and $10.00 for clothes, doctor, and medicines . . . if family has more than two children, the prepayment should be increased proportionately."[33] Finally, Mexicans were advised to ensure that "at least two people you trust accompany you to speak with the *terrateniente*."[34]

To be sure, whether or not women earned "direct" wages, they nonetheless worked just like and just as much as their male counterparts did: on average women picked anywhere between 100 to 150 pounds of cotton a day, and some up to 200 pounds.[35] Besides picking, women hoed and chopped, baled hay, and plowed. As one contemporary investigator explained, "from these Mexican peon women comes cheap labor for the farm and factory. With them, we can raise cotton, cheap cotton; in fact, we can meet almost any price the market will pay and still produce cotton, even though to do it we have to bring across the Rio Grande fresh supplies of labor each year."[36] This worker influx from Mexico included large numbers of women.

The kinds of gendered labor issues raised by Jovita Idar and others resonated with the large numbers of Mexican women workers even after the military phase of the Revolution had ended. In October 1918 ethnic Mexican women employed in the commercial laundry business in El Paso vehemently protested the dismissal of two fellow female workers due to their union activism. The workers, who had recently founded a local of the International Laundry Workers Union, objected to the dismissal of one sorter and one marker from the Acme Laundry in El Paso.[37] As Acme stepped up efforts to control the labor force, close to five hundred obreras from six different laundries walked off the job.[38] Ethnic Mexican women's act of abandoning difficult-to-secure jobs took on special meaning in El Paso. As the late historian Irene Ledesma has argued, "Anglo El Pasoans regarded Mexicans as foreigners, regardless of their citizenship status."[39] To protest working conditions in an era of intense antiforeign sentiment and in a highly patriarchal society involved certain risks. Moreover, as violence crossed the border, Texas Rangers, vigilante groups, and even some affluent Mexican

Americans frequently labeled Mexicans as "bandits." Thus, any uprising against authority or representatives of authority was seen as a transgression, and swift action could be taken to quell it.[40]

Nativist movements would continue to create obstacles to Mexican-based labor organizing throughout the 1920s in West Texas.[41] In that part of the state, as the historian Miguel Levario has documented, ethnic Mexicans, including women, were not spared direct violence by Texas Rangers.[42] However, residents on both sides of the border would resume their labor activism. Shortly after the Revolution ended, AFL-organized obreras struck once again. The decision came quickly after a *mítin,* or rally; within a week after the plan took shape, the women struck; they "asked for money to survive, food and work."[43] The activism showcased by the female laundry workers in El Paso formed part of a labor network that extended throughout the borderlands. The walkouts organized by women took place within the wider context of revolutionary upheaval reflecting the decline of Mexican social, political, and economic power on both sides of the river.

The postrevolutionary period, particularly the late 1920s and 1930s, ushered in a new era of labor activism, much of it influencing Mexican immigrant women. One of the most important pieces of labor legislation enacted as a result of the Mexican Revolution was Article 123 of the Constitution of 1917. At the national level, the article called for the establishment of labor arbitration boards under the purview of the Mexican Department of Labor, a tripartite entity consisting of representatives from industry, labor, and the state. Beginning with the first labor dispute presented to the Junta Central de Conciliación y Arbitraje (located in Monterrey) and the Junta Local de Conciliación y Arbitraje (located in various municipalities), the documentation of all cases reviewed has been preserved. The principal labor arbitration board, established in 1918 in Monterrey, received the highest number of grievances, including cases from other municipalities that could not be resolved.[44]

As Ledesma has pointed out, "labor union activity in the United States increased enormously in the 1930s because of economic conditions and encouragement from the national government in the form of the Wagner Act."[45] Across the Río Grande, Mexican labor union activity also intensified, especially with the passage of the Ley Federal del Trabajo (1931). Despite opposition to the law from industrialists, labor activists in Monterrey "quickly developed an intimate familiarity with specific clauses and the broader implications of Article 123."[46] The Confederación Regional de Obreros Mexicanos (CROM), founded by the labor leader Luis Morones in 1918, had little backing in Monterrey and in the state. By the late 1920s, the CROM had entered a steady decline, but it had laid the foundation for large labor organizations. In Nuevo León, while labor unionism had strengthened during the Revolution, it declined and remained weak during the 1920s. Unionism remained weak principally due to industrialists' implementation of paternalistic practices that gained the support and respect of many norteño workers; they often joined *sindicatos blancos,* or company-sponsored unions. In fact, in large factories such as Cervecería Cuauhtémoc, which employed a substantial number of women in the bottling department, these "white unions" thrived. In the 1920s these company unions appeared in major industrial sectors, including steel, glass, cement, and beer, as noted by Michael Snodgrass, and had organized under the Federación de Sindicatos Independientes de Nuevo León (FSINL).[47] Early labor organizations like the steelworkers' union and other groups applied pressure to finally implement the federal labor law of 1931 in Nuevo León. The labor arbitration boards did not fully function until 1924.

Labor arbitration board members often viewed workers through a paternalistic lens, explaining in many of their opinions that "the claimant is not an enlightened person . . . he/she cannot defend himself/herself . . . the company must pay for their work value and expenses incurred." However, when presented with enough evidence, arbitration board members often sided with labor, at least until the early 1940s.[48] In Tamaulipas, however, the emergence of Emilio Portes Gil and his Partido Socialista Fronterizo (PSF) brought a resurgence of radical political activity that, as Heather Fowler-Salamini has pointed out, was among one of the stronger regional labor movements. It effectively rivaled the power of the central government and "represented a viable, reformist, regional alternative to the fulfillment of the goals of the Mexican Revolution."[49] Soon, however, the PSF would take on a more corporatist role and become the blueprint for the future party of the Revolution: the National Revolutionary Party. Despite the accomplishments of the PSF as a cross-class social-political organization, "no women received a party position."[50] Still, in the 1920s a minimum wage and the right to strike would become part of state labor law. It was not until the early 1930s that the labor arbitration boards received a steady number of cases involving punitive firings, unpaid wages, claims regarding diseases acquired at the workplace, and other work-related grievances.[51]

Indeed, both the Wagner Act and the Ley Federal del Trabajo signaled a turning point in labor relations in the greater borderlands. Mexican women wage earners stepped up efforts to organize. Like their *cigarrera* and *costurera* counterparts in Linares, Montemorelos, and Monterrey, Mexican women cigar makers and pecan shellers in the El Paso and San Antonio regions rallied to voice demands regarding their dire economic situation. Emerging from the San Antonio region, a fiery young community labor organizer and former LULAC member named Emma Tenayuca combined the rhetoric of communism, feminism, and revolutionary ideology to organize cigar rollers and pecan shellers. Earning an average of $2.25 a week, pecan-shelling obreras worked in unsanitary conditions: the workrooms lacked proper ventilation, workers sat on backless benches, and the only tools they had for crushing pecan shells were their own hands.[52] Tenayuca, referencing revolutionary leaders like the Flores Magón brothers, later recalled the conditions of Mexican workers. She explained, "I started going to the plaza and political rallies when I was 6 or 7 years old. . . . You had the influence of [the] Flores Magón brothers . . . you had *enganchadores,* contractors who came in and took people out to the Valley. I was exposed to all of that." She continued, "I had a basic underlying faith in the American idea of freedom and fairness. I felt there was something that had to be done . . . and I went out on the picket line. That was the first time I was arrested."[53] Tenayuca's exposure to radical ideas emanating from Mexico and the revolutionary struggle there and her understanding of "American" rights combined to produce a unique perspective on issues of labor and women's rights in the region.[54]

Ties between Mexicans and their counterparts in Texas grew stronger precisely because a pro-labor agenda existed among workers on both sides of the border. This cooperation aided activists in setting up conferences advancing binational labor. Just one year before the El Paso women workers walked off the job at the commercial laundries, there was a binational labor conference in Laredo attended by Mexican, Mexican American, and Anglo American labor representatives.[55] The more radical sectors of organized Mexican labor had previously decided not to support or participate in the conference because of AFL leader Samuel Gompers's pro-war stance and the networking organizations' failure to address jailed supporters of the PLM. The conference finally took place in Laredo in 1918. Identifying themselves as the Confederación Obrera Pan Americana (COPA), the conference attendees called for "the improvement of Mexican immigrants' labor situation in the United States. . . . We should fight to make the wages of immigrants the same as [those] of US workers." They also stressed the "fraternal and solidarity ties among workers on both sides of the border." The binational organizers advocated a transnational worker autonomy that would not be "under the tutelage of either government."[56]

That a labor conference took place at this crossroads points to how the revolutionary rhetoric about labor rights influenced working-class ideologies on both sides of the border. Labor organizers in Texas, including Clemente N. Idar, kept abreast of changing labor laws in Mexico and functioned as border labor brokers. Idar made it a point to disclose any new information about Mexican organizing activity to organizations in the United States. As he explained to the AFL-affiliated Bakery and Confectionery Workers' International Union in Chicago, "I have . . . gained considerable knowledge of the labor laws of Mexico as contained in the Federal Constitution and State Constitutions." In the spring of 1922, Clemente Idar found himself in Torreón, in northern Mexico. He was instrumental in organizing the locals of the United Brotherhood of Carpenters and Joiners of America, as well as tailors and common laborers.[57] He would later continue aiding ethnic Mexicans throughout the United States.[58] This binational labor activism continued well into the 1930s. Like Clemente Idar and Emma Tenayuca, Manuela Solis Sager also organized agricultural and garment workers in the greater South Texas region, including Laredo and San Antonio. Sager's efforts continued throughout the 1930s.[59]

Collective organizing intensified from the mid-1920s to late 1930s as workers faced increasing economic pressures. In Xicotencatl, for example, in the southern region of Tamaulipas, twenty campesinas came together to form a "Fraternidad Femenil" (union of women workers) and a *cooperativa agrícola* (agriculture cooperative) that came to include two hundred women—the shareholders of the cooperative. They presented their elaborate twenty-seven-article *estatutos* or stipulations. That the women included in Article 27 a "*caja de ahorro*" points to the way in which the idea of a communal bank and *cooperativismo* still resonated among workers even during the 1920s.[60] Within weeks, the central labor arbitration board in Victoria had replied that their union was recognized and officially registered in the state.[61] Other obreras followed suit, organizing collectives and *sindicatos:* waitresses from Tampico formed the Sindicato de Meseras in 1924, and domestic servants from the area formed similar unions.[62] Others participated in the predominantly male oil labor struggles, supporting their strikes (in 1924 against El Aguila and La Corona, and in 1925 against Mexican Gulf).[63] Tampico had been a hotspot for activist movements and radical organizations such as the Gremio Unido de Alijadores, and women also took part in these movements and groups. In 1932 Tampico native Esther Tijerina Chapa emerged as a leader in the national women's movement. She helped to organize the Frente Unico Pro-Derechos de la Mujer (FUPDM) in 1935, and the group grew to a membership of fifty thousand, spread throughout twenty-five sectors.[64] Between 1935 and 1938 the FUPDM functioned as a "national umbrella group for working, middle, and upper-class women from throughout the country."[65] Chapa, a practicing physician, was a leading proponent for women's rights, and, unlike other feminists of that time, she argued that because women engaged in the same kinds of activities that "[brought] men to political consciousness," women thus possessed the same rights and should be allowed to vote.[66] However, women like

Chapa were in the minority; throughout the region in places like Tampico and Monterrey, more radical women could be found who had aligned themselves with the early anarchist or communist movements. As the historian Jocelyn Olcott has argued, the FUPDM had become an organ of the official party, the Partido de la Revolución Mexicana, by the early 1940s.[67]

Not being associated or affiliated with a union did not mean lack of activism. Particularly for working women who were not in a union, alternative cultural practices helped them to cope with labor issues. The practice of petitioning authorities for aid survived the Revolution.[68] To cope with job loss, gain assistance for children, or resolve family-related issues, women submitted *peticiones* to both local and national authorities or to labor groups or *mutualistas*. In El Paso, for example, Guadalupe Garza wrote to the president of the Sociedad "Melchor Ocampo." She wrote about her "*necesidades*" and asked for any help possible for her little girl, who was ill. She explained that "*porque soy una mujer sola*" (because I am a single woman), "*no tengo a quien aclamar*" (I have no one to rely on). She closed by stating that she "awaited a favorable response."[69] The organization received similar petitions, including some from women in Piedras Negras, Coahuila.[70] Labor organizations continued to receive petitions and have transnational appeal.

Immigration and the transnational nature of many labor and mutual-aid organizations after the Revolution extended the new discourse on women's labor to those living north of the border. Organizations welcomed women workers and addressed general women's issues. For example, the Sociedad Mutualista "Melchor Ocampo" in 1930 organized a "cultural conference" in their social hall in Eagle Pass, Texas, where "noted speaker" and *licenciado* Paulino Rubio from the sister border town of Piedras Negras delivered a lecture entitled, "Mutualismo, La Mujer y el Hogar."[71] Other organizations began to include more coverage on women's labor issues in their publications.

With the Revolution came the modernization of society and labor relations, as well as the modernization of gender. In the postrevolutionary period, as the historian Susie Porter has argued for Mexico City, "female sexuality, sexual morality, and honor continued to inform women's daily work."[72] Women's social identities as workers and their labor demands became increasingly defined within the context of domesticity and femininity.[73] As noted by Mary Kay Vaughan, "stabilization and development required the modernization of patriarchy," and while the postrevolutionary governments, particularly the Cárdenas administration, were advocates for labor rights and encouraged women's participation in unions, the nation-state promoted their domestic roles and tied them to the health and strength of the nation. Women were now "*compañeras*" and not "slaves," and men were encouraged to stand strong to support their modern new revolutionary families.[74] This shift was part of the greater effort to reconstruct the borderlands, particularly Tamaulipas and the Nuevo León countryside, through the support of small farmers and *ejidatarios* "dedicated to commercial cotton agriculture," which was the primary focus of agrarian policies in the region during the late 1920s and 1930s.[75] The discourse of reconstruction through *compañerismo* specifically defined women as key to the grand project of nation and state building. State-sponsored literature of the period explained women's central role to the nation in gendered terms, emphasizing their roles as "mothers," "wives," and "*compañeras*" as a way to promote solidarity and unity and to prevent yet another massive uprising.[76] As Vaughan has explained, the postrevolutionary period involved the "rationalization of domesticity"; women's social roles included "nurturing . . . healthy bodies for purposes of defense and production."[77]

As a gendered discourse to promote nationalism gained strength in the postrevolutionary period in Mexico, a similar discourse influenced the labor of women in Texas, particularly given its proximity to the border. Women workers, wives of fellow obreros, and even their children were spoken of in gendered terms. Women workers were also part of the larger modern working-class Mexican family. Local tailor unions and the Hermandad Unida de Carpinteros y Ensambladores formulated specific gendered messages to aid the "*gran familia*" of tailors.[78] There would be a union creed for women, one for men, and one for the children; the entire "family was tied to the male union members." Integrating women and children became a top priority for the union: "We have not given women and children much priority. If we have them on our side, helping them understand what we understand with regard to the aspirations, doctrines and principles that form the basis of our labor movement . . . our work will be more efficient and fruitful."[79]

The Brigada Cruz Azul, which included women who had participated in the Revolution, articulated a gendered discourse to promote ideas of nationalism and was an advocate for Mexican immigrant women in the postrevolutionary period. A. P. Carrillo, president of the organization, poignantly argued in a speech to the group that "those of us who had to leave our nation to come to work honorably and with dignity . . . need to respect this nation's flag . . . but we should never forget to honor our own flag." He included women in his message, expressing that "for you Mexican mothers, that is your task to instruct your children . . . to honor that tri-color flag, which is the symbol of our beloved Mother nation, which is the mother of our parents, the mother of our grandparents, the mother of our heroes, the mother of all of us, that is the Mother country!"[80]

Female members of the group were also encouraged to continue working and helping the poor, widows, and orphans. Women were spoken of in terms of their "power" and position as mothers first, then as workers. One activist from Laredo argued that "it was absolutely indispensable to educate women from our *raza* so that she can further have an influence on her children's intelligence."[81] Another activist, Hortencia Moncayo, who spoke ardently against lynching, was compared to Mexican independence heroine Josefa Ortíz de Domínguez, known as "La Correjidora," and Leona Vicario.[82] In this way, women's roles as wives, mothers, and protectors of the family were underscored and became part of the state discourse on reconstructing the region.

By the 1930s the Great Depression had hit Texas and was affecting northern Mexico. As the historian Julia Kirk Blackwelder has shown, ethnicity would play a crucial role in the kinds of occupations to which women had access. Of particular significance was Mexican American women's low labor participation. Blackwelder points out that "largely unskilled, geographically segregated, and greeted with prejudice, prospective Hispanic workers had few job choices."[83] Indeed, work was limited, and hundreds of thousands of Mexican American women and their families would face deportation. Mexican immigrant and Mexican American women workers who had contributed to the Texas economy in the early twentieth century and during the Revolution now faced their forced return to Mexico.[84] For those women who remained in their jobs in the United States, technological innovations and sophisticated machinery gradually replaced them, as was the case in factories and tobacco establishments throughout northeastern Mexico.

The Revolution, for women, had been a moment for creating, sustaining, and promoting ideas about worker autonomy, fair wages, and gender equity. Women had taken advantage of the environment produced by the war to formulate radical ideas about their rights, and this radicalization had led to a "renaissance" for women, to quote the historian Emma Pérez. Others continued to sell their labor, contributing to the expansion and modernization of the borderlands. Building on the ideas espoused during the Revolution, women and their activism shaped the larger conversation about labor and labor rights. However, the Revolution did not fix the widespread gender inequities present in the borderlands. It did, however, modernize those gender inequalities by defining the modern Mexican woman as a person who was central to the development of the nation-state. Yet, it did so by underscoring women's roles as wives, mothers, daughters, and sisters and by highlighting their responsibility to the country. Although the activism of women during the Revolution helped to bring women's labor issues to the forefront, women's work was still gender specific, despite the advances made by women like Jovita Idar and Emma Tenayuca in the postrevolutionary period. Even in the agricultural fields, where the backbreaking labor was considered family work, only a handful of women earned wages directly. It would take another "renaissance" for women—a massive movement concerned with issues that went beyond labor—decades after the Revolution to address the gendered, racial, political, and economic inequalities that continued to shape and affect their lives at work and at home.

Chapter Six

Class, Gender, and Power in the Postrevolutionary Borderlands

Trabajo a domicilio [I work from home]. I never stepped inside a factory.

MARÍA LUISA CORONA, CIGAR WORKER, 1937

We want a society without classes.

SINDICATO UNICO DE OBRERAS DE LA INDUSTRIA CIGARRERA EN LINARES, 1937

SEVEN YEARS AFTER THE REVOLUTION ENDED, Linares resident Rafaela Hernández began working at Refugio García Garza's Compañía Cigarrera de Linares. Cigarrera de Linares was one of five *tabacaleras* in that town, and Rafaela was one of more than one hundred *cigarreras* who labored in the tabacaleras there. Working alongside married and single women, she rolled and packaged cigars and soon "identified [herself] as a worker." Rafaela, like many other cigarreras, performed work at the factory and at home, frequently leaving the shop to secure *hojas,* or paper used for rolling cigars. She had been working for more than a decade when Soledad González and Cruz Olivo invited her to join the Sindicato Unico de Obreras de la Industria Cigarrera de Linares (SUOICL). Shortly after Rafaela joined the union, she faced dismissal from her job; García Garza alleged she had left the tabacalera without securing permission. Backed by the SUOICL, Rafaela confronted Garza as she presented her case to the Linares labor arbitration board regarding the alleged "unfair dismissal."[1] During the course of the labor dispute, Rafaela, her *compañeras,* and company representatives all presented testimony. Rafaela's union representative argued that she had in fact secured permission from Rafaela García, the *trabajadora de confianza,* whose role was to supervise the cigarreras and who thus worked closely with the factory owner. The union representative further claimed that "since the founding of the red [independent] union SUOICL, the owners of the tabacaleras of this city in general, and the Compañía Cigarrera in particular, have been disregarding the rights [of union members] guaranteed by the Ley del Trabajo." It took more than a year to resolve the case, and, finally, in 1937, Rafaela received 150 pesos as a settlement from Compañía Cigarrera.[2]

Like the various formal grievances of *obreras* found in the labor dispute records of Nuevo León, Rafaela's *testimonio* as a cigarrera in the aforementioned labor dispute is part of the larger but little-known history of the obreras who rolled and packaged cigars in the tabacaleras of northern Mexico. Tabacaleras have been relegated to the margins of the history of the region because these businesses were not considered part of the major industrial presence in the region, as well as because tabacaleras relied on tobacco imported from the interior of the country. Tabacaleras were also gendered work sites where women could assume positions of authority, power, and leadership, particularly as trabajadoras de confianza.

Cigarreras' labor contributions and their union participation reveal that they were mostly active in unions not sponsored by companies and that they used the labor arbitration boards as a vehicle to claim labor rights after the Revolution. The case of the cigarreras shatters the long-held idea of an autonomous, norteño, male working class that embraced company paternalism.[3] Labor unionism would work as a double-edged sword, however. While unions and the right to submit labor grievances via the boards provided a space for women to articulate labor demands, they were subjected to male labor leaders who controlled the larger unions to which the smaller, independent cigarrera unions were attached. Even if these were all-female unions, male labor leaders often acted as their representatives during labor arbitration hearings. While cigarreras' activism was in line with revolutionary syndicalism and tabacaleras were dominated by female labor, obreras were frequently represented by male labor leaders in disputes and found that modern labor relations rarely altered entrenched gender ideologies. Thus, although obreras were now part of the labor conversation, their role as workers was defined in terms of *compañerismo* and tied to their role as mothers and wives, in short, their reproductive roles. If modernizing the borderlands involved increased wage labor and reliance on a permanent labor force, then it also "modernized gender inequality," to borrow from the historian Susan Besse.[4]

Tabacaleras were gendered work environments inasmuch as they were places where collective ideas of class could flourish. Cigarreras played an important role in the revolutionary syndicalism movement in a region where a large number of workers opted for company paternalism, given its benefits. Cigarreras also worked off-site, rolling and packaging cigars in their own homes—performing *trabajo a domicilio* as they had since the colonial period. Their labor outside of the factory walls, while important, has also been left out of the larger labor narrative of norteño history, and there are several reasons for this neglect.

Workers' contributions to the rise of industrialization in the region, principally in Monterrey, have been amply documented. Yet, this historiography has been associated with "*industrias pesadas*" (heavy industries) dominated by male labor.[5] Given the focus on steel production, mining, modern breweries, and glass production, labor studies have zeroed in on male steel workers, miners, and beer and glass workers—organized into either "red" (independent, non-company-sponsored) or "white" (company-sponsored) unions. For the same reason, the tabacaleras of Nuevo León (there were only three tabacaleras in Tamaulipas), which catered to the needs of a burgeoning population, have not received scholarly attention. A look at the daily work of obreras in tabacaleras, as well as their labor grievances in the form of firsthand testimony, reveals a hidden history of norteño or *regiomontano* labor. The labor identity so celebrated by norteños, even to this day, has been that of a masculine and autonomous workforce that either took pride in joining company unions or embraced revolutionary syndicalism. Analyzing these records, however, reveals a more complex norteño labor identity based on women's work and their activism in red unions. It also points to the limits of women's activism in a postrevolutionary state that came to control the power of unions through their consolidation in the massive Confederación de Trabajadores de México (CTM) overseen by regional trade union patriarchs.

For the most part, cigarreras' labor activism took place in red unions, given women's service in small to medium-sized tabacaleras, whereas women in the expansive leading brewery in Monterrey, Cervecería Cuauhtémoc, were sympathetic to the company union. Those cigarreras who were organized belonged to red unions affiliated with the colossal CTM, which promoted collective action along class lines. Unlike the demands outlined by members of the Frente Unico Pro-Derechos de la Mujer (FUPDM), including "gender equity in labor and land reform," before its consolidation by the Cárdenas government, members of the CTM-sponsored cigarrera unions rarely demanded gender equity in the workforce. Even as they found themselves in all-female work environments, organized obreras spoke in terms of their position as workers and called for class-based solidarity. As the historian Jocelyn Olcott and others have argued, despite the concentration of female workers in sectors such as tobacco, cigarreras were usually represented by men from the parent labor organizations.[6] In the case of the cigarreras of Nuevo León, their unions were linked to the Federación Regional de Obreros y Campesinos de Linares, which in turn reported to the Federación de Trabajadores de Nuevo León (founded in 1936)—the local affiliate of the CTM.

Historians have studied industrial development and its associated consequences in Nuevo León, particularly its industrial hub in Monterrey. Monographs have addressed the emergence of heavy industries, company paternalism, urbanization, and migration. Juan Mora-Torres, Javier Rojas Sandoval, and Michael Snodgrass have expanded the historiography of industrial development, capital, and labor in that state. Save for a chapter by Snodgrass on women in the brewery sector of Monterrey and his analysis of masculinity and obreros, the subject of women's labor and their labor activism, as well as the way in which gender informed such activism, has not been addressed. Further, the way in which gender ideologies intersected with those of class has not been the focus of scholarly debate in northeastern Mexico.[7] While Latin American historians have made advances in the area of women's labor, historians studying Nuevo León continue to neglect women, because "most women in the cities have worked in the tertiary sector," as the historian Emilia Viotti da Costa argued in 1989. Although she made this observation some time ago, working women's experiences in the Mexican Northeast still have not received adequate attention.[8]

As the historian Dawn Keremitsis has argued, women in the Mexican frontier region had access to economic opportunities that may not have been available to them in the southern part of the country.[9] The growth of the female labor force in light industries coincided with the growth of a national market. The expansion of commercial agriculture, smelter operations, and oil industries propelled large numbers of women wage laborers into the workforce by the late nineteenth century, yet this growth in female wage labor occurred only in selected industries. Women found themselves in sectors that historically employed female labor because the work environments in those sectors theoretically offered a safer environment. Tabacaleras employed women of all ages from the countryside and growing urban centers. This predominantly female environment supported the idea that it protected women's morality.[10] As an examination of labor dispute cases will show, the tabacaleras were not insulated or isolated and they offered women both flexibility and a certain degree of independence.

The 1930s was a period of renewed interest in revolutionary syndicalism. As pro-labor Pres. Lázaro Cárdenas took office in 1934, popular organizing was encouraged while non-company-sponsored unions were met with repression. Labor unions emerged quickly to gain the recognition of the pro-labor government and reap the benefits of a "legitimate," registered union. The Cárdenas administration also encouraged women to organize. Some women began to form their own unions, often becoming affiliated with the massive CTM under the aegis of the administration.[11] The available evidence indicates that the few female unions that existed were "red" and also linked to the CTM. As Olcott has argued, Cárdenas saw women as potential allies in accomplishing the agenda of his administration, and he further encouraged women's organizing. Women's earlier efforts at organizing were evident in large-scale events such as the

First National Congress of Women Workers and Peasants, in 1931, and they also formed a sector of the Partido Nacional Revolucionario (PNR) (later named Partido de la Revolución Mexicana, or PRM, and then the Partido Revolucionario Institucional, or PRI), which came to represent the Revolution in its institutionalized form and ruled continuously until the year 2000.[12]

The female-dominated tobacco industry in the Northeast remained labor intensive during the Porfiriato and up through the 1920s, with advanced technology not arriving until the mid- to late 1930s. While tabacaleras such as El Buen Tono became known for introducing mechanization in central Mexico, the factories in the North lagged behind.[13] In fact, the way work was performed by cigarreras during the Porfiriato remained largely unchanged after the Revolution, except for volume. Tobacco industry employment was traditionally based on *destajo* (piecework), with cigar rollers expected to complete a certain number of weekly *tareas* (tasks); during the Porfiriato the typical goal was fifteen boxes a week, and by the postrevolutionary period the target had increased to more than twenty boxes per week.[14] As factories emerged in the North, the standard workday consisted of twelve and a half hours, with thirty minutes to an hour for lunch. Wages were higher in this sector; cigarreras could earn two to two and a half pesos on average for approximately twelve hundred rolled cigars, which amounted to an average weekly income.[15] The national wages for female workers in the cigar industry were about the same: two pesos, six centavos, while male workers in this sector earned three pesos, nine centavos.[16]

While cigarreras were among the best paid female workers, as compared to domestic servants, *tallanderas* in ixtle haciendas and *piloncilleras* in sugar mills, bakers, candy makers, and textile and garment workers, they found themselves in front of labor arbitration boards submitting claims for unpaid wages, violations of work contracts, diseases acquired at the workplace, and unfair dismissals. Presenting grievances to the labor boards allowed women the opportunity to claim labor rights through a formal process. As early as 1918, when the Nuevo León board was created, women were utilizing the arbitration boards, further redefining the conversation about labor and labor rights. As Snodgrass has pointed out, "the labor law became effective to the extent that working-class mobilizations pressured the government to make it so."[17] The cases of cigarreras described below are mainly those processed during the 1930s. While these cases cover only a little more than a decade, they nonetheless shed light on labor conditions, as well as labor relations among workers, factory owners, and trabajadoras de confianza, and they illustrate the active participation of women in labor arbitration activities. The cases also point to women's active involvement in red unions as opposed to those controlled by industrialists.[18]

In the 1920s the cigarrera Rafaela Hernández, whose story introduced this chapter, had received and accepted an invitation to join the CTM-affiliated SUOICL. She had been working at Cigarrera Linares for more than ten years when in 1936 she found herself in a labor dispute with the factory owner, Refugio García Garza. Her experiences as an obrera reflected the changes felt by many during those transitional first decades of the twentieth century. Rafaela had been working alongside other obreras, and her experiences as a cigarrera helped her identify as an obrera, as she explained in her testimony to the labor board.[19] As the historian Heather Fowler-Salamini has argued regarding female Veracruz coffee sorters, their close association with one another, often spending more time with each other than with their families, created a strong sense of camaraderie.[20] Cigarreras, too, found themselves in a community-based environment of female workers. Through *pláticas* (conversations) with other obreras, Rafaela became aware of the SUOICL, and by 1936 she had joined it. Soon thereafter, García Garza fired Rafaela. In García Garza's testimony, he claimed Rafaela had not obtained written permission to leave the factory in search of *hojas* (cigar paper). Rafaela's representative, Juan González, appointed by the CTM to assist her, argued that it was Rafaela's involvement in "*sindicalismo revolucionario*" that led García Garza to fire her.[21] When Rafaela protested the "unwarranted dismissal," SUOICL and non-organized cigarreras testified on her behalf, arguing that in fact García Garza had fired Rafaela because she belonged to a union. During the labor dispute, González claimed that García Garza used "different pretexts to fire female workers who distinguish themselves as real advocates of revolutionary syndicalism."[22] In other words, Rafaela belonged to a red union and thus was considered a troublemaker.

The fact that cigarreras such as Rafaela joined red unions is significant and critical to our understanding of the working class in Nuevo León.[23] These red unions fared better in smaller factories, where company paternalism was not strong. Given that most women worked in light industrial sectors and smaller factories as compared to men employed in the large Fundidora de Monterrey or Vidriera Monterrey, revolutionary syndicalism usually thrived and did not face the same threats by the large white unions (which were the most organized and successful unions and represented more than 50 percent of the workers).[24] Red unions eventually came to pose a real threat to white unions. The Nuevo León working class was not a homogenous mass attracted solely to company paternalism. While many workers took pride in belonging to company unions—often a pride couched in the language of regionalism espousing a "unique" *regiomontano* tradition, as Snodgrass has pointed out—there were those workers who also took pride in not supporting industrialists and creating independent organizations. These more radical unions were the ones that cigarreras created and joined.[25]

Unlike research findings on women's labor in textiles and related industries in Guadalajara and Puebla, in the Northeast there was no real concerted effort to remove female workers from the workplace; there was no discussion about women displacing male workers.[26] In the tabacaleras, there had always been a female labor force, and while these workplaces had been dominated by obreras since the colonial period, there is little evidence of a male- (or female-) led movement to push obreras out of these industries. However, while there was no concerted effort to oust women from work sites, there was a gendered discourse promoting ideas of femininity and domesticity as well as appropriate and "ladylike" behavior in the tabacaleras.

In the postrevolutionary period, as explained earlier, the rhetoric of *compañerismo* and "*cooperación de los sexos*" was advanced to reconstruct the nation by acknowledging women's roles as workers but in feminine, domestic terms. However, women's lived experience as workers, as labor claims reveal, rarely point to women "behaving properly."[27] The case of María Díaz, a young campesina from Linares, illustrates how women pressured authorities to enforce their labor rights. On June 10, 1936, María left a small tabacalera in the countryside to present a grievance to the Linares labor board. She was not part of a union when she submitted her grievance. María was one of two dozen workers employed by La Esmeralda, a small tabacalera that required each worker to roll seventy-two hundred cigars a week to complete six *tareas*.[28] To cut production costs, the factory owner, Arturo Alaníz, reduced some of the workers' tareas, including María's, to one per week. For four months, María and her fellow obreras felt the repercussions of the reduction, earning only about two pesos daily and working only a few days of the week. María took her case to the labor board, arguing that Alaníz had "failed to abide by the work contract and [had] suspended work assignments."[29] After six months of deliberations by the board, Alaníz signed a contract with the obreras pledging to assign the same tareas continuously. María had taken matters into her own hands by demanding that her rights as a worker be acknowledged.[30] During the proceedings she met with the cigarreras, and these daily interactions among the obreras, as well as their discussions about labor conditions, encouraged others to submit related grievances. By the time the board resolved the case, María, along with other cigarreras, had created the first female cigar workers' union in Nuevo León, the SUOICL. By the following year the SUOICL had extended Rafaela Hernández an invitation to join.

The initiative taken by María and her coworkers to submit grievances against their *patrón* Alaníz demonstrates both women's continuing practice of voicing concerns as well as their decision to take advantage of the legal tools available to them in the new era of postrevolutionary labor relations. In Alaníz's tabacalera, cigarreras had to cope with market fluctuations that directly affected their livelihoods throughout the 1930s. As the historian Susie Porter has argued, the continued "subcontracting, mechanization, and a continued reliance on outwork kept a downward pressure on wages."[31] Besides having to contend with declining wages, obreras faced changing market demand. When Alaníz reduced their workload and pay, the obreras came together to outline their demands collectively. Adelina Díaz, Francisca Prieto, Guillermina Constante, Petra Cuellar, Josefina Martínez, Santos Palacios, Anastacia Palacios, Josefa Alameda, Jacinta Alameda, Virginia Soto, and Guadalupe Almaráz joined forces for a "society without classes" and founded the SUOICL. Numerous signatures and a series of thumbprints filled the labor claims they submitted to the labor board.[32] The SUOICL quickly moved to recruit other cigarreras, and it extended aid to other organized workers from various sectors during labor conflicts.

Women who were considered troublemakers could in fact be blacklisted and had difficulty securing employment in other factories. They thus put their livelihood and that of their family on the line when they claimed labor rights. Whether organized or not, women's actions demonstrated that, while work often consumed their lives, factories did not control them. They often missed several months of work when they submitted petitions to the labor boards. For those complaining about unjust firings, awaiting resolutions could mean a long period without real wages.[33]

Cigarreras frequently developed respiratory illnesses, as was the case with Consuelo Flores, who worked at Manuel González Garza's Fábrica de Cigarros de Hoja La Quintana in Linares. After more than five years rolling cigars and working as an *encajitalladora* (packager), Consuelo acquired *tabacosis infectada,* a respiratory condition.[34] Consuelo went to Monterrey to present her case to the Junta Central de Conciliación y Arbitraje. After an eight-month ordeal, including an examination by a board-appointed doctor, she managed to obtain compensation for her "professionally acquired disease." The board granted Consuelo eighty-five pesos for wages lost during the eight-month ordeal "for the inability to work due to the disease she contracted at work."[35] During the quest to receive compensation for her medical condition, Consuelo also insisted that González Garza acknowledge the national minimum daily wage of one peso, fifty centavos. Consuelo had been paid only seventy-five centavos for rolling twelve hundred to eighteen hundred cigars per day. She argued that, "in all virtue, I have the right to ask for unpaid wages from January through the last day of my employment because I only earned [i.e., received in payment] seventy-five centavos." However, Consuelo received only a sum that equaled four months of lost wages, which amounted to more than the required three months' severance pay. Fortunately for the veteran cigarrera, the board ordered González Garza to pay for her medical expenses as well.[36] Recovering lost wages or receiving aid for medical expenses was crucial for family survival. Consuelo's family depended on her wages to help pay the rising costs of basic food and clothing. Acquiring a respiratory disease could end a cigarrera's career and seriously reduce the family income. Consuelo's case not only reveals how local industrialists disregarded national labor laws but also points to the perseverance of women when their new labor rights were violated.

Still, others dropped their labor complaints because of distance. Celia García Falcón, a worker at the Fábrica de Cigarros La Violeta, had presented a case to the board in Linares, accusing the factory owner, Anselmo Perales, of unjustly firing her and violating her work contract. However, she retracted her petition because "it was impossible to travel to Monterrey." Celia's financial situation, lack of transportation, or a combination of other factors might have prevented her from pursuing the case.[37]

Cigarreras from other towns also organized unions in order to pressure authorities to enforce labor laws. Obreras from the Fábrica La Violeta created the Sindicato de Obreras de la Fábrica La Violeta (SOFLV). Soon after the union was registered, the SOFLV moved to align itself with local unions. The group proceeded to intervene in a local labor matter involving organized male glass workers from a factory owned by the elite Garza Sada family of Monterrey. Led by Josefina González and Ludivina Sánchez, cigarreras from SOFLV petitioned the president himself, Lázaro Cárdenas, arguing that supervisors from Vidriera Monterrey mistreated the glass workers and that these "poor" and "defenseless obreros" needed his intervention.[38] Soon, Emilia Cortez and Elena Moreno from the Sindicato de Obreras "La Esmeralda" (SOLE), from La Esmeralda tabacalera in Linares, joined SOFLV in its gesture of solidarity and also wrote on behalf of the glass workers.[39] The harsh work conditions under which the overwhelmingly male labor force toiled at Vidriera Monterrey created opportunities among workers for class solidarity that cut across gender lines.

CTM-affiliated Nuevo León federations also seized the opportunity to solidify bonds based on similar working-class experiences. The fact that gender inequality was prevalent at work sites and in communities did not always lead to divisions based on gender. As historian Thomas Miller Klubock explains for the Chilean mining community known as El Teniente, organized miners and Communist Party members encouraged women to join in "the labor and political struggles around class-based issues."[40] A similar discourse circulated in the Mexican northeast, in the tabacaleras. However, the rhetoric employed by the organized cigarreras was shaped by their own ideas about gender. In the obreras' petition on behalf of the male workers at Vidriera Monterrey, the men appeared weak in relation to the local authorities and their factory bosses, and, according to the obreras, the men needed their help. The cigarreras' written and verbal protests demonstrated that the women could intervene in labor matters involving male workers. Their demands also underscored their role as strong, vocal leaders fighting against some of the most powerful capitalists in Monterrey (the Garza Sada and Garza García families). The cigarreras sought the assistance of the organized compañeras from one of the largest bread and pasta factories, La Industrial; the La Industrial obreras were members of a mixed-sex union. Shortly thereafter, obreras from the bakery La Superior and various all-female garment workers' unions joined the effort to support the male glass workers. The obreras' unions emphasized their commitment to "social justice, harmony, and progress" in their petitions to Cárdenas on behalf of the Vidriera Monterrey workers.[41]

While class solidarity could cut across gender lines and work to the advantage of labor in its struggle against capital, or at least in enforcing labor laws, gender was not entirely subsumed—it never was.[42] In the case of the SUOICL, while women such as Soledad González and Cruz Olivo held leadership positions (general secretary and conflict manager, respectively), the affiliations of the union with the parent Federación Regional de Obreros y Campesinos de Linares, which in turn reported to the Federación de Trabajadores de Nuevo León (FTNL), forced it to function under the purview of male-dominated organizations. Thus, capable cigarreras who were organized and for the most part literate were frequently represented by a male union member. In the SUOICL petitions to the labor boards, local CTM-affiliated labor leader Juan G. González represented the women. In a letter to members of the local board in Linares, Soledad González notified them that Mr. González was to "advise" the obrera Rafaela Hernández in her grievance submitted against Compañía Cigarrera de Linares. González was to also assist Gloria Sandoval, a cigarrera who was asked to give testimony during Rafaela's hearing. While the archival record does not specifically indicate why Juan G. González was appointed and asked to offer counsel to the women, we know that the SUOICL rarely represented its members directly in labor disputes. Both the SUOICL and male members of either the Federación Regional de Obreros y Campesinos de Linares or the FTNL promoted a "society without classes," as evidenced in the many letters, petitions, and speeches by labor leaders, and they followed the class-based agenda promoted by the CTM. These groups fell under the purview of the CTM, which sought to promote class-based discipline and which, by 1938, had consolidated its power and begun to push women's issues into the margins. While the SUOCIL, the Federación Regional de Obreros y Campesinos de Linares, and the FTNL rarely issued calls for gender equity, the fact that women's labor issues were no longer central weakened women's greater labor struggle in the region and throughout the country. None of the labor cases presented by organized cigarreras between 1936 and 1940 called for gender equity.[43] The cases were instead brought forward in support of the working class.[44] Despite the activities of numerous female labor leaders, CTM representatives attended to the cases of the obreras. The women's labor movement was co-opted and now subject to a modernized patriarchal state.

Community Work Culture and *Trabajo a Domicilio*

While large numbers of women rolled cigars in factories, other cigarreras performed the work at home. Cigarreras who worked *a domicilio* have not been part of the story of norteño industrialism. Given the unevenness of industrial development, heavy industries such as petroleum, steel, and its associated sectors expanded more quickly in terms of technological advancements due to higher levels of capital investment. Light industries such as tabacaleras remained labor intensive, relying on women workers until the 1940s.[45]

Cigarreras came from small villages, ranches, haciendas, and from the city, and they worked both inside and outside factory walls. María Luisa Corona, a single woman, joined the ranks of obreras who rolled cigars at home "*trabajando a domicilio* . . . never stepping inside a factory," as she testified in a labor dispute.[46] It was customary for factories to provide obreras with the required materials to perform tasks at home, and it was quite common for obreras to provide their own transportation when purchasing other materials. The nature of cigar rolling gave women home workers greater flexibility, autonomy, and an opportunity to remain close to their families all while protecting, in the popular view, women's morality. Frequently, women gathered in one home and worked together, which helped to strengthen a community-based work culture. Women also chose when they wanted to work, perhaps doing so when the family's financial situation became severely strained or opting to remain at home to care for children and family members.[47]

It was quite common for cigarreras to leave their posts and not return "for four hours or more" while going out to purchase cigar paper. When the "paper was not given to us," testified Francisca Prieto, we "purchased it from the *comerciantes* who sell it." The ability to leave work sites made it easy for women to use time away from the factory to address personal or family needs.[48]

Rural women's work experiences in the Nuevo León countryside include the representative examples of Francisca Prieto and her female relatives and the Alameda sisters. It was common practice for the owners of tabacaleras to hire some individuals who did their assigned tasks at home. Francisca Prieto, along with her mother and sisters, performed this type of "home work" for Arturo Alaníz, owner of La Esmeralda, a small cigar factory with some eighteen (in-house) workers who completed from three to nine *tareas,* or boxes of cigars, per week. The Alameda sisters—Josefa, Jacinta, and Guadalupe—worked inside the factory, together producing fifteen tareas per week. Prieto family members also collectively produced fifteen boxes. A regular workweek for the Prieto sisters and their mother Guadalupe consisted of rolling more than ten thousand cigars at home. Once the work was completed, the obreras usually relied on local women operating as labor intermediaries to deliver the finished products to the main factory.[49]

Performing home work instead of working within factory walls did not prevent women from submitting complaints to the labor boards or joining unions. The cigarrera Francisca Prieto was known in the region for her labor activism and leadership in the SUOICL. In fact, Francisca, a married woman, had been working as a cigarrera for more than sixteen years before she filed a complaint. Along with fellow worker María de la Cruz, Francisca's activism in the SUOICL and the CTM elevated Francisca to a respected position in her community.[50]

Two other siblings, Cruz Olivo and Cristina Miranda, also performed some home work for Compañía Cigarrera de Linares, with which La Esmeralda partnered. The sisters were assigned four and six tareas, respectively, for work done in the factory and from home.[51] When the women submitted a case to the local labor board regarding unpaid wages, Alaníz, the factory owner, explained that "the obreras work at home voluntarily and their work is paid based on the number of cigars rolled."[52] He argued that he paid only for what the workers produced, and he claimed to have counted fewer cigars than the figure reported by the sisters. The case involved testimony from both parties, but when women home workers presented grievances, it was difficult to win a case given the fact that there was not a substantial labor force that could potentially speak out on behalf of the claimant or claimants. Thus, union membership and mutual aid was crucial to their success in claiming labor rights. While home work or "outwork" provided some flexibility for women, it frequently became a pretext for factory bosses to employ unfair labor practices, as demonstrated in the numerous labor dispute cases presented to both the municipal and the central labor board in Monterrey. Factory management could penalize workers for late delivery of goods or accuse them of shoddy workmanship and easily dismiss them.[53]

TABLE 8. Cigarrera labor force in Nuevo León, 1900

Municipality	*Females*	*Males*
Allende	10	
Cadereyta Jiménez	11	3
Cerralvo	1	
Doctor Arroyo	1	8
Doctor Coss	1	
Doctor González	2	
Galeana	1	10
García	27	
Garza García	1	
General Bravo	1	
General Terán	20	11
General Zuazua	1	
Guadalupe	4	
Hualahuises	9	1
Iturbide	3	1
Juárez	1	
Lampazos	2	4
Linares	123	49
Los Herrera	1	
Marin	2	
Mina	6	
Montemorelos	58	13
Monterrey	192	27
Parás	2	
Pesquería Chica	1	
Rayones	5	1
Sabinas Hidalgo	7	
San Nicolás Hidalgo	60	1
Santa Catarina	10	
Santiago	16	
Villaldama	8	
Total	586	130

Source: Adapted from "Población Según la Ocupación Principal," 1900–1902, Sección Estadística, Secretaría de Gobierno de Nuevo León, in Memorias de Bernardo Reyes, AGENL.

Class, Power, and Gender and the *Trabajadoras de Confianza*

While some women gained a sense of having a "worker" identity based on shared experiences with female coworkers at the factories or by working from home or joining unions, others' work identity and experience were shaped by their positions of considerable power as *trabajadoras de confianza.* In the tabacaleras, as in some of the garment factories in the area, obreras could assume these positions that offered opportunities for leadership, power, prestige, and, of course, conflict with workers.[54] As the historian Elizabeth Quay Hutchison has observed for Chile, the cigar industry in particular offered women the opportunity to assume positions of authority.[55] In contrast to the collective action of women found in organizations like the SUOICL, the complex power relations that developed between trabajadoras de confianza and their fellow cigarreras underscore the interplay of class, power, and gender.[56] With these roles, women could assume positions of authority and leadership, particularly in sectors dominated by female labor. Trustworthy employees often had several years of experience and knew the terrain—the geographic and the labor landscape—given their key roles as labor brokers. They often oversaw a large female labor force, particularly in cigar and garment establishments. The tabacaleras throughout Latin America provided opportunities for women to improve their socioeconomic status and offered them a chance to supervise other female workers. Hutchison writes that in Chile "women managers were most likely to be found in textile (9 percent), tobacco (16 percent), and clothing (19 percent) factories."[57] In Nuevo León, the pattern was similar with regard to the tobacco sector and was consistent with national figures.[58] Although these positions gave cigarreras the opportunity to gain respect from male bosses, the workers they directly oversaw often responded with contempt.[59]

At La Violeta, another Linares-based cigar factory, Simona Navarro became a trabajadora de confianza. As a labor broker, she had confianza status that gave her the right and responsibility to assign tasks to other women. She was an experienced cigarrera who assumed a high level of authority, which often increased when factory *patrones* were away. Simona hired obreras; she assigned tasks to the workers and could also dismiss them.[60] In other parts of the country women workers also assumed positions of authority in a variety of other business sectors. Fowler-Salamini explains that in the coffee region of Veracruz, in towns such as Córdoba and Coatepec, these *empleadas de confianza* were quite common. In fact, female union members won the right to appoint their own *encargada* (overseer) with the passage of the Ley Federal del Trabajo in 1931.[61]

At Compañía Cigarrera de Linares, factory owner Refugio García Garza also gave Dolores Olvera a confianza position. She helped to secure the labor force for García Garza by recruiting and hiring women, including Rafaela Hernández, from the Nuevo León countryside to provide services for factories in urban Monterrey and in Linares. Dolores oversaw the obreras' assigned tasks and submitted daily reports of their performance. Her position earned her the reputation of being a well-established labor broker. A labor dispute involving the cigarrera María Luisa Corona, who performed home work for Compañía Cigarrera de Linares, illustrates the opportunities for leadership available to women and how they challenged gendered expectations held by male owners and managers.[62] Dolores's responsibility as a contract negotiator for Cigarrera de Linares involved visiting *rancherías* and villages in search of female workers. Shortly after María Luisa began her tenure as a cigarrera, she presented a case to the labor board regarding unpaid wages. In her testimony, María Luisa referred to Dolores as her *patrón* and not as her *patrona;* factory workers hardly ever encountered male factory owners directly.[63] Thus, cigarreras' use of the masculine term *patrón* to refer to their female supervisor is noteworthy. While it is possible that trabajadores de confianza were called patronas in everyday labor relations, in official labor dispute cases the term remained in its masculine form. Eventually, María Luisa's case was resolved in her favor. Later, in 1939, María Luisa and several other obreras presented further complaints against Cigarrera de Linares for unjust firing and unpaid vacation time; after more than a year passed María Luisa and her "*socias*" finally won their case against the factory.[64]

María Luisa's case reveals much about women's work and power. Unlike El Buen Tono, the large tabacalera that usually assigned a male overseer to help "keep women [workers] silent," the factories in the North, for the most part, placed women in supervisory positions. The work relationship between Dolores and María Luisa redefined the traditional male boss/female laborer relationship.[65] Trabajadoras de confianza often testified against obreras, as can be seen in the records of numerous cases in which these intermediaries testified in support of García Garza and Cigarrera de Linares.[66] Obreras continued submitting grievances against García Garza and the factory. In 1940 Ana María Rodríguez, another cigarrera working for García Garza, submitted a complaint for unjust firing and lost wages; the labor arbitration board ordered García Garza to pay her 250 pesos.[67]

EMPLOYED IN LIGHT INDUSTRIES that produced items including tobacco, bread and pasta, and textiles and garments, as well as in selected departments of glassworks and breweries, women sold their labor to businesses that served the basic consumer needs of a growing population.[68] Historians' focus on the region's heavy industries has led both to the assumption that the norteño working class was a homogenous mass of men and to the relative absence of women in the larger labor historiography of the region. Examining women's experiences and labor activism from a "gendered-class" perspective leads to the necessity of recasting our view of how this particular borderlands region developed.[69]

The complaints that cigarreras presented before the labor arbitration boards provide a window into the complexity of labor relations among women. That obreras assumed positions of authority both inside and outside the factory, even if in a predominantly female work environment, accentuates the dynamics of women's socioeconomic status. These cases also show how gender and class ideologies were constantly changing and negotiated. Further, they point not only to how class solidarity could trump gender alliances but also how class was shaped by notions of gender. Women who assumed positions of authority often did so after many years of service, and their new status brought them extra responsibilities. These confianza workers point to the complexity surrounding women's labor experiences as they helped to recruit and discipline members of the labor force while complicating gender norms of authority and power. They played a key role in the resurgence of industrialization in the region, particularly in Monterrey during the 1920s and 1930s in the second wave of industrialization. At the same time, they helped to validate the sexual division of labor and the suppression of female workers when they sided with male management in labor disputes. This practice often had the effect of strengthening worker bonds among cigarreras.

Obreras' labor contributed to the emergence of Monterrey as the industrial nucleus of the greater Mexican borderlands. While women did not lay railroad tracks, drill for oil, or work in the smelters' production departments, they nonetheless labored in the expanding light industries that addressed the growing population of the Northeast, particularly Monterrey.

Unlike the research findings by Snodgrass regarding marriage and work in Cervecería Cuauhtémoc, this study shows that marriage did not keep women away from the tabacaleras. While we have limited testimony by cigarreras who married and continued on the job, we know from the documentation of labor disputes that many cigarreras were married and employed. In fact, married cigarreras had on average ten years or more on the job. The case of women brewery workers in Monterrey reveals certain pressures involved in working for large factories where company paternalism prevailed and thrived. The experiences of cigarreras gradually replaced by advanced technology in the

1940s and 1950s foreshadowed those of obreras in the Cervecería Cuauhtémoc bottling and packaging division, which increased mechanization in the 1970s. Across the country, sectors that had historically employed large numbers of women were now shifting to more modern production techniques, which often meant replacing women with men based on the perception that men were better at operating machinery.[70] Women did remain in clerical positions in the brewery. However, "as in earlier times, marriage marked the end of the secretaries' careers."[71] Company paternalism provided schools, health benefits, and shopping savings that encouraged households to get by on one income while extending benefits that offered financial stability for the entire household. However, cigarreras who worked in small to medium-sized tabacaleras seldom had such benefits. The pressure for such women to continue working remained, and, due to the relatively small and intimate workforce typical in such workplaces, women could then practice a more independent labor activism, one more in line with revolutionary syndicalism. Obreras who submitted grievances in the 1930s fared better than those few workers who presented claims in the late 1920s. During the Cárdenas presidential administration, Nuevo León labor boards featured labor delegates who were critical of the white unions.[72]

Revolutionary syndicalism, however, would soon be co-opted by the state; by the end of Cárdenas's term the government increasingly controlled labor. As Fowler-Salamini argues with regard to the female Veracruz coffee workers, "they were part of a paternalistic workplace culture and an emerging Mexican post-revolutionary state" that was intent on consolidating and controlling organized labor.[73] Cigarreras, too, would face this new environment. Labor dispute cases submitted by obreras and their male counterparts became difficult to win. As the nation-state expanded, it co-opted union leaders and made decisions on behalf of labor and in step with new government policies. Moreover, women's work in the manufacturing sector began to decline as regional union leaders fought against each other and as advanced machinery replaced women's work.[74] Still, women's labor had contributed to the development of the northeastern borderlands from the Porfiriato through the height of unionism in the 1930s. As a result, women have received acknowledgment as paid laborers and as key to reconstructing the borderlands after the Revolution.

By the mid-1930s the state had advanced a discourse of development that underscored the triumph of the Revolution, the principles of which had become institutionalized. This discourse of revolutionary nationalism promoted gendered class ideologies similar to those that marked labor relations during the Porfiriato but under the guise of modernity. Women were now "compañeras" and not "*siervas*"; they were part of the great Mexican family—on both sides of the border, since the same rhetoric, as carried by labor organizers such as Clemente Idar and others, was used to create a sense of national pride and unity among Mexicans who had gone to the United States. Women laborers in tabacaleras, commercial agricultural estates, and in a variety of other sectors, organized or not, were perceived and defined as members of a nation-state that proudly recognized labor and encouraged unionism. Ironically, much of the rhetoric of modernization and progress espoused by regional elites and foreign investors to make the borderlands "productive" now functioned to make workers—men and women—into loyal supporters of the new revolutionary state. Women's labor became acknowledged as their labor activism became part of the institutionalized revolution.

By the 1940s, as the revolutionary government entered its second decade of rule in the midst of a global war, a significant number of norteñas witnessed a massive migration of their sons, brothers, fathers, grandfathers, and husbands. They would enlist in the Bracero Program, a binational labor program created to alleviate labor shortages due to World War II, and one of the largest contingents of workers involved in it came from Tamaulipas and Nuevo León. When the Bracero Program came to an end in the mid-1960s, norteñas, joined by *mexicanas* from the interior, would come to dominate the emerging manufacturing sector along the border. Labor activism in these assembly plants, or *maquiladoras,* would face numerous obstacles, from the post-1960 period to the present day.

Epilogue

The *obrera* recognizes her rights, proudly raises her head and joins the struggle, the time of her degradation is over, she is no longer a slave sold for some coins, she is no longer a servant, but the equal of a man.

JOVITA IDAR, LAREDO, TEXAS, 1911

Mujer te doy por compañera y no sierva. [Woman, you are now a companion, a compatriot, not a slave.]

EL SURCO (VICTORIA, TAMAULIPAS), 1925

Muy pronto me identifique como obrera. . . . empecé a trabar en la fábrica [Cigarrera Linares] en 1927. [Soon I identified myself as a worker. . . . I began to work in the factory (*Cigarrera Linares*) in 1927.]

RAFAELA HERNÁNDEZ, 1937

AS I REFLECT ON THE EXPERIENCES of the *tallandera de ixtle* Ursula Tapia, the *cigarrera* Rafaela Hernández, and the *jornalera* Petra Vásquez, I am bombarded with news about kidnappings and tortures, as well as chilling pictures of decapitated Mexicans. Four women and five men were hanged at a major intersection in Nuevo Laredo, a place that has become a hotspot for frenzied violence in this borderland. That same border town where the writer and activist Jovita Idar expressed her concerns and demanded rights be extended to women was long ago contested and the site of the bloodiest revolution of the twentieth century.

This corner of Mexico—long viewed as a center of political liberalism and autonomy—experienced a profound socioeconomic transformation during the early years of the Porfiriato. It was a period of change that would help bring Mexico into the global capitalist economy with a harder but not impenetrable border. Outright contestation has always characterized the region, and it was in the borderlands that state-enacted policies were contested, rejected, or modified to fit local needs.[1] While certainly not at the scale of the drug cartel war, violence was a by-product of many of the transformations that residents such as Ursula Tapia, Jovita Idar, and Rafaela Hernández experienced and helped to shape. The process of land transfer from shared use to concentration in the hands of foreign investors and regional elites unfolded not only in the Northeast of Mexico but also on the north bank of the Río Grande.

Residents of the borderlands, however, would negotiate and contest such dramatic and profound change. The long-standing historiographical tradition of the region has underscored the availability of higher wages. However, as the cases of the tallanderas and jornaleras at the expanding commercial haciendas of the region reveal, workers earned some of the most depressed wages in the country, and in many cases these workers suffered physical abuse. This type of experience spurred workers to leave in search of better paid work on nearby rural estates, in urban factories, or in Texas, all in the effort to support their families. Further exacerbating the situation for already impoverished *norteños* was the physical abuse and debt peonage that had developed as early as the eighteenth century and had become widespread at the height of the Porfiriato.

This form of labor control intensified as competition for labor increased along with the rise of industrial capitalism and the emergence of heavy and accompanying light industries that required a more permanent labor force. Given the relatively low population density in the region, despite an influx of migrants from nearby regions, women were seen as viable, necessary, and cheap wage laborers. While women did not lay railroad tracks, drill for oil, or work in the production departments of ore smelters, they nonetheless labored in the expanding light industries that played a key role in the growing population of the Northeast and elevated the status of Monterrey such that it became the industrial nucleus of the borderlands.

While there was no concerted effort to push women out of wage work, their labor and associated identities as workers were always defined in gendered terms. Yet, women addressed their position as workers and their labor conditions by renegotiating class and gender boundaries. Cigarreras in small tabacaleras spoke the language of class and radical revolutionary syndicalism, creating all-female unions along "red" lines as opposed to the "white" unions aligned with company management. That they engaged the state by claiming their labor rights through formal appeals to the labor arbitration boards shatters the long-held idea of an autonomous, male norteño working class. Further, unlike many norteño workers, *obreras* did not receive the benefits extended by company paternalism, given that women workers were concentrated in small fábricas or were working from home. Unlike some major factories in the central part of the country, many facilities in the Northeast were places where women had opportunities to assume positions of leadership, authority, and power, as in the case of *trabajadoras de confianzas,* who, based on their years of experience, took on extra responsibilities, including the supervision of large numbers of obreras. This work arrangement reveals that class solidarity could in fact trump gender alliances. These *confianza* workers who helped to recruit and discipline labor point to the complexity surrounding women's labor experiences as they relate to gender norms of authority and power. At the same time, however, when these women sided with male management in labor disputes, their work experiences helped to validate the sexual division of labor and the suppression of female workers. This dynamic often strengthened the communal bonds among workers, as in the case of cigarreras.

The transformations that began during the Porfiriato were constantly contested and negotiated by residents and lessons were learned. The Revolution incorporated much of the radical thought of people like Jovita Idar. Norteños used their *vecino* status and its associated privileges to their benefit during the colonial period and the Porfiriato, and the Revolution then further popularized and modernized this practice. When obreras were dismissed or laid off due to a decrease in production, they resorted to the old cultural practice of the *petición,* they migrated to places with more opportunities, or they presented grievances to the state-established labor arbitration boards. The numerous cases brought to the labor boards by urban workers and preserved in documents housed at the Tamaulipas and Nuevo León state archives include language that reveals workers' own perceptions of their role in the postrevolutionary state as they claimed their "rights as *obreros* and citizen[s]" as "gained by the Revolution."[2]

Residents petitioned for land, demanded access to agricultural credit, and continued to organize. Emilio Portes Gil's ascension to power and the presidency was seen as good for organized labor, and in that period of the 1920s "key articles of the Constitution of 1917 [were implemented] in the area of education, labor, agrarian reform, control of the church, and restrictions on foreigners."[3]

Tallanderas, jornaleras, and *piloncilleras,* however, were concrete reminders of the unevenness of the modern vision for the region. In addition, there were campesinos who continued to enter into verbal contracts and thus were at the mercy of landowners.[4] As campesinos joined unions, the more seasoned workers encouraged their newer fellow members to use the labor boards when necessary. With written contracts, workers had a better chance at gaining favorable *dictámenes,* or decisions. Campesinos looked to unions because their economic hardships were increasing. Through the Lázaro Cárdenas administration, the number of sharecroppers was declining, and in certain sectors, such as the citrus-growing region of southern Nuevo León, sharecroppers' rents were set at more than 30 percent. With limited access to arable land and credit (most of the land available to sharecroppers required irrigation to produce crops), campesino families had few options.[5] By the late 1930s, cities were growing while the countryside, where hacienda or company stores could still be found, was continuing to decline.[6] In short, the result of modernization in the region was a borderland whose incorporation remained incomplete.

While the Mexican Revolution provided an opportunity for women and some progressive men to define women workers as legitimate laborers pushing for full-fledged labor rights, as the Revolution came to a close and as state-building resumed, women workers and their labor issues would be defined within the parameters of the modern revolutionary state. In effect, women were encouraged to work and to organize, but these new worker identities were still defined in very gendered terms, with women workers still considered separate and still encouraged to perform work "appropriate" for women. These new gendered identities, ideologies, and expectations worked in tandem with the larger efforts to reconstruct the nation-state.

Women's labor was imperative to sustaining the new modernized borderlands, and women's new roles were seen as supporting those of male workers. Labor issues and worker identities were couched within the context of a modernized nation-state that used the memory of the Revolution to create a unified country and emphasize the "*cooperación de los sexos para el bien de la nación.*" By creating a sense of national pride, the state proceeded to consolidate the various labor ideologies and different kinds of workers into the massive Confederación de Trabajadores de México. Labor was not simply recognized; it became an organ of the government.

Although now under the purview of the state, union activism continued. By the 1960s, labor relations had once again been altered. New but limited opportunities for women in repetitive, detail-oriented manufacturing jobs in the *maquila* industry emerged. Women would find themselves in an anti-union, predominantly female work environment in which highly patriarchal and exploitative labor relations predominated. By the 1990s these once border-restricted jobs were gradually opening up in the greater borderlands, in places such as Monterrey and Ciudad Victoria.[7] Indeed, women's work in foreign-owned assembly plants would open up another chapter in the history of labor relations in this region.

It is my hope that *Working Women into the Borderlands* not only brings a renewed sense of understanding to one of the highly contested peripheries of Mexico but that it also provides a starting point for a new history of the Mexican borderlands that acknowledges the contributions of both women and men to the building, sustaining, and ever-changing crossroads of Mexico and the United States.

Appendix One

Selected Mutual-Aid Societies and Related Collective Organizations in the Mexican Northeast, 1880–1910

Organization	*Location*	*Purpose*	*Year founded*
La Sociedad para Mujeres Arepentidas	Monterrey, N.L.	To help women who have left the "bad life"	n.d.
La Sociedad Concordia Cosmopolita de Auxilios Mutuos	Brownsville, Tex.	Mutual support	n.d.
La Sociedad Pedagógica Mutualista	Monterrey, N.L.		1887
La Sociedad Hermana Obrera	Linares, N.L.	To support women workers from Linares	1896
Sociedad Obreos de Linares	Linares, N.L.	To support obreros	1888
Sociedad de Beneficencia Mutua "Servando Canales" La Sociedad Unión Fraternal Obreros de Brownsville	Reynosa, Tamps., and Brownsville, Tex.	To support workers	1892
Sociedad Mutualista Hijos de Hidalgo	San Diego, Tex.	Mutual support	1902?
Sociedad Mutualista Hidalgo y Juárez	Monterrey, N.L.	Mutual support	
Círculo Patriótico y Literario "Martir de Guilapan"	Monterrey, N.L.	To honor Gen. Vicente Guerrero and assist several mutual-aid societies and literary and scientific organizations	1904

Organization	*Location*	*Purpose*	*Year founded*
Sociedad Juárez de Obreros	Juárez, Chih.	To support workers	1893
La Sociedad Benito Juárez de Auxilios Mutuos	Soliseño, Tamps.	Mutual support	ca. 1900
Sociedad Mutualista Juárez	Doctor Arroyo, N.L.	Mutual support	n.d.
Sociedad Recreativa Porfirio Díaz	Monterrey, N.L.		n.d.
Sociedad Unión México-Texana	Brownsville, Tex.	Mutual support	1900?
Sociedad Cooperativa El Porvenir de la Unión	Monterrey, N.L.	To offer aid to and a "*caja de ahorros*" for poor workers and members	1900
Sociedad José Ma Morelos de Auxilios Mutuos	Monterrey, N.L.	To support the study of law	1874
Gran Círculo de Obreros	Monterrey, N.L.	To support obreros and obreras	1874
Sociedad Cooperativa de Obreros de Monterrey	Lampazos, N.L.		n.d.
Sociedad Pedagógico-Mutalista	Monterrey, N.L.		1896
Sociedad Científica Artística y Recreativa "Porfirio Díaz"	Monterrey, N.L.	To promote the sciences, arts, and literature and an awareness of moral issues in society	ca. 1880
Sociedad Hidalgo para Auxilios Mutuos	Sabinas Hidalgo, N.L.	Obreros "helping one another"	ca. 1907
Sociedad Josefa Ortíz de Domínguez	Monterrey, N.L.	To help obreros and improve women's condition	1885

Organization	*Location*	*Purpose*	*Year founded*
Sociedad Benito Juárez de Señoras de Matamoros	Matamoros, Tamps.	Help society	n.d.
Sociedad "Concordia" de Protección Mutua	Nuevo Laredo, Tamps.		1901?
Sociedad de "Amigos del País"	Monterrey, N.L.		n.d.
Sociedad de "Amigos de la Unión"	Monterrey, N.L.		1886
Sociedad Amigos del Trabajo	Monterrey, N.L.		n.d.
Sociedad Hijas de Juárez	Monterrey, N.L.	Help society	ca. 1900
Sociedad Obreras de Nuevo León	Monterrey, N.L.		ca. 1900
Gremio de Cigarreros	Matamoros, Tamps.	Help cigar workers	n.d.
Sociedad Obrera Progresista "Unión, Progreso y Tolerancia"	Victoria		ca. 1900

Source: Compiled from information in AGENL, AGET, and the Prieto Papers, NLB.

Appendix Two

Selected Organizations in Texas Affiliated with the Partido Liberal Mexicano, 1911–1917

Organization	*Location*	*Year founded*
Grupo Regeneración	San Antonio, no. 25	1911
Grupo Regeneración "Tierra y Libertad"	San Antonio, no. 25	1911
Grupo Regeneración "Tierra y Libertad"	San Antonio, no. 131	1913
El Grupo Liberal Mexicano Práxedis G. Guerrero	Strawn, no. 25	1911
Grupo Regeneración	Gonzales, no. 35	1911
Grupo Regeneración Práxedis G. Guerrero	Amarillo, no. 35	1911
Grupo Regeneración "Pan Tierra, y Libertad"	Brady, no. 40	1911
Grupo Regeneración Guillermo Stanley, Blo.	Grove, no. 40	1911
Grupo Regeneración de Agricultores	Fentress, no. 81	1912
Grupo Regeneración "Tierra y Libertad"	Beaumont, no. 81	1912
Grupo Femenino "Aspiraciones Libres"	Morin, no. 81	1912
Grupo Regeneración "Ignacio Zaragoza"	Raton, no. 81	1912
Grupo Regeneración "Práxedis Guerrero"	Cameron County, no. 83	1912
Grupo Regeneración "Blas Salinas"	Knippa, no. 87	1912
Grupo Regeneración "Tierra y Libertad"	Austin, no. 89, no. 107	1912
Grupo Regeneración "Tierra y Libertad"	Austin, no. 149	1913
Grupo Regeneración Del Valle	Rio Grande Valley, no. 89	1912
Grupo Regeneración de Hutto	Hutto, no. 89	1912
Grupo Regeneración de Kyle	Kyle, no. 89	1912
Grupo Regeneración "Práxedis Guerrero"	San Marcos, no. 89	1912
Grupo Regeneración "Práxedis Guerrero"	San Marcos, no. 162	1913
Grupo Regeneración "Tierra y Libertad"	Uhland, no. 89	1912

Organization	*Location*	*Year founded*
Grupo Regeneración "Práxedis Guerrero"	Garfield, no. 89	1912
Grupo Regeneración "Tierra y Libertad"	Bluff Springs, no. 96	1912
Grupo Regeneración "Rebeldes sin Hogar"	Alba, no. 96	1912
Grupo Regeneración "Rebeldes sin Hogar"	Alba, no. 131	1913
Grupo Regeneración "Benjamín Canales Garza"	Malakoff, no. 98	1912
Grupo Regeneración "Vencer o Morir"	Como, no. 99, no. 110	1912
Grupo Regeneración "Vencer o Morir"	Como, no. 131	1913
Grupo Regeneración "Higinio Tanguma"	Riesel, no. 103	1912
Grupo Regeneración "Tierra y Libertad"	Weir, no. 103	1912
Grupo Regeneración "Tierra y Libertad"	Weir, no. 149	1913
Grupo Regeneración "Tierra y Libertad"	Waxahachie, no. 107	1912
Grupo Regeneración "Bandera Roja"	Gonzales, no. 130	1913
Grupo Regeneración "Prismas Anarquistas"	Burkett, no. 148	1913
Grupo Regeneración "Solidaridad Perpetua"	Brownsville, no. 149	1913
Grupo Regeneración "Amor y Justicia"	Coleman, no. 149	1913
Grupo Regeneración "Praxedis Guerrero"	Hondo, no. 187	1914
Grupo Regeneración "Libertad o Muerte"	Rio Grande Valley, no. 257	1917
Grupo Regeneración "Juárez y Lerdo"	Reagan, no. 257	1917

Source: Adapted from Alcayaga Sasso, "Librado Rivera y los Hermanos Rojos."

Appendix Three

Selected Estatutos *(By-Laws) and* Artículos *of the Unión de Obreras "Fraternidad Femenil" (Xicotencatl, Tamaulipas)*

To the Junta de Conciliación y Arbitraje,

Ciudad Victoria, Tamaulipas

(Citing Article 109 from La Ley del Trabajo) . . . we attach the document that is required.

Primer Acta

In the Villa of Xicotencatl on September 23, 1924, at three o'clock in the afternoon a group of twenty female workers came together in the home of Antero Morales. In the *compañero*'s house on Hidalgo number 37 we agreed to organize ourselves in a Unión de Obreras . . . seeing the years of slavery to which the oppressed class has been subjected up to this day. We seek moral and intellectual betterment for its members.

Having agreed that it will carry the name of Unión de Obreras "Fraternidad Femenil," we adopt our slogan, "Liberty and Emancipation," followed by the appointment of the executive committee made up by four members:

General Secretary, Miss María de la Luz Ysaguirre
Secretary of the Interior, Mrs. Eulalia González
Secretary of the Exterior, Mrs. Juana J. de Hernández
Secretary of Treasury, Miss Encarnación Vega

This was followed by the majority of votes agreeing to hold the sessions on Thursdays and pay ten centavos as our dues. Being that there were no other pending issues we concluded the meeting at five p.m. Colleagues, we also have the honor of informing you that on the fifth of the present month it was concluded that our *Cooperativa Agrícola* was formed, and hope that while you are in office, you will continue to support us and hope for the success of this *cooperativa.* Having met all legal requirements we respectfully submit,

"Liberty and Emancipation"
Xicotencatl, Tamaulipas, August 11, 1925
the Executive Committee

General Secretary
María de la Luz Ysaguirre

Secretary of the Treasury
María Ynocencia Vega

Capítulo Primero

Foundations for the Unión de Obreras "Fraternidad Femenil," Xicotencatl

ARTICLE ONE

It is determined that for the formation of the *Cooperativa* the quantity of 2,000 pesos in *oro nacional* will serve as the basis. . . . Its 200 . . . *socias* who constitute this organization will pay two pesos biweekly.

ARTICLE TWO

. . . Each member cannot hold more than six shares.

ARTICLE THREE

The organization's capital can be increased with new members and reduced if there is a death or expulsion of a member. . . .

ARTICLE FOUR

Both the admission and expulsion of a member will be resolved by a general assembly made up of the shareholders. . . .

Capítulo Segundo
On the admission, retirement, and expulsion of the members

ARTICLE TEN

In order to be admitted as a member of the society it is required of the member to leave any job that is in conflict with the goals of the organization. . . .

ARTICLE ELEVEN

Every member who does not cover the dues will be dismissed by the board of Directors. . . .

ARTICLE TWELVE

A member could also be excluded when she fails to follow through with her contractual obligations. As a member and a worker belonging to the organization, even if she remains as a volunteer . . . she has an obligation to contribute her personal labor for the good of the organization. . . .

ARTICLE THIRTEEN

In case of voluntary retirement . . . the organization will reimburse the expenses incurred for handing over their shares. . . . reimbursement will remain in the organization's treasury until it is verified and approved. . . .

ARTICLE FOURTEEN

In case of separation by death or voluntary retirement, her heirs and beneficiaries will only have the rights to the amount of the shares in the form and terms set in the previous article.

ARTICLE FIFTEEN

No member can retire before six months after their admission.

Capítulo Tercero
From the assembly

ARTICLE SEVENTEEN

The general assembly of shareholders will take place on ordinary and extraordinary bases . . . every year, in the board of directors [hall]; except in case that the final part of the article is required, one or other assemblies should come together at least eight days in advance. . . . All should be notified sufficiently in advance and be informed of date and hour . . . for consideration and resolution by the assembly.

ARTICLE EIGHTEEN

The shareholders should identify themselves as such to the audience in the assembly, stating their title. . . .

ARTICLE NINETEEN

In order for a general assembly to take place there should be present at least half and one more of the shareholders. . . . Whatever the issues may be, they should be addressed during the order of the day and resolved in session by the majority vote of the shareholders.

ARTICLE TWENTY

The general assembly will be presided over by the president of the board of directors, manager, or in the case that the president is absent the vice president will preside and in the absence of both, the board will designate someone. The president will have the right to break a tie after the votes are verified[;] the votes given will carry out functions of the secretary, it is bestowed on the board and in the result that the name of the person or member that should, precede the assembly...

Capítulo Cuarto
From the Board of Directors

ARTICLE TWENTY-FOUR

The organizing committee is in charge of a Board of Directors formed by elected members . . . the board members will serve one year, and they can be reelected if the general assembly of shareholders sees it beneficial. From these five board members the first will be a president, one vice president, one secretary of treasury, and one member, Director, and Manager. . . . Their work is as follows. . . .

ARTICLE TWENTY-SEVEN

A *caja de ahorros* will be organized to aid the members. . . .

Notes

PUBLISHED WORKS INCLUDED in the bibliography are cited here in shortened author/title format. Archival materials are initially cited in full-length format, with the original cataloging information and abbreviations. At subsequent citations, collections will generally be cited with a shortened name, and archives cited multiple times will be referred to by their acronyms. Acronyms used in the notes, including some traditionally used to cite particular items, are listed alphabetically below. Full information about each archive, including location, is included in the bibliography.

AGENL	Archivo General del Estado de Nuevo León
AGET	Archivo General del Estado de Tamaulipas
AGN	Archivo General de la Nación
AHM	Archivo Histórico de Matamoros
AHR	Archivo Histórico de Reynosa
AHT	Archivo Histórico de Tampico Carlos González Salas
AMC	American-Mexican Claims Commission
INEHRM	Instituto Nacional de Estudios Históricos sobre la Revolución Mexicana
JCCA	Junta Central de Conciliación y Arbitraje
JLCA	Junta Local de Conciliación y Arbitraje
MDA	M. D. Anderson Library
NLB	Nettie Lee Benson Latin American Collection

INTRODUCTION

Epigraphs: Anzaldúa, *Borderlands/La Frontera,* 154–55 (Anzaldúa dedicated her poem "A Sea of Cabbages" to those who have worked the fields); Ana María Sánchez to Junta Local de Conciliación y Arbitraje, July 3, 1937, caja 110, expediente 9, Fondo: Junta Central de Conciliación y Arbitraje, AGENL.

1. Teodora Cepeda, Monterrey, to Governor, Nuevo León, Sept. 24, 1892, Fondo: Trabajo, Asunto: Sirvientes, AGENL; Response to Teodora Cepeda's petition, Sept. 26, 1892, Fondo: Trabajo, Asunto: Sirvientes, AGENL.

2. Here, I employ the term *norteño* to refer to people residing in northern Mexico, including Mexicans who migrated to the region in search of employment and remained

there. While there is literature that addresses the term *norteño* with regard to identity, I employ this term to signify a group of people occupying a shared geographical space.

3. See the introduction to Truett and Young, *Continental Crossroads,* 1–34.

4. On the various theoretical interpretations of modernization, modern, modernism, and modernity, see AHR Roundtable, "Historians and the Question of 'Modernity.'"

5. French, *Peaceful and Working People,* 5–8. On the concept of the *vecino* as a member of a community, see Radding, *Wandering Peoples.* See also Shelton, *For Tranquility and Order.*

6. The idea and practice of cooperativism formed part of the broader socioeconomic agenda of the Mexican Revolution. Many of the integral features of cooperativism had been promoted by the early mutual-aid societies on both sides of the Río Grande. The practice of cooperativism can be traced to pre-industrial Mexico (e.g., *cajas de ahorro,* or communal banks). See Rojas Coria, *Tratado del cooperativismo en México,* 2nd ed. See also Hart, "Evolution of the Mexican and Mexican American Working Classes"; and Hart, *Revolutionary Mexico.*

7. Truett, *Fugitive Landscapes.*

8. Rojas Coria, *Tratado del cooperativismo,* 335. On the conditions in the region that facilitated industrialization prior to the 1880s, see Cerutti, *Burguesía, capitales, e industria en el norte de México.*

9. Katz points to industrial capitalism and the gradual shift to widespread free wage labor as a more relevant factor in the formation of the Mexican North as opposed to the simple drawing of a geopolitical boundary between the United States and Mexico. See Katz, *Secret War in Mexico,* 4–10. Hastings Donnan and Thomas M. Wilson, in *Borders, Frontiers of Identity, Nation and State,* explain borderlands as a phenomenon that emerged with the rise of nation-states. See also Truett, "Transnational Warrior," and other articles in the *Continental Crossroads* volume edited by Truett and Young. Other important works include those by Gloria Anzaldúa on borders and borderlands, particularly *Borderlands/La Frontera;* Adelman and Aron, "From Borderlands to Borders"; Baud and van Schendel, "Toward a Comparative History of Borderlands"; Sahlins, *Boundaries;* Jiménez, "El Lejano Norte español"; Cuello, *El norte, el noreste y Saltillo en la historia colonial de México;* St. John, *Line in the Sand;* and Hernández, "Borderlands and the Future History of the American West."

10. For a literary perspective on distinguishing between border and frontier, see Barrera, "Border Places, Frontier Spaces." See also Gutiérrez and Young, "Transnationalizing Borderlands History."

11. Truett and Young, *Continental Crossroads,* 16.

12. Chassen López, "'Cheaper Than Machines,'" 28. See also Chassen López, "Más baratas que las máquinas."

13. William E. French has studied the transition to a "culture of capitalism" and addressed competing cultural perspectives held by various social classes. See the introduction in French, *Peaceful and Working People.* On the same period in the state of Chihuahua, see Lópes, "Crisis económica y desorden social en Chihuahua en vísperas de la revolución."

14. Herrera Pérez, *Breve historia de Tamaulipas,* 34–39; Alonso, *Thread of Blood,* 15–20. See also the essays by Martha Rodríguez, Isidro Vizcaya Canales, and Cuauhtémoc

Velasco Ávila on the extermination of indigenous peoples in the Mexican Northeast in *Historia del noreste mexicano.*

15. For example, see the case of *abuso de confianza* submitted by one Lino Rubio, who is described as Angela Vásquez's *mozo,* or servant. Vásquez was the owner of a cantina and bakery in Monterrey in 1908. Case against Angela Vásquez, June 24, 1908, Monterrey, ca. 17, num. 430, Sección: Justicia, Asunto: Abuso de Confianza, AGENL.

16. Katz, *Secret War in Mexico;* Hart, *Empire and Revolution.*

17. Cerutti, "Monterrey and Its Ambito Regional." The idea of an *ámbito regional* appears in Cerutti's several pre-1990 publications, including Cerutti, *Economía de Guerra.*

18. Cerutti, "Monterrey and Its Ambito Regional." Cerutti, *Economía de Guerra.* The focus is on Tamaulipas, Nuevo León, and South Texas, with some references to northern Veracruz, northern San Luis Potosí, and Coahuila. For an earlier treatment of this region, as conceptualized in this book, see Chapa, *Texas and Northeastern Mexico.*

19. Responding to anglophile history popularized by Frederick Jackson Turner and his students, Bolton, and later a new generation of "Boltonians," laid the foundation for the study of the region encompassing the present-day US Southwest and present-day northern Mexico. Bolton dedicated his life to researching and writing the history of the Spanish in the region. He wrote about Spanish explorers, settlers, and missionaries, emphasizing the northward move as the English and French moved westward. Bolton and Marshall, *Colonization of North America; Greater America: Essays in Honor of Herbert Eugene Bolton.* Bolton's students, particularly John Francis Bannon, continued expanding the field, contributing to the history of the Floridas and early settlements in Texas and California. By the 1970s the field had justified Spanish exploration, settlement, and Christianization. Bannon, *Bolton and the Spanish Borderlands.* See also Hurtado, *Herbert Eugene Bolton.*

20. Weber, *Spanish Frontier in North America.* See also Weber, *Mexican Frontier;* Gutiérrez, *When Jesus Came the Corn Mothers Went Away;* and Adelman and Aron, "From Borderlands to Border." Regrettably, Adelman and Aron do not draw from northern Mexican history to illuminate their discussion on the Río Grande region. See also Tinker Salas, *In the Shadow of the Eagles.*

21. In 1983 Guillermo Beato and Domenico Sindico published an article on the early industrialization of the region. The authors focused on the smelting sector in Monterrey, and their findings supported Cerutti's conclusions with regard to how steel production transformed Monterrey and the regional economy. However, like Cerutti, they omitted the repercussions of the economic changes on the larger nonelite population. Beato and Sindico, "Beginning of Industrialization in Northeast Mexico"; González Quiroga and Cerutti, "Guerra y Comercio en Torno al Rió Bravo." For a discussion of the effects of capital accumulation on elite families who controlled most of the industries in Monterrey, see Saragoza, *Monterrey Elite and the Mexican State.* See also Maíz and Olvera, *La nueva historia de Nuevo León,* which includes an article by Javier Rojas Sandoval on the *hojalatera* (tin) industry.

22. Rojas Sandoval, *Monterrey,* 73.

23. Flores Torres, *Burguesía, militares, y movimiento obrero en Monterrey.*

24. Adelson, "Cultural Roots of the Oil Workers' Unions in Tampico." On Tampico

history, see González Salas, *Acercamiento a la historia del movimiento obrero de Tampico;* and González Salas, *El casino tampiqueño.*

25. Matamoros and Nuevo Laredo are discussed in Ramón Ruiz's *On the Rim of Mexico* (1998) and in Milo Kearney and Anthony Knopp's *Border Cuates* (1995). Discussions of the cities' roles in their respective states have been included in Herrera Pérez, *Breve historia de Tamaulipas;* and Juan Fidel Zorilla, *Historia de Tamaulipas.* Other studies offer background information on the region; see, for example, Vizcaya Canales, *Los orígenes de la industrialización de Monterrey* (first published in 1969; AGENL released a third edition in 2001); and Roel Melo, *Apuntes históricos de Nuevo León.* For a history of the Union of Industrial Workers in Matamoros in the post-1930 period, see Guerrero Miller and Ayala, *¡Por eso!*

26. Saragoza, *Monterrey Elite and the Mexican State;* Snodgrass, *Deference and Defiance in Monterrey.*

27. Mora-Torres, *Making of the Mexican Border.* For Monterrey workers, see also Rojas Sandoval, *Monterrey;* Rojas Sandoval, "Minería en Nuevo León"; and Morado Macias, "Empresas mineras y metalúrgicas en Monterrey." For Tampico workers, see Adelson, "Cultural Roots of the Oil Workers' Unions." Glenn D. Kuecker offers an excellent interpretation of the transition of Tampico to modernization and Tamaulipas governor Alejandro Prieto's role in this process; see Kuecker, "Alejandro Prieto." The exception here is Snodgrass, *Deference and Defiance in Monterrey,* particularly the chapter on women in the brewing industry of Monterrey. For an excellent interpretation of gender, modernization, and state formation in northern Mexico focusing on Chihuauha, see Alonso, *Thread of Blood.*

28. Mallon, *Defense of Community in Peru's Central Highlands.*

29. Truett and Young, *Continental Crossroads.*

30. Zorilla, *La mujer en Tamaulipas;* Aguilar Belden de Garza, *Una ciudad y dos familias.*

31. Sieglin, *Mujeres en el campo a finales del siglo XX.*

32. See also Rangel, "Participación de las mujeres marginadas."

33. Snodgrass, *Deference and Defiance in Monterrey,* chap. 3.

34. Olcott, *Revolutionary Women in Postrevolutionary Mexico.* See also French, *Peaceful and Working People.*

35. Goldsmith, "Sindicato de trabajadoras domésticas en México."

36. Santiago, "Women of the Mexican Oil Fields."

37. Fowler-Salamini, "Gender, Work, and Working-Class Women's Culture in the Veracruz Coffee Export Industry."

38. Ramos Escandón, "Gender, Labor, and Class Consciousness in the Mexican Textile Industry."

39. Porter, *Working Women in Mexico City.* See also Farnsworth-Alvear, *Dulcinea in the Factory;* Hutchison, *Labors Appropriate to Their Sex;* and Olcott, *Revolutionary Women in Postrevolutionary Mexico,* for a similar approach.

40. González, *Refusing the Favor.*

41. See Anzaldúa, *Borderlands/La Frontera,* for a feminist/Chicana approach to the study of the borderlands; see also an essay by Ernesto Chávez, "Is Aztlán in the Borderlands?," shared with La Colectiva (a student group at the University of Houston) in 2002;

Chávez questioned the lack of Chicano/a history in the field of borderlands history. Essay in possession of author. See also Truett and Young, introduction to *Continental Crossroads;* and Deena González, "Gender in the Borderlands," in *Frontiers: A Journal of Women Studies* 24 (2003), a special issue on gender and the borderlands, as well as the introductory essay by the guest editor Antonia I. Castañeda in the same issue.

42. Fernández Aceves, "Once We Were Corn Grinders"; Fowler-Salamini, "Gender, Work, and Working-Class Women's Culture in the Veracruz Coffee Export Industry."

43. González Sánchez, *Vallecillo, Nuevo León.*

44. Radding, *Wandering Peoples;* Jiménez, "Popular Organizing for Public Services."

45. García Martínez, "El espacio del (des)encuentro."

CHAPTER ONE. SELLING THE *NORTEÑO* BORDERLANDS

I would like to thank Jim Case, who offered comments on parts of chapters 1 and 4 (which were originally combined into one and presented at the Newberry Library Conference on Labor and Transnationalism, Chicago, Sept. 18–20, 2008). Parts of this chapter were read by the Writing across the Curriculum group at the University of Texas–Pan American, and I thank group members Mark Noe and Dan Knight for their insightful comments.

Epigraph: A. W. Gifford, president, Imogene Mining Company (Saint Louis) Operating Gold Properties in Tamaulipas, to Alejandro Prieto, governor of Tamaulipas, July 22, 1889, in Alejandro Prieto Papers, Nettie Lee Benson Latin American Collection, University of Texas at Austin (hereafter, Prieto Papers, NLB).

1. *Tovar González, "Extranjeros en el Soconusco,"* 32–33.

2. Hart, *Empire and Revolution,* 221.

3. Cerutti, *Economía de guerra;* Tyler, *Santiago Vidaurri and the Southern Confederacy.* For an excellent overview of events during the mid-nineteenth century, see Octavio Herrera Pérez, *Tamaulipas en tiempos de Benito Juárez* (Victoria, Tamps., 2006).

4. For a discussion of the development of "capitalist cotton agriculture," see Walsh, *Building the Borderlands.*

5. See Cerutti, *Economía de guerra.*

6. Quoted in Rangel Frías, "Años de Caudillo," 243–44, 246, 253–55.

7. E. L. Doheny interview, Apr. 16, 1918, Washington, D.C., File K, E. L. Doheny Research Foundation Collection, Mary Norton Clapp Library, Occidental College, Los Angeles, Calif. (hereafter, Doheny Research Foundation Collection, OC).

8. Olvera Guerrero, *Reseña histórica del municipio de Ocampo,* 13.

9. "Memoria Administrativa del Estado de Tamaulipas," 1892–93, Fondo: Memorias Administrativas del Estado de Tamaulipas, caja s.n., 176, Archivo General del Estado de Tamaulipas, Ciudad Victoria (hereafter, AGET).

10. For wages of peons or farmhands and seamstresses, as well as other occupations, see the various wage tables in Memorias de Bernardo Reyes, Comisión Nacional Agraria (Secretaria de la Comisión Agraria), AGENL. See also "Wage lists for Southern Tamaulipas," Tampico, Consular Dispatches, United States, Records Relating to the Internal Affairs of Mexico (Record Group 812), M. D. Anderson Library, University of Houston

(hereafter, US Consular Dispatches, MDA). Seymour Taylor was the American owner of the large orchard mentioned.

11. Mora García, *El General Alberto Carrera Torres,* 79.

12. Ibid., 58. See chap. 3 on campesina/o petitions to state and local officials.

13. Hart, *Empire and Revolution,* 168.

14. Cavazos Garza, "Jeronimo Treviño," 243–44, 246.

15. Cerutti, *Economía de guerra;* Alvarado Mendoza, *Tamaulipas,* 16–17. This pattern of concessions and transnational commerce began in the 1860s, during the American Civil War.

16. Rangel Frías, "Años de Caudillo," 260. See also Hernández, *Mexican American Colonization during the Nineteenth Century,* for a discussion on colonizing the Mexican North.

17. Rangel Frías, "Años de Caudillo," 261.

18. Toscano Hernández, *Haciendas ixtleras,* 9–11.

19. Hart, *Empire and Revolution,* 168; Cavazos Garza, "Jeronimo Treviño," 245; Thompson, *Cortina,* 224–25.

20. Traffic and Industrial Departments of the National Railways of Mexico, *Facts and Figures about Mexico,* 7, in NLB.

21. Ibid., 7; O'Brien, *Revolutionary Mission,* 37. See also Morado Macías, *Nuevo León en el siglo XX,* vol. 1.

22. Traffic and Industrial Departments, *Facts and Figures about Mexico,* 8. Spaniards involved in the business ventures included Valentín Rivero and Hermanos Hernández.

23. Rojas Coria, *Tratado del cooperativismo en México,* 337. For mining in the Texas-Coahuila region, see Calderón, *Mexican Coal Mining Labor in Texas and Coahuila.*

24. Iturriaga, *La estructura social y cultural de México,* 20–25; Anderson, *Outcasts in Their Own Lands;* Hart, *Empire and Revolution.*

25. Parkes, *History of Mexico,* 306.

26. Traffic and Industrial Departments, *Facts and Figures about Mexico,* 8.

27. Ibid.

28. Fifty centavos was the equivalent of approximately seventy-five US cents.

29. "El Zapupe Tamaulipeco: su importancia como planta textil, terrenos apropriados para plantarse, su cultivo," *Pan American Magazine, Tamaulipas,* 1907, 63–66. The wages were described as low compared to those offered in the United States, thus allowing investors to earn more profits in Mexico. However, the wages offered in agricultural estates in the North were "higher than anywhere else in Mexico," according to Katz, "Labor Conditions on Haciendas in Porfirian Mexico," 32.

30. N. O. Winter, "Mexico and Her People To-Day," in "Sanitation—Personal Uncleanliness," Nov. 26, 1917, File L–Life of the People, Doheny Research Foundation Collection, OC.

31. "Peon Women," in Percy F. Martin, *Mexico of the Twentieth Century* (London: Edward Arnold, 1907) in File–Life of the People 400–500/LI-803, Doheny Research Foundation Collection, OC.

32. Edward Doheny, Mexican Petroleum Co., interview, May 20, 1918, File L, Doheny Research Foundation Collection, OC.

33. Occupations of women according to the census of 1910, *Boletin de la Dirección*

General de Estadística, no. 5 (1914): 95, in File I–Labor, Doheny Research Foundation Collection, OC.

34. "Drawn work, Matamoros," in *Commercial Relations of the United States with Foreign Countries, 1908,* vol. 3 (Washington, D.C., 1909), in File I–Labor L-804–1599, Doheny Research Foundation Collection, OC.

35. Ibid.

36. "British Diplomatic and Consular Reports, Mexico, July 1905," no. 3429, Vice-Consul Wilson on Ixtle, File I–Labor, Doheny Research Foundation Collection, OC.

37. "El Zapupe Tamaulipeco," 156–57.

38. Doheny interview, May 20, 1918.

39. *Discursos leídos por el Señor Gobernador del estado de Tamaulipas, Ingeniero Alejandro Prieto al H. Congreso del Mismo* (Victoria, Tamps.: Imprenta de "El Eco del Centro," 1891), 24–25, in Prieto Papers, NLB.

40. Ibid.

41. Truett, *Fugitive Landscapes,* 257.

42. Alejandro Prieto to Presidente Porfirio Díaz, July 31, 1903, Prieto Papers, NLB.

43. For a history of Alejandro Prieto and his efforts at modernizing Tampico, see Kuecker, "Alejandro Prieto." See also Kuecker, "Desert in the Tropical Wilderness."

44. "El auge de los Ferrocarriles–Estado de Tamaulipas," in *El florecimiento de México,* ed. Francisco Tretini (Mexico City: Tipografía de Bouligny y Schidt, Sucs., 1906), reproduced in Zorilla, Miro Flaquer, and Herrera Pérez, *Tamaulipas,* 88–90; Coatsworth, *Growth against Development;* Gamboa, "Los momentos de la actividad textil," 226. Mexico had 11,500 kilometers of track in 1896. Hart, *Revolutionary Mexico,* 133

45. "El auge de los Ferrocarrileros–Estado de Tamaulipas," 88–89; Graf, "Economic History of the Lower Rio Grande Valley," 116–17. See also Zorilla, *Tamaulipas.*

46. "El auge de los Ferrocarriles–Estado de Tamaulipas," 88–89.

47. Toscano Hernández, *Haciendas ixtleras,* 25.

48. *Carretones* were large carts used to transport goods.

49. Olvera Sandoval, *Monterrey y sus caminos de hierro,* 20–22.

50. Aguayo, *Estampas ferrocarrileras: fotografía y grabado,* 60–61; Olvera Sandoval, *Monterrey y sus caminos de hierro,* 21–23. Ferrocarril de Monterrey al Golfo was also known as the Tampico Railroad.

51. Kuntz Ficker, "La mayor empresa privada del Porfiriato," 39–40, 53; US Consul, Monterrey, to William Hunter, Second Assistant Secretary of State, United States, Oct. 28, 1880, US Consular Dispatches, MDA. The central station was 1,074 kilometers from Mexico City, 497 kilometers from San Luis Potosí, and 269 kilometers from Nuevo Laredo. *Monterrey 1893: visión y progreso desde el ferrocarril.*

52. *Ferrocarril al Golfo,* exhibition, Antigua Estación de Golfo, Casa de la Cultura, Monterrey. Seven hundred peons were hired for rail construction work. Several years before the completion, the two lines, Monterrey al Golfo and Ferrocarril Internacional, merged with the goal of creating a rail route to the US border. Cerutti, *Burguesía, capitales, e industria,* 122; Olvera Sandoval, *Monterrey y sus caminos de hierro,* 13; Loria, *La política ferrocarrilera de México.*

53. "Contrato celebrado entre Manuel Fernández, Oficialía Mayor de la Secretaría

de Fomento, en representación del Ejecutivo de la Unión, y el Sr. James Sullivan, como agente y en representación de la Compañía Constructora Nacional Mexicana para la Construcción de los Líneas de Ferrocarril, una de México a la Costa del Pacífico, y la otra a la Frontera del Norte," Sept. 13, 1880, wallet 26, 1880, Secretaría de Fomento, Colonización, Industria, y Comercio, NLB; Hart, *Empire and Revolution.* The other land concession was for the construction of a rail line crossing through Durango, Guanajuato, and El Paso. "Contrato celebrado entre Manuel Fernández, Oficialía Mayor de la Secretaría de Fomento, en representación Ministerio de Fomento, Colonización, e Industria, y C. Andrés Treviño como representante de la Cía. del Ferrocarril de Matamoros a Monterrey para construcción de un ramal entre Mier y Cerralvo termine en N. Laredo," Dec. 10, 1872, caja 10, exp. 99, Secretaría de Comunicación y Obras Publicas, Departamento del Trabajo, Archivo General de la Nación, Mexico City (hereafter, AGN).

54. Rojas Sandoval, "Minería en Nuevo León," 18–19. Mining activities in the Sierra de San Carlos in Tamaulipas lasted from 1890 to 1908. See Herrera Pérez, *Breve historia de Tamaulipas,* 210. The Ley Minera de 1892 favored capitalists by granting investors subsoil rights.

55. Rojas Sandoval, "Minería en Nuevo León," 187; Morado Macías, *Nuevo León en el siglo XX,* 56–58; Mora-Torres, *Making of the Mexican Border,* 263; Hart, *Empire and Revolution,* 14.

56. Meyer and Beezley, *Oxford History of Mexico,* 419.

57. Enrique Quiroga, "Sobre la historia del petróleo en México, Petroleros Británicos perdieron 'Casiano' y 'Cerro Azul' por erróneos informes," *Revista Tamaulipas,* no. 256 (1977): 53–55, in Special Collections, Lower Rio Grande Valley, University of Texas–Pan American Library, Edinburg, Tex.

58. Muir, *Geology of the Tampico Region,* 2. Autry later invested in a wide variety of industries in Tampico. See Fondo: Tesorería (particularly the Libro de Causantes or taxpayers registry), Archivo Histórico de Tampico Carlos González Salas, Tampico (hereafter, AHT); "En el umbral de la industria," *La Revista Peninsular,* no. 464, Sept. 11, 1998, http://www.larevista.com.mx/pemex3.htm. Autrey (some sources use Autrey instead of Autry) was the lawyer for Texaco. Ocasio Meléndez, *Capitalism and Development,* 100. Meléndez notes that Autrey was an Irish American. See also Adelson, "Cultural Roots of the Oil Workers' Unions," 36–57; Pan American Petroleum & Transport Company, *Mexican Petroleum.*

59. Herrera Pérez, *Breve historia de Tamaulipas,* 211; Aguilar Camín and Meyer, *In the Shadow of the Mexican Revolution,* 14; Ocasio Meléndez, *Capitalism and Development,* 116; Hart, *Revolutionary Mexico,* 147.

60. Samuel E. Magill, Tampico, to US Department of State, Mar. 18, 1901, US Consular Dispatches, MDA; Hart, *Empire and Revolution,* 155–56; O'Brien, *Revolutionary Mission,* 254. See also Ansell, *Oil Baron of the Southwest;* Ocasio Meléndez, *Capitalism and Development,* 107; Hart, *Empire and Revolution,* 38, 156.

61. Arguelles, *Reseña del estado de Tamaulipas,* 200, 299; Alarcón, *Evolución y dependencia en el Noreste,* 37–39.

62. Quoted in Vázquez Juárez, "Joseph Andrew Robertson empresario norteamericano," 5; Mora-Torres, *Making of the Mexican Border,* 86–87; Cronon, *Nature's Metropolis.*

63. Vázquez Juárez, "Joseph Andrew Robertson empresario norteamericano," 5.

64. See Olvera Sandoval, "La citricultura en Montemorelos," 158.

65. Ibid., 13. Joseph Robertson was born in Bakers, Tennessee, in 1849. He arrived in Monterrey in 1887. See also Saragoza, *Monterrey Elite and the Mexican State.* Emeterio de la Garza also helped the Guggenheims with a concession for a smelter in Chihuahua. He was a close friend of Porfirio Díaz. Wasserman, "Foreign Investment in Mexico," 8.

66. Cavazos Garza, "Jeronimo Treviño," 243–44.

67. Ibid., 255.

68. Ibid., 256.

69. Ibid. See also Saragoza, *Monterrey Elite and the Mexican State,* on strategic marriages in Monterrey.

70. Olvera Sandoval, *Monterrey y sus caminos de hierro,* 16–17, 25; Hart, *Empire and Revolution,* 248.

71. Cavazos Garza, "Jeronimo Treviño," 245–46.

72. W. F. Cummins, geologist, to William Kelly, Esq., president, Compañía de Terrenos y Minas en el Estado de Tamps., S.A., "Report of the Hacienda el Sacramento," May 1917, Hart Collection, Houston, Tex.; Coatsworth, *Growth against Development,* 169–89; Montejano, *Anglos and Mexicans in the Making of Texas,* 22.

73. Montejano, *Anglos and Mexicans in the Making of Texas,* 22, 97–99. Compared to Stillman and King's circle of investors (which included giants such as William Rockefeller and John Stewart of the United States Trust Company, New York), Kelly was a small-scale investor. Hart, *Empire and Revolution,* 186. On the numerous interethnic marriages that solidified business ventures, see Monday and Vick, *Petra's Legacy.*

74. "Una muestra de gratitud de los alijadores," *El Sol de Tampico,* Nov. 30, 2005.

75. This assessment is based on information in the *cartas-peticiones* in the AGENL.

76. Walsh, *Building the Borderlands,* 69.

77. Lic. Julio Guerrero, Mexico City, to Senador Alejandro Prieto, Feb. 17, 1905, Prieto Papers, NLB.

78. Onofre Zambrano, Monterrey, to Alejandro Prieto, Tampico, June 4, 1903, Prieto Papers, NLB.

79. "Compañía Manufacturera Singer," *El Progresista* (Victoria, Tamps.), Apr. 24, 1904.

CHAPTER TWO. PEASANT WOMEN'S WORK IN A CHANGING COUNTRYSIDE DURING THE PORFIRIATO

Epigraphs: "Memorandum in the case of Mrs. H. A. Woolman," Apr. 20, 1896, Tampico, US Consular Dispatches, MDA; "Testimony of Mrs. H. A. Wooman, p. 8, May 6, 1896, Tampico, US Consular Dispatches, MDA.

1. *Mrs. Herbert's Scientific System of Dress-Cutting, for Self-Instruction.*

2. There is slightly more research on sectors typically dominated by women's labor during the second industrialization period (1920s) in the region, particularly in Monterrey. See, for example, Rojas Sandoval, *El patrimonio industrial histórico de Nuevo León;* and Elizondo Elizondo, "Bajo la mirada de la sospecha," on businesswomen/brothel owner Soledad Padrón de Chávez and other Monterrey residents during 1868–1870. See also

Sonia Hernández, "*Las Obreras de Monterrey:* Women's Work in Garment Factories during the Second Industrialization" (manuscript).

3. Fowler-Salamini and Vaughan, introduction to *Women of the Mexican Countryside.*

4. Mining was also an important economic activity in both Tamaulipas and Nuevo León. Vizcaya Canales, *Los orígenes de la industrialización de Monterrey,* xiv–xv; Samuel E. Magill, Consulate of Tampico, to David J. Hill, secretary of state, Sept. 26, 1902, US Consular Dispatches, MDA; John Farwell, US consul in San Luis Potosí, to Samuel E. Magill, US consul in Tampico, June 5, 1900, US Consular Dispatches, MDA. Among the ixtle producers in central and southern Tamaulipas was the Compañía Anglo-Mexicana of San Luis Potosí. The company shipped ixtle to New York through its agent in Tampico, J. Hess. "Industria ixtlera," *Revista Ferronales* (1960): 40, NLB; Primera Convención de la Liga de Comunidades Agrarias y Sindicatos Campesinos del Estado de Tamaulipas, Mexico City, 1926, 11, in Instituto Nacional de Estudios Históricos sobre la Revolución Mexicana, Mexico City (hereafter, INEHRM); Mora-Torres, *Making of the Mexican Border,* 92. The history of ixtle has not received as much attention as henequen in the Yucatán region (and the history of *ixtleros* even less). See Joseph, *Revolution from Without;* Alston, Mattiace, and Nonnenmacher, "Coercion, Culture, and Contracts"; and Evans, *Bound in Twine.*

5. "Industria ixtlera," *Revista Ferronales* (1960): 40, NLB.

6. "Memoria Administrativa del Estado de Tamaulipas," 1892–93, caja s.n., 209, Fondo: Memorias, AGET.

7. Rivera Estrada and Osnaya Rodríguez, "Repercusiones del asentamiento colonial," 486–87.

8. Zebadúa, "La lucha por la tierra en la región citrícola," 185.

9. "Estado que manifiesta las producciones agrícolas de cada una de las municipalidades en el estado de Nuevo León," no. 32, US consul, Monterrey, July 31, 1879, US Consular Dispatches, MDA.

10. Chassen López, "'Cheaper Than Machines.'" See also Tuñón Pablos, *Women in Mexico.*

11. Toscano Hernández, *Haciendas ixtleras,* 11; Mora-Torres, *Making of the Mexican Border,* table 3.4. As noted by Juan Mora-Torres, the naming of properties/estates as *haciendas* in Nuevo León did not always correspond to the actual type of property. "The problems of using the labels '*hacienda*' and '*rancho*' in Nuevo León is that many *comunidades* called their properties *haciendas* and *ranchos.*" Mora-Torres, *Making of the Mexican Border,* 105. Mora-Torres also notes that, as compared to haciendas in Coahuila (and, I would add, Tamaulipas), haciendas in Nuevo León were quite small. We should also note Casey Walsh's definition of the word *rancho*—it also meant a group of people and/or a place. In Tamaulipas, ranchos were similar to farms with up to thirty residents. Walsh, *Building the Borderlands,* 79.

12. Zebadúa, "La lucha por la tierra," 186.

13. Zebadúa, "Las Comunidades Campesinas," 403–404.

14. Zebadúa, "La lucha por la tierra," 186.

15. Herrera Pérez, "El ixtle en Tamaulipas," 50, 60.

16. Mora García, *El General Alberto Carrera Torres,* 91.

17. Ibid., 50.

18. Ibid., 91.

19. Toscano Hernández, *Haciendas ixtleras,* 12.

20. Ibid., 14.

21. Ibid., 18–19.

22. "Memoria Administrativa del Estado de Tamaulipas," 1892–93, caja s.n., 208, Fondo: Memorias, AGET.

23. These production figures are for 1903. Toscano Hernández, *Haciendas ixtleras,* 18–19.

24. "Memoria Administrativa del Estado de Tamaulipas," 1892–93, caja s.n., 208, Fondo: Memorias, AGET.

25. Toscano Hernández, *Haciendas ixtleras,* 26.

26. Comité Directivo del Sindicato "El Porvenir" del Obrero Textil to José Zorilla, Hacienda las Pilas, Aug. 12, 1925, caja s.n., exp. 11, no. 40, Fondo: Junta Central de Conciliación y Arbitraje, AGET. *Tallanderas* could also be *mediera/os* (a type of sharecropper).

27. Toscano Hernández, *Haciendas ixtleras,* 23.

28. Ibid., 23–24.

29. Keremitsis, "Latin American Women Workers in Transition," 498.

30. Quoted in Toscano Hernández, *Haciendas ixtleras,* 20–24, 54.

31. Toscano Hernández, *Haciendas ixtleras,* 54.

32. See Cerutti, *Agua, tierra, y capital en el Noreste de México;* and Toscano Hernández, *Haciendas ixtleras.*

33. Unión de Obreros "El Despertar del Esclavo" to Federación Obrera de Tampico, June 1, 1925, Xicotencatl, caja 3, exp. 3, no. 20, Fondo: Junta Central de Conciliación y Arbitraje, AGET.

34. Unión de Obreras "Fraternidad Femenil" to Junta Central de Conciliación y Arbitraje (Tamaulipas), Aug. 11, 1925, caja 3, exp. 3, Fondo: Junta Central de Conciliación y Arbitraje, AGET.

35. "Anuario Tamaulipas, 1910–1911," Fondo: Anuarios Estadísticos del Estado de Tamaulipas, AGET.

36. Mora-Torres, *Making of the Mexican Border,* 116.

37. Esiquio Martínez to Juez Segundo del Ramo Penal (Monterrey), Mar. 28, 1898, caja 809, no. 151, Sección: Justicia, Asunto: Falta a la Moral, AGENL.

38. See the various *censos industriales* by *municipio* in the AGENL and the *anuarios,* or annual reports, in AGET. Both indicate low numbers of women in the agricultural sector, where they were mainly classified as *jornaleros* or *peones de campo.*

39. Hart, *Revolutionary Mexico,* 282, 295.

40. Dixie R. Reid and James R. Clayton, claimants, May 19, 1931, Docket no. 1551, Hart Collection; *Anuario Estadístico del Estado de Tamaulipas* (Victoria: Establecimiento Tipográfico del Gobierno, 1912), 225, in AGET. See Hart, *Empire and Revolution,* 511–25, for a partial list of large American landholdings in Mexico between 1910 and 1913; and González Filizola, *Una victoria perdida,* 107.

41. Olvera Guerrero, *Reseña histórica del municipio de Ocampo,* 13.

42. F. Legorreta, Cd. Victoria, to Alejandro Prieto, Tampico, Feb. 23, 1904, Prieto Papers, NLB; Onofre Zambrano, Monterrey, to Alejandro Prieto, Tampico, Apr. 22, 1904,

Prieto Papers, NLB. Blalock was born Mar. 24, 1855, and died Nov. 23, 1925, according to the inscription on his tomb in Chamal cemetery, Chamal Viejo, Tamaulipas, author's fieldwork.

43. Lic. H. Dávila, notario público, Tampico, to Alejandro Prieto, Aug. 17, 1904, Prieto Papers, NLB; Hart, *Empire and Revolution,* app. A. For census data, see Anuario Estadístico del Estado de Tamaulipas, 1910–11, AGET; see also Mora García, *El General Alberto Carrera Torres,* 67.

44. Mora García, *El General Alberto Carrera Torres,* 67. The haciendas in Ocampo (formerly Santa Barbara), Tamaulipas, during the Porfiriato included Buenavista, El Chamal, El Pencil, El Platanito, El Tigre, La Mula (present-day Santa María de Guadalupe), Puertecitos (Providencia, present-day Librado Rivera), San Francisco, and San Lorenzo. Olvera Guerrero, *Reseña histórica del municipio de Ocampo.*

45. International Land and Investment Company, Sept. 16, 1944, American-Mexican Claims Commission (hereafter, AMC) Docket no. 80, Hart Collection.

46. Descendants of George W. Hanna, n.d., AMC Docket no. 20, Hart Collection. María Zebadúa notes that corn and brown sugar (*piloncillo*) were major goods and that beans and squash were grown on a lesser scale. Zebadúa "La lucha por la tierra," 186.

47. Descendants of George W. Hanna, n.d., AMC Docket no. 20, Hart Collection.

48. Blanco Caballero, "Problema agrario en Tamaulipas," 111, 122. On the agrarian situation during and after the Revolution in Nuevo León, see the numerous documents found in the Fondo: Archivo de la Comisión Agraria (Secretaría de la Comisión Agraria), AGENL.

49. Hart, *Empire and Revolution,* app. 1.

50. Mora-Torres, *Making of the Mexican Border,* 119.

51. John Farwell, Tampico, to Samuel E. Magill, San Luis Potosí, May 28, 1901, US Consular Dispatches, MDA. Industrial development also brought with it a flurry of foreigners specializing in "professional" trades and interacting with natives on a daily basis. For instance, in 1907 the American doctor Charles F. Graham, from Texarkana, set up a practice in Reynosa specializing in the care of women and girls. A male foreign doctor thus competed with female *parteras* or midwives. See "Partidos" (1907), Fondo: Epoca Actual, Sección: Presidencias, Archivo Histórico de Reynosa (hereafter, AHR).

52. McGary, *American Girl in Mexico.*

53. Ibid.

54. Hart, *Empire and Revolution,* 219. American foremen were paid a yearly salary of fifteen hundred dollars in US currency on the Townsend estate. Cora Townsend's father was Gideon Townsend, and her mother had business connections to the Canal Bank of New Orleans. A handful of American women traveling in Mexico, usually accompanied by husbands, parents, or siblings, wrote about their experiences in Mexico and revealed racial and cultural prejudices against Mexicans. See Hahner, *Women through Women's Eyes,* especially the piece from Fanny Chambers Gooch, "Keeping House in Northern Mexico."

55. Toscano Hernández, *Haciendas ixtleras,* 54.

56. "Censo industrial: cuadro de estadística, secretaría de fomento, colonización," caja 17 (1903), Fondo: Secretaría General de Gobierno, Serie: Estadísticas, Asunto: Monterrey y otros municipios, AGENL; Hart, *Empire and Revolution,* 219.

57. Hart, *Empire and Revolution,* 225–26.

58. "Censo industrial: cuadro de estadística, secretaría de fomento, colonización" (1903).

59. Ibid.

60. Mora García, *El General Alberto Carrera Torres,* 87.

61. Herrera Pérez, "El ixtle en Tamaulipas," 52.

62. J. W. Fiske, J. L. Mott Iron Works, New York, to Alejandro Prieto, Feb. 6, 1895, Prieto Papers, NLB.

63. Herrera Pérez, "El ixtle en Tamaulipas," 52. For a discussion of liberalism and women, see Tuñón Pablos, *Women in Mexico,* 60–62.

64. Zorilla, *La mujer en Tamaulipas,* 44–45.

65. Keremitsis, "Latin American Women Workers in Transition," 498.

66. Male workers at Guido Moebius's shops earned eighty-seven centavos a day. "Censo Industrial: Cuadro de Estadística, Secretaría de Fomento, Colonización" (1903).

67. Section on Arramberi, "Censo industrial: cuadro de estadística, secretaría de fomento, colonización" (1903).

68. For an overview of cigar factories in other parts of Mexico, see Camacho Morfín and Pichardo Hernández, "La cigarrera 'El Buen Tono,'" 86–87; Deans-Smith, *Bureaucrats, Planters, and Workers;* González Sierra, *El monopolio del humo.* For Nuevo León, see Dicken, "Monterrey and Northeastern Mexico," 150.

69. Vizcaya Canales, *Los orígenes de la industrialización de Monterrey,* 98; Leal Ríos, *Linares: visión del siglo XX,* 22.

70. The estimate is based on the production values of two factories. In 1910 Montemorelos had two cigar factories—branches that belonged to one of the major companies in Linares. The factories in Montemorelos raked in profits of five thousand to eight thousand pesos a month. Cipriano Ordaz, Montemorelos, to Governor, Nuevo León, Jan. 26, 1910, caja 46, exp. 48, Fondo: Correspondencia de Alcaldes, Sección: Montemorelos, AGENL. Since most cigar factories were in Linares and Monterrey, it is likely that women living in surrounding pueblos commuted to these centers for work, particularly after the availability of rail transportation.

71. Mora-Torres, *Making of the Mexican Border,* 241. The value of goods produced (in pesos) is based on Walker, "Mexican Industrial Revolution and Its Problems," table 6. Textiles alone constituted one of the leading industries in the nation. In Nuevo León three major textile companies merged in 1908, forming a nine-million-peso enterprise. Ibid., 6; Guttman, *Work, Culture, and Society in Industrializing America.*

72. Snodgrass, "Contesting Identities," 8. For a discussion of women in garment factories, see Hernández, "*Las Obreras de Monterrey*" (manuscript).

73. Quoted in Hutchison, *Labors Appropriate to Their Sex,* 52. See also Porter, *Working Women in Mexico City,* on women's labor and morality.

74. Deans-Smith, *Bureaucrats, Planters, and Workers,* 258. The author notes that this was the "same proportion as at the end of the colonial period." Ibid.

75. "Población según la ocupación principal," Secretaría de Gobierno del Estado de Nuevo León, Sección de Estadística, Memorias de Bernardo Reyes, 1899–1903, AGENL.

76. Vizcaya Canales, *Los orígenes de la industrialización de Monterrey,* 98; "Población según la ocupación principal," Secretaría de Gobierno del Estado de Nuevo León, Sección Estadística, Memorias de Bernardo Reyes, 1900–1906, AGENL.

77. Saldaña, *¿Y que hicimos?*, 83.

78. See the Censo Industrial for Nuevo León for various municipalities.

79. See Censo Industrial for Nuevo León, and the numerous cases found in the JCCA in the AGENL.

80. "Anuario 1910–1911," caja s.n., Fondo: Anuarios Estadísticos del Estado de Tamaulipas, AGET.

81. Wages for the early 1900s are based on Camacho Morfín and Pichardo Hernández, "La cigarrera 'El Buen Tono.'" It is very likely that the wages during this time period were higher in the northern part of the country than elsewhere. The earliest information on wages I have found for cigarreras in the northern region dates to 1900, based on the JCCA, AGENL; Saldaña, *¿Y que hicimos?*, 83. In 1885 cigarreras earned approximately four reales for every twenty-four hundred cigars rolled. See Ramos Escandón, "Señoritas Porfirianas," 158–59.

82. Lopes, "Del taller a la fábrica," 264–65. Male workers earned one peso per day.

83. Patricia Moctezuma Yano, "Las actividades de subsistencia en México frente a la globalización: los piloncilleros de la huasteca potosina," 7–9, http://lasa.international.pitt.edu/Lasa2001/MoctezumaYanoPatricia.pdf (accessed May 10, 2010).

84. "Talladores de ixtle: El Pillo Barrón Carmona los explota," *El Janambre*, Nov. 25, 2009, http://www.janambre.com.mx/?p=605.

85. "Censo industrial: cuadro de estadística, secretaría de fomento, colonización" (1903).

86. Ibid. Further research is needed on female landowners in northern Mexico; clearly, there were women who owned land, rented land, and were considered both *latifundistas* and *minifundistas* (small landholders). See Kanter, "Native Female Land Tenure and Its Decline in Mexico"; Deere and Magdalena, *Rural Women and State Policy;* and Kellogg, *Weaving the Past.*

87. "Censo industrial: cuadro de estadística, secretaría de fomento, colonización" (1903).

88. See the numerous cases in Fondo: Justicia, Sección: Justicia, Asuntos Falta a la Moral and Asunto: Abuso de Confianza, AGENL, for evidence of female business owners.

89. Interview with "Ana María," in Arenal, *Mujeres de tierra y libertad*, 43.

90. Interview with "Juanita" in Arenal, *Mujeres de tierra y libertad*, 23.

91. Juan G. González to JLCA, Aug. 31, 1937, caja 12, exp. 7, Fondo: Trabajo, Asunto: Junta Local de Conciliación y Arbitraje, AGENL.

92. "Anuario 1910–1911," Fondo: Anuarios Estadísticos del Estado de Tamaulipas, AGET.

93. Tuñón Pablos, *Women in Mexico*, 75. Julia Tuñón Pablos writes, "In 1885, 183,293 women or 26.5 percent of the economically active population worked. By 1890 this number had risen to 210,566, and the number of women wage earners surpassed that of domestic servants." Ibid.

94. Sieglin, "Agua, acumulación de capital, y burguesía," 54.

95. Ibid.

96. "En busca de mayor fortuna" Caso Ordinario escrito sobre entrega de una niña ("In search of better fortune," Regular Case regarding custody of child), Juana Vásquez, versus

Ismael Pérez Maldonado, caja. 14, ex. 28, 1887, Sección: Justicia, Asunto: Abuso de Confianza, AGENL.

97. Ibid.

98. "Memorandum in the case of Mrs. H. A. Woolman," Apr. 20, 1896, Tampico, US Consular Dispatches, MDA.

99. Ibid.; W. C. Whitefield, San Luis Potosí, to Consul, Tampico, May 4, 1896; "Testimony of William de Burgh Coxen, British citizen," in Mrs. H. A. Woolman's case against María and Altagracia Gómez, Apr. 20, 1896, Tampico, both in US Consular Dispatches, MDA. Woolman also makes reference to the fact that the system she introduced in Mexico was the same as O. H. de Lamarkons's system in the United States.

100. "Testimony of Mrs. H. A. Woolman," May 6, 1896, 8, Tampico, US Consular Dispatches, MDA.

101. Ibid. The use of the word *gringo* by Mexicans is also found in an account of the murder of an American near Tampico. Adam Lieberknecht, Tampico, to Assistant Secretary of State, United States, Aug. 22, 1893, US Consular Dispatches, MDA.

102. "Testimony of Mrs. H. A. Woolman," May 6, 1896, 8.

103. "Compañía Manufacturera Singer," *El Progresista* (Victoria, Tamps.), Apr. 24, 1904. On Catarino Garza's various occupations, see Young, *Catarino Garza's Revolution.*

104. McGary, *American Girl in Mexico,* 9.

105. See Pratt, *Imperial Eyes.*

106. Santiago, "Women of the Mexican Oil Fields," 96.

107. Carlos Morton, claimant, AMC Docket no. 667, Aug. 3, 1925, Hart Collection.

108. Andrea Bayless and Ana María Fernández (Mrs. W. R.) Johnson, claimants, Docket no. 106, Aug. 29, 1939, Hart Collection. See also the Mexican American Claims Commission (partial list), NLB.

109. *Anuario Estadístico del Estado de Tamaulipas* (Victoria: Establecimiento Tipográfico del Gobierno, 1912), 223, in Fondo: Anuarios Estadisticas del Estado de Tamaulipas, AGET.

110. Ibid., 225. Another interethnic/interracial marriage was that between Manuela Martínez and John Breckenridge Hibler, from the Hacienda de Pablillo in Galeana, Nuevo León. Hart, *Empire and Revolution,* 299–300. Patricio Milmo and sons also owned a property near Doña Sara. Ibid.

111. Warren P. Sutton, Matamoros, to Second Assistant Secretary of State, United States, Apr. 12, 1882, US Consular Dispatches, MDA; "Defunciones de Extranjeros habidas en 1899," adapted from Anexo no. 16 in Memorias de Bernardo Reyes, 1899–1903, AGENL.

112. Ben F. Moats, to Samuel E. Magill, Tampico, Mar. 1, 1899, US Consular Dispatches, MDA; "Agrarian Dotation from Lands of the Estate of the Late Ingerbrick O. Brictson," O. Brictson, claimant, AMC Docket no. 53, June 18, 1943, Hart Collection.

113. McGary, *American Girl in Mexico,* 68.

114. Ibid., 54. See ibid., chap. 4, for comments on marriage and courtship and a description of Elizabeth McGary's short-lived courtship with a Mexican man by the name of Eduardo.

115. P. Rueda, Mexico City, to Emilio Portes Gil, Mexico City, Mar. 22, 1922, caja 2 bis. Serie II (1 carpeta), Archivo Histórico Particular de Emilio Portes Gil, AGN (hereafter,

Archivo Emilio Portes Gil, AGN). Emilio Portes Gil was the legal consultant for the Ferrocarriles Nacionales. Hart, *Empire and Revolution,* 224; Adelson, "Cultural Roots of the Oil Workers' Unions." See also Olvera Rivera, "Identity, Culture, and Workers' Autonomy."

116. Hart, *Empire and Revolution,* 224.

117. "Summary of the Antecedents of the Oliver Case," from Howard Taylor Oliver, claimant, Docket no. 34, Sept. 14, 1938, Hart Collection.

118. Ibid. Oliver also organized a company, Oliver American Trading Company, Inc. (1915–22).

119. See official registration of the all-female union, Unión de Obreras "Fraternidad Femenil," sent to JCCA (Tamaulipas), Aug. 11, 1925, caja 3, exp. 3, Fondo: Junta Central de Conciliación y Arbitraje, AGET.

120. Herrera-Pérez, "El ixtle en Tamaulipas," 52.

121. Sieglin, *Mujeres en el campo a finales del siglo XX,* 4.

122. Ibid., 55.

CHAPTER THREE. "WE CANNOT SUFFER ANY LONGER FROM THE *PATRÓN*'S BAD TREATMENT"

Epigraphs: Manuel Aguilar to Governor, Nuevo León, Dec. 13, 1889, Fondo: Trabajo, Asunto: Sirvientes, caja 1859–1929, AGENL; Sociedad Hermana Obrera de Linares to Governor, Nuevo León, Oct. 5, 1888, Fondo: Trabajo, Asunto, Asociaciones Organizaciones y Sindicatos, AGENL.

1. [Name illegible], Tuxpan, to Secretario de Agricultura y Fomento, Mexico City, Feb. 14, 1922, caja 2 bis, exp. 1, Archivo Emilio Portes Gil, AGN.

2. Historian José E. Iturriaga explains that an urban population in 1910 was classified as one with more than two thousand inhabitants. In 1940 that figure rose to twenty-five hundred. Iturriaga, *La estructura social y cultural de Mexico,* 6–7.

3. The original Spanish text is as follows: "Iba a trabajar unos días para hacerse de recursos y poder seguir para Estados Unidos." Case against Miguel Martínez for "delito de abuso de confianza, por parte de Hernán Gila Guillen, presentado al Mariano Alcalde, Ciudad Linares, N.L.," June 30, 1913, caja s.n., Sección Justicia, Asunto: Abuso de Confianza, AGENL.

4. The historian Miguel Angel González Quiroga has written extensively on labor control mechanisms in northern Mexico, particularly in Nuevo León. See esp. González Quiroga and Cerutti, *Texas y el norte de México (1848–1880).* Also, see the numerous cases involving debt peonage and campesinos' plans to abandon hacienda employment for work in factories in Fondo: Trabajo, Asunto: Sirvientes, AGENL. Historically, the Mexican North competed with US landowners and business leaders for unskilled Mexican labor. Texas received three-fourths of all immigrants entering the United States, a large number of them from northeastern Mexico. Taylor, "Notes on Streams of Mexican Migration," 287–88.

5. For an examination of the citrus region in southern Nuevo León (Montemorelos region), see Sieglin, "Agua, acumulación de capital, y burguesía." See also the classic work by François Chevalier, *Land and Society in Colonial Mexico,* 278–79, in which the author

notes that the northern haciendas were among the first to create a large permanent labor force, mainly through debt peonage.

6. Hart, *Revolutionary Mexico,* 259; "Relación de las haciendas y ranchos existentes en el Estado, con expresión de sus principales productos," in *Anuario Estadístico del Estado de Tamaulipas, formado por la dirección general técnica* (Victoria: Establemiento Tipográfico del Gobierno, 1912), and "Informe de la Sauteña," Oct. 27, 1906, both in Hart Collection. El Chamal (Colonia Americana) in the municipio of Ocampo also was a major sugar producer. See Arguelles, *Reseña del estado de Tamaulipas,* 214. The Hacienda Sauteña dates back to 1789. See Herrera Pérez, *Breve historia de Tamaulipas,* 210.

7. The firm of Reid and Clayton managed the Hacienda El Caracol. In 1902 James R. Clayton and his sister Dixie R. Reid, wife of John M. Reid, purchased the hacienda from the firm. Sworn testimony of James R. Clayton, n.d. (ca. 1917–18?), Hart Collection. See also González Filizola, *Una victoria perdida.*

8. Arguelles, *Reseña del estado de Tamaulipas,* 210–12.

9. In Linares, located approximately seventy-five miles south of Monterrey, a sugar company, Compañía Azucarera Mexicana, owned by Francisco Armendaiz, used *maquina moderna,* or modern technology, and employed seventy workers to produce from 200,000 to 250,000 kilograms of sugar and 30,000 liters of alcohol. Charles W. Parker was granted a concession to establish the company. See also Permisos y Concesiones, AGENL; Olvera Sandoval, "La citricultura en Montemorelos," 18–19. Sixty-six percent of the total workforce of Nuevo León labored in the agricultural sector in 1910. For the citrus region, see Sieglin, "Agua, acumulación de capital, y burguesía."

10. See the many documents related to this company, esp. "Expediente de la demanda presentada por Estefano de la Rosa en contra de la *The Bernal Orchard Co.,*" Sept. 1925, caja 4, exp. 1, Fondo: Junta Central de Conciliación y Arbitraje, AGET.

11. "Estimated Annual Cost of Operation," Tampico Sugar Company, Samuel E. Magill, Tampico, to US Department of State, Sept. 22, 1904, US Consular Dispatches, MDA.

12. Hart, *Empire and Revolution,* 220–24.

13. Ibid., apps. 1 and 2.

14. "Wage lists for Southern Tamaulipas," Tampico, US Consular Dispatches, MDA. An American, Seymour Taylor, owned the largest orchard in Tamaulipas. See also items in American-Mexican Claims Commission, NLB.

15. Adapted from Sieglin, "Agua, acumulación de capital, y burguesía"; Zebadúa, "La lucha por la tierra"; and Katz, "Labor Conditions on Haciendas in Porfirian Mexico."

16. Katz, "Labor Conditions on Haciendas in Porfirian Mexico." Katz writes that "after 1917 . . . peonage had been legally and to a large degree practically abolished." Ibid., 13. For an overview of *tiendas de raya* (hacienda or company stores) in other regions, see Aurora Gómez-Galvarriato, "Myth and Reality of Company Stores during the Porfiriato: The *tiendas de raya* of Orizaba's Textile Mills," http://www.helsinki.fi/iehc2006/papers2/Gomez.pdf (accessed July 2, 2008). Katz identified four main sources for the study of haciendas: "accounts by contemporary journalists and social reformers; parliamentary debates, some during the Díaz period but mainly from the Madero years; local historical and anthropological surveys; [and] reports by foreign diplomats." Katz, "Labor Conditions on

Haciendas in Porfirian Mexico," 12. I would add *cartas-peticiones* and petitions for *amparo,* or aid, as a fourth source, given that these were frequently submitted by workers and shed light on the labor relations and conditions in the countryside and urban centers in the northern region of the country.

17. Saldaña, *¿Y que hicimos?,* 9–10; see also chap. 2.

18. Alejandro Prieto to Timoteo Castañeda, May 11, 1903, Prieto Papers, NLB.

19. Timoteo Castañeda to Alejandro Prieto, Feb. 29, 1904, Prieto Papers, NLB.

20. Gómez Castillo, *Esbozo biográfico del consolidador del Sindicato y Cooperativa del Gremio Unido Alijadores,* 10–13. Isauro Alfaro Otero later founded the Cooperativo de Alijadores.

21. Rowley's partners were also American: George W. Clynes and Harry Dalin. Marcial Ocasio Meléndez refers to Rowley as "Edwin Rowley" in *Capitalism and Development,* 142–43, whereas Carlos González Salas refers to him as "Edward" in *Acercamiento a la historia del movimiento obrero de Tampico.*

22. Gómez Castillo, *Esbozo biográfico del consolidador del Sindicato y Cooperativa del Gremio Unido Alijadores,* 15.

23. Ibid.

24. Ibid., 17.

25. Guerrero Miller and Ayala, *Por eso!* 25. Tampico became one of the major recruiting centers for another labor organization, the Casa del Obrero Mundial, founded in 1915.

26. Gremio Unido de Alijadores de Tampico to José Etienne, Tampico, June 7, 1912, caja 10, exp. 6, Dirección General de Gobierno, AGN.

27. González Salas, *Acercamiento a la historia del movimiento obrero de Tampico,* 16–17.

28. Ibid.

29. "Una muestra de gratitud de los alijadores," *El Sol de Tampico,* Nov. 30, 2005; Ocasio Meléndez, *Capitalism and Development,* 145.

30. "Tampico," *El Eco,* Jan. 1, 1922, Sección Noticias de los Estados Tamaulipas y Nuevo León, Hispanic Recovery Project, University of Houston; Gómez Castillo, *Esbozo biográfico del consolidador del Sindicato y Cooperativa del Gremio Unido Alijadores,* 18. By 1921 the GUA had taken control of all of the work on the docks. The following year, in May 1922, the machinery once owned by Rowley was for sale at a price of 800,000 pesos, and the GUA did not have money to purchase it. The governor of Tampaulipas lent the GUA money so that it could acquire machinery. A year and a half later, the GUA "era ya una sociedad cooperative rentable," in other words, it could contract itself. See "Una muestra de gratitud de los alijadores," *El Sol de Tampico,* Nov. 30, 2005.

31. The GUA later became the Sindicato del Gremio Unido de Alijadores de Tampico y Doña Cecilia.

32. Gremio Unido de Alijadores de Tampico, to José Etienne, Tampico, June 7, 1912, caja 10, exp. 6, Dirección General de Gobierno, AGN.

33. Testimony of "P.R.," in *Los pobres de Monterrey.*

34. Saldaña, *¿Y que hicimos?,* 16–17; Walker, "Mexican Industrial Revolution and Its Problems," 25.

35. See Adelson, "Historia social de los obreros industriales de Tampico," chapter on migration.

36. Warman, *"We Come to Object,"* 7.

37. Manuel Aguilar to Governor, Nuevo León, Dec. 13, 1889, Fondo: Trabajo, Asunto: Sirvientes, 1859–1929, AGENL; Ma. Del Carmen Jiménez Villanueva, *Escribanos Públicos: 1824–1910,* no. 7 (Monterrey: Colección Alberto Galván Rentería, 1990), in Biblioteca Ricardo Covarrubias, AGENL.

38. Porter, *Working Women in Mexico City,* 133.

39. See note 37.

40. Quoted in Arzola, *Una historia vivida,* 12–13.

41. Mora García, *El General Alberto Carrera Torres,* 74n109.

42. Quoted text in ibid., 116–17.

43. Katz, "Labor Conditions on Haciendas in Porfirian Mexico," 13; Sieglin, "Agua, acumulación de capital, y burguesía," 38.

44. Sieglin, "Agua, acumulación de capital, y burguesía," 37–39.

45. Zebadúa, "La lucha por la tierra en la región citrícola," 187.

46. Ibid., 187–88.

47. Pedro Salas, to Governor, Nuevo León, Mar. 10, 1910, no. 632, Fondo: Trabajo, Asunto: Sirvientes, AGENL.

48. Federico de los Ríos, to Governor, Nuevo León, Mar. 10, 1910, s.n., Fondo: Trabajo, Asunto: Sirvientes, AGENL.

49. Testimony of "E. G." in *Los pobres de Monterrey.* Many of the day laborers working on the railroads also worked in the smelters, particularly in the Fundidora de Monterrey, and in the Tampico oil sector. This transient population had gained valuable experience by migrating to different labor centers in the Mexican Northeast, and, in many cases, to the United States. At age twenty-two, Esteban Garza married a woman from Monterrey and brought home one and a half pesos a day—substantially higher than his father's daily wage. After working on the railroads and in the brewery, Esteban retired in Monterrey, where he worked alongside his wife on a commercial dairy farm.

50. Andres Rodríguez, to Governor, Nuevo León, Oct. 23, 1896, Fondo: Trabajo, Asunto: Sirvientes, AGENL.

51. Ibid.

52. Response to Andres Rodríguez's petition, Monterrey, Oct. 29 and 31, 1896, Fondo: Trabajo, Asunto: Sirvientes, AGENL.

53. Snodgrass, *Deference and Defiance in Monterrey,* 39.

54. Municipalities in the *región citricola* of Nuevo León include Allende, Cadereyta Jiménez, General Terán, Hualahuises, Linares, and Montemorelos.

55. Similar patterns of migration occurred in Texas. See Pastrano, "Bureaucratic Origins of Migrant Poverty"; Olvera Sandoval, 169–79.

56. Olvera Sandoval, "La citricultura en Montemorelos," 169–79. Olvera Sandoval also notes that a crate of these oranges sold for 2.50 pesos in Corpus Christi and 3.50 to 3.75 pesos in Phoenix; there were also shipments to Kansas City.

57. Teodora Cepeda, Monterrey, to Governor, Nuevo León, Sept. 24, 1892, Fondo: Trabajo, Asunto: Sirvientes, AGENL.

58. Response to Teodora Cepeda's petition, Sept. 26, 1892, Fondo: Trabajo, Asunto: Sirvientes, AGENL.

59. Teodora Cepeda, Monterrey, to Governor, Nuevo León, Sept. 24, 1892, Fondo: Trabajo, Asunto: Sirvientes, AGENL.

60. Donnan and Wilson, *Borders, Frontiers of Identity, Nation and State,* 63; James Scott, *Weapons of the Week.*

61. Severiano Flores and Eduardo Herrera, representing Sociedad Unión Regiomontana de Monterrey, to Governor, Nuevo León, Apr. 17, 1888, Fondo: Trabajo, Asunto: Asociaciones, Organizaciones y Sindicatos, AGENL; Severiano Flores and Eduardo Herrera representing Sociedad Unión Regiomontana de Monterrey, to Gran Círculo de Obreros, Monterrey, and Sociedad Mutualista de Señoras, Monterrey, Apr. 1888, Fondo: Trabajo, Asunto: Asociaciones, Organizaciones y Sindicatos, AGENL.

62. Ibid.

63. Ibid. See also Rojas Coria, *Tratado del cooperativismo en México.* The Gran Círculo de Obreros was founded in 1871 in Mexico City.

64. Sociedad Mutualista de Señoras y Señoritas, Monterrey, to Bernardo Reyes, Monterrey, May 1, 1886, Fondo: Trabajo, Asunto: Asociaciones, Organizaciones y Sindicatos, AGENL. Organizations used this "honorary member" political strategy so that their groups would appear to be pro-government, and they often simultaneously were circulating proclamations criticizing that same government. Mutualistas organized by men adopted similar strategies. See Sociedad Mutualista "Pedro Jose Mendez" Victoria, Tamaulipas, and the naming of Alejandro Prieto as their *socio honorario,* Greto Valderas representing Sociedad Mutualista "Pedro Jose Mendez," to Alejandro Prieto, Jan. 9, 1889, Prieto Papers, NLB. In its most basic form, the word *amparo* refers to legal protection or aid. The word and the practice of *amparo* refer to both the judicial procedure of filing a *juicio de amparo* for legal protection (made available to Mexicans with the Constitution of 1857) and *amparo* in the form of asking for aid through a petition or *protesta* (protest or *queja*). For a brief history of the *juicio de amparo,* see Sánchez Mejorada, "Writ of Amparo." For a legal analysis, see Baker, *Judicial Review in Mexico,* 148–49. For a structural, juridical interpretation, see Arnold, "Vulgar and Elegant." There were also all-female mutualistas that did not comprise working-class women exclusively; most of the members were educators or the wives of businessmen. See Sociedad Cooperativa Violeta, Reynosa, Tamaulipas, to Salvador Guevara, Reynosa, June 27, 1925, Fondo: Epoca Actual, Sección: Juzgado Penal, Asunto: Sindicatos, Sociedades y Agrupaciones, AHR. Other examples of such organizations include the popular Club Femenil Violeta and Club Blanco, and many more; see Fondo: Presidencia (Actas de Cabildo, 1920–30), Archivo Histórico de Matamoros (hereafter, AHM). See also Cuellar, "La Recreación en Matamoros," 2000, a copy of which was provided by Mr. Cuellar, former director of the AHM. For upper-class women in mutualistas, see Zorilla, *La mujer en Tamaulipas.*

65. Sociedad Mutualista de Señoras, to Bernardo Reyes, Monterrey, Aug. 24, 1886; Sociedad Mutualista de Señoras y Señoritas, to Governor, Nuevo León, Sept. 15, 1886; Sociedad Mutualista de Señoras y Señoritas, Monterrey, to Governor, Nuevo León, Sept. 19, 1886, all in Fondo: Trabajo, Asunto: Asociaciones, Organizaciones y Sindicatos, AGENL.

66. The Sociedad Mutualista de Señoras y Señoritas used the physical space belonging to the Gran Círculo de Obreros for meetings and special events. Two women from

Ciudad Victoria—Irene Passemente de Arguelles and Josefa C. de Guerra—organized the Sociedad Femenil Cooperativa de Victoria on Feb. 17, 1906. The women emphasized family values. Passement was the wife of the governor of Tamaulipas.

67. Vizcaya Canales, *Los orígenes de la industrialización de Monterrey,* 122.

68. Olivares Arriaga and Altair Tejeda de Tamez, *Mujeres que han dejado testimonio en Tamaulipas,* 43–44. Aminta Blanco de Mainero organized Sociedad Hijas de Hidalgo in 1910.

69. "Al los Señores Secretarios de la Cámara de Diputados del Departamento de Trabajo," Sept. 22, 1911, caja 1, exp. 1, Departamento de Trabajo, AGN.

70. French, *Peaceful and Working People,* 88.

71. See Porter, *Working Women in Mexico City.* See also Ramos Escandón, *Presencia y transparencia;* and Martin, *Governance and Society in Colonial Mexico.* For a description of women street vendors, see McGary, *American Girl in Mexico.*

72. Sociedad Hermana Obrera de Linares to Governor, Nuevo León, Apr. 21, 1892, July 16, 1892, July 7, 1894, Jan. 8, 1895, Feb. 23, 1895, July 13, 1896, July 15, 1896, all in Fondo: Trabajo, Asunto: Asociaciones, Organizaciones y Sindicatos, AGENL; Young, *Catarino Garza's Revolution.*

73. Sociedad Hermana Obrera de Linares to Governor, Nuevo León, Apr. 21, 1892, July 16, 1892, July 7, 1894, Jan. 8, 1895, Feb. 23, 1895, July 13, 1896, July 15, 1896, all in Fondo: Trabajo, Asunto: Asociaciones, Organizaciones y Sindicatos, AGENL; "Población según ocupación principal," Sección: Peones de Campo, Comerciantes, Cigarreras, Lavanderas, Criados o Sirvientes, y Población total, all in Memorias de Bernardo Reyes, 1899–1903, AGENL. There were 9,647 males and 9,716 females in Linares, as reported in the 1890 census. Of the males, 2,791 were considered *peones de campo* (countryside peasants), 223 males were *comerciantes* (merchants), while 9 females were *comerciantes.* Another 200 women performed (paid) domestic work. The term "public washers" refers to women employed in commercial laundries or working at public washing sites.

74. Sociedad de Obreros de Linares, to Governor, Nuevo León, Oct. 5, 1888, Fondo: Trabajo, Asunto: Asociaciones, Organizaciones y Sindicatos, AGENL.

75. Leal Ríos, *Linares: visión del siglo XX,* 207–208.

76. Sociedad de Obreros de Ciudad Juárez, to Governor, Nuevo León, Sept. 12, 1893, Fondo: Trabajo, Asunto: Asociaciones, Organizaciones y Sindicatos, AGENL; Gómez Castillo, *Esbozo biográfico del consolidador del Sindicato y Cooperativa del Gremio Unido Alijadores,* 7; Marin Peña and E. Herrera representing Gran Círculo de Obreros, Monterrey, to Secretary, Nuevo León, Jan. 13, 1898; Andrés Quintanilla representing Gran Círculo de Obreros, Monterrey, to Governor, Nuevo León, Nov. 12, 1889, both in Fondo: Trabajo, Asunto: Asociaciones, Organizaciones, Sindicatos, AGENL.

77. See app. 1.

78. Vicente Cavazos, president of Sociedad Cooperativa "El Porvenir de la Unión," Monterrey, to Governor, Nuevo León, Oct. 26, 1900, Fondo: Trabajo, Asunto: Asociaciones, Organizaciones y Sindicatos, AGENL. Some of the first *cajas de ahorro* appeared as early as the 1840s. Hart, "Evolution of the Mexican and Mexican-American Working Classes," 6; Hart, "Nineteenth-Century Urban Labor Precursors," 303. One of the first *bancos cooperativos* was the Banco Social del Trabajo, founded in November 1877, and the

Cooperativa de Consumo in Tampico, founded in 1900. See Rojas Coria, *Tratado del cooperativismo en México.*

79. Unión de Obreras "Fraternidad Femenil" to JCCA (Tamaulipas), Aug. 11, 1925, caja 3, exp. 3, Fondo: Junta Central de Conciliación y Arbitraje, AGET; see also app. 2.

80. Hart, *Anarchism and the Mexican Working Class;* Parlee, "Impact of United States Railroad Unions on Organized Labor," 451. See the many cases involving the detention and imprisonment of workers who publicly spoke against the government in Fondo: Falta de respeto a la autoridad, AGENL.

81. The ixtle boom lasted from 1890 to 1908. Herrera Pérez, *Breve historia de Tamaulipas,* regional economy map, 210.

82. Jesús Peña, Cd. Victoria, to Jesús Tarrega, Reynosa, May 15, 1929, Fondo: Epoca Actual, Sección: Juzgado Penal, Asunto: Sindicatos, Sociedades y Agrupaciones, AHR; López Olivares, *Presidentes municipales de Reynosa.*

83. Leoncio Torres, Cd. Victoria, to Presidente Municipal, Cd. Victoria, Jan. 5, 1934, Fondo: Epoca Actual, Sección: Juzgado Penal, Asunto: Sindicatos, Sociedades y Agrupaciones, AHR; Arguelles, *Reseña del estado de Tamaulipas,* 104.

84. Sociedad Obreros Progresista, Cd. Victoria, to Presidente Municipal, Reynosa, Jan. 2, 1904, Fondo: Epoca Actual, AHR; José L. García, president, Sociedad Benito Juárez de Auxilios Mutuo, to Governor Bernardo Reyes, Sept. 14, 1900, caja 1880–1904, Fondo: Trabajo, Asunto: Asociaciones, Sindicatos y Organizaciones, AGENL.

85. See Iturriaga, *La estructura social y cultural de Mexico,* for a lengthy discussion on the transition to urbanization in the country.

86. [Name illegible], Tuxpam, Veracruz, to Secretario de Agricultura y Fomento, D.F. Feb. 14, 1922, caja 2 bis, exp. 1, Archivo Emilio Portes Gil, AGN.

87. Leal Ríos, *Linares: capital de Nuevo,* 66, 204.

88. Hart, *Revolutionary Mexico,* 237–43; Young, *Catarino Garza's Revolution.*

89. Telegram from Tula authorities to Alejandro Prieto's office, Dec. 19, 1887; telegram from Jaumave authorities to Alejandro Prieto's office, Dec. 20, 1887, both in Prieto Papers, NLB.

90. "Al los Señores Secretarios de la Cámara de Diputados del Departamento de Trabajo," Sept. 22, 1911, caja 1, exp. 1, Departamento del Trabajo, AGN.

91. Alejandro Prieto, "Mi último discurso al H. Congreso Primero de Abril, 1896," 9, Prieto Papers, NLB.

92. Olvera Sandoval, "La citricultura en Montemorelos." Olvera Sandoval notes that there were thirty-one US citizens in Montemorelos in 1903 (seventeen men and fourteen women). Ibid., 158.

93. Sieglin, "Agua, acumulación de capital, y burguesía," 55.

94. Herrera Pérez, "El ixtle en Tamaulipas," 50.

95. Nuncio, Mexico City, to Secretaría de Fomento, Colonización, y Industria, Sept. 12, 1911, caja 1, exp.1, Departamento del Trabajo, AGN.

96. "Informe a Diputados del Congreso de Tamaulipas," undated report, undated folder, box 1905–17, Prieto Papers, NLB.

97. Saldaña, *¿Y que hicimos?,* 15–16.

98. Aguilar Camin and Meyer, *In the Shadow of the Mexican Revolution,* 10; Rojas Sandoval, *Monterrey,* 35–38.

99. *Visión histórica de la frontera norte,* 63.

CHAPTER FOUR. (EN)GENDERING REVOLUTION IN THE BORDERLANDS

Epigraphs: "El Movimiento Avanza: Proclama (desde el campo de operaciones, estado de Tamaulipas)," *La Bandera Roja en Tamaulipas,* Sept. 29, 1911, in NLB; "Expediente relativo a la queja hecha por el Sr. Luis Dibildox Contra Los Responsables de Atropellos," Luis Dibildox, to Governor, Nuevo León, Sept. 4, 1925, caja 6 (1925), Archivo de la Comisión Agraria, AGENL.

1. This research indicates that about 15 percent of some seventy-five petitions were favorably answered; that is, the petitioner gained help in contacting a poor people's lawyer, received a recommendation for a job, or received funding for school supplies (especially in the postrevolutionary period). See the cases in both the AGET and the AGENL.

2. Olvera Sandoval, *Monterrey y sus caminos de hierro,* 28–29.

3. Parkes, *History of Mexico,* 310; Aguilar Camín and Meyer, *In the Shadow of the Mexican Revolution,* 12–13, 15.

4. Marín, *Recuerdos de la Revolución Constitucionalista;* Marín, *La rebelión de la huertista en Tamaulipas;* Soto, *Emergence of the Modern Mexican Woman,* 48–49.

5. Bernardo Reyes, Monterrey, to Club Reyista, Aug. 28, 1911, no. 315–3a; Bernardo Reyes, Monterrey, to Juez Primero de Letras del Ramo Penal, Aug. 22, 1911, no. 315; Generoso Garza, to F. González Garza, Nuevo León, Sept. 19, 1911, all in Fondo: Trabajo, Asunto: Asociaciones, Organizaciones y Sindicatos, AGENL.

6. Leobardo Chapa, Nuevo León, to Ministro de Gobernación, Mexico City, Aug. 24, 1911, Fondo: Trabajo, Asunto: Asociaciones, Organizaciones y Sindicatos, AGENL.

7. Report on the demonstrations by Club Liberal Anti-Reyista 2 de Abril de 1903, Inspector General de Policía, Monterrey, to Leobardo Chapa, Nuevo León, Aug. 21, 1911, Fondo: Trabajo, Asunto: Asociaciones, Organizaciones y Sindicatos, AGENL; "Documento XIX Leyes de Amnistía," anexo no. 274, Apr. 2, 1903, Memorias de Bernardo Reyes, 1899–1903, AGENL. Although Pablo Benítez Leal occupied the governorship (1900–1902), Reyes exercised power as minister of war in the state from 1900 to 1903. Similar demonstrations took place in Doctor Arroyo, Nuevo León, in March 1903. See *Visión histórica de la frontera norte,* 63.

8. Classic works on women and the Mexican Revolution include Salas, "Soldadera in the Mexican Revolution," and other essays in Fowler-Salamini and Vaughan, *Women of the Mexican Countryside, 1850–1990; Las mujeres en la revolución mexicana;* Macías, *Against All Odds;* Mendieta Alatorre, *La mujer en la revolución mexicana;* Ramos and Lau, *Mujeres y revolución, 1900–1917;* Reséndez Fuentes, "Battleground Women"; and Soto, *Emergence of the Modern Mexican Woman.*

9. *Las mujeres en la revolución mexicana,* 124–25.

10. See the various articles on the Revolution in the *Brownsville Herald* during the month of March 1913; and Ramos Aguirre, *Mujeres de armas tomar.*

11. "Brave Matamoros Girls," *Brownsville Daily Herald,* May 16, 1913.

12. Case against Guadalupe Barrera for slander, May 28, 1913, c. 810, no. 112, Sección: Justicia, Asunto: Falta a la Moral, AGENL.

13. Palomo Acosta and Winegarten, *Las Tejanas,* 76–77.

14. For a discussion of the intersections of "text" or "narrative" and "action" or "politics," see Young, *Catarino Garza's Revolution,* particularly chap. 1.

15. Pozas Horcasitas, "La evolución de la política laboral mexicana," 93.

16. Pérez, *Decolonial Imaginary,* 56.

17. Ibid., 56–58; Teresa Palomo Acosta, "Sara Estela Ramírez," *Handbook of Texas Online,* http://www.tshaonline.org/handbook/online/articles/fra60 (accessed Sept. 18, 2009); Cynthia E. Orozco, "Mexican-American Women," *Handbook of Texas Online,* http://www.tshaonline.org/handbook/online/articles/pwmly (accessed Sept. 18, 2009). See also Melero, "Sara Estela Ramírez and Andrea Villarreal González." See also Zamora, "Sara Estela Ramírez."

18. Lomas, "Articulation of Gender in the Mexican Borderlands," 294; see also Lomas, "Transborder Discourse."

19. See Lawhn, "Mexican Revolution and the Women of *México de Afuera*"; Hart, *Anarchism and the Mexican Working Class,* 92–93.

20. Hart, *Anarchism and the Mexican Working Class,* 293–97.

21. Ibid., 300.

22. Ibid., 91–95.

23. González Salas, *Acercamiento a la historia del movimiento obrero de Tampico,* 65–68; Higinio Tanguma, "Proclama Floresmagonista," in Zorilla, Miro Flaquer, and Herrera Pérez, *Tamaulipas.*

24. Hernández, "Military Activities in Matamoros during the Mexican Revolution," 6.

25. "El Movimiento Avanza: Proclama (desde el campo de operaciones, estado de Tamaulipas)," *La Bandera Roja en Tamaulipas,* Sept. 29, 1911, in NLB.

26. Ibid. See also Pérez, *Decolonial Imaginary,* chap. 3.

27. "El Movimiento Avanza." Some of the adherents of the PLM also became supporters of the revolutionary manifesto known as the Plan de San Diego. See the various chapters on the topic in De León, *War along the Border.*

28. While Mora-Torres does not focus on *obreras* he acknowledges the lower wages they received in the textile industry. The Magón brothers also called for a minimum national pay of thirty centavos for children and seventy-five centavos for men (in the textile industry). See Mora-Torres, *Making of the Mexican Border.*

29. In states such as Utah and California, for example, women made strides with regard to improvement of wages and general work conditions. The Utah State Federation of Labor Convention "declared in favor of a minimum wage law for women." In California, unionized theater workers pressed for equal pay when they discovered that theatrical managers planned to substitute women for male operators in their motion picture theaters. Given men's activism in unions, the theatrical managers saw women as cheaper alternatives and as passive and nonthreatening workers. However, the female operatives' actions

contradicted this idea; in a cross-gender solidarity movement, their issues were made public, leaving theater managers with no other alternative than to heed their demands. "Unions Favor Women's Minimum Wage," and "Organized Labor Protects Women," *Pan American Labor Press / El Obrero Pan-Americano,* órgano de la confederación obrera Pan-Americana (San Antonio, Tex.), Oct. 9, 1918, box OS1, Clemente N. Idar Papers, NLB (hereafter, Idar Papers, NLB).

30. Zamora, "Sara Estela Ramírez."

31. Alcayaga Sasso, "Librado Rivera y los Hermanos Rojos," 107.

32. Mexican Realty Company, claimant, July 18, 1924, Agency no. 2152, Docket no. 526, Hart Collection. The Mexican Realty Company had acquired Hacienda La Victoria in 1909.

33. Blalock Colony, claimants, AMC box 155, Hart Collection. Later, in 1935, Otto Brictson lost 1.25 million acres (i.e., Hacienda San José de las Rusias) in a government expropriation.

34. Hart, *Revolutionary Mexico,* 286–88.

35. Mexican Realty Company, claimant, July 18, 1924, Agency no. 2152, Docket no. 526, Hart Collection. The practice of squatting was a useful strategy employed by many campesinos seeking lands. The Hacienda Rascón in southern Tamaulipas also came under attack in 1913. A group of rebels demanded weapons, money, and horses. Wilbert L. Boney, San Luis Potosí, and Dr. Rafael Cepeda, San Luis Potosí, Feb. 26, 1913, as annexed in Roy Cunningham, claimant, Agency no. 2195, Hart Collection. Even in the 1940s and 1950s, Mexicans were squatting on lands and pressuring the government to continue granting land plots. A member of my own family (the Véliz-Morado family) who belonged to the Confederación de Trabajadores Mexicanos (CTM), Río Bravo branch, camped near San Fernando, Tamaulipas, and was able to acquire lands from the government in this way. The Véliz-Morado family still owns land in an *ejido* (communal landholding) in San Fernando.

36. "Discurso, Grupo Regeneración 'Prismas Anarquistas' de Burkett, Texas," in *Regeneración,* no. 147, June 28, 1913, Archivo Electrónico de Ricardo Flores Magón, www.archivomagon.net/Periodico/Regeneracion /CuartaEpoca/ . . . / e4n147.pdf (accessed Nov. 30, 2009).

37. Alcayaga Sasso, "Librado Rivera y los Hermanos Rojos," 138.

38. Palomo Acosta and Winegarten, *Las Tejanas,* 211–12.

39. *Album conmemorativo de las Comisiones Honoríficas y Brigada Cruz Azul* (1925), 61, microfilm reel 1, Eustacio Cepeda Papers, NLB (hereafter, Cepeda Papers, NLB).

40. Ibid.

41. Bacha-Garza and the San Juan Economic Development Corp., *Images of America,* 102.

42. Transcription of Jovita Idar speech by Clemente N. Idar, n.d., folder 14, box 9, Idar Papers, NLB.

43. Limón, "El Primer Congreso Mexicanista de 1911," 95.

44. Quoted in ibid., 95, 98. Women also continued to participate in mutual-aid societies in the 1930s. Dolores Charó represented the Club Social Recreativo "Latino Americano," a mixed-sex organization in Robstown, Texas. Women also participated in the various

activities of the Sociedad Mutualista "Hijos de Hidalgo," also in Robstown. See "Notas de Robstown," in *El Paladín:* Órgano de L.U.L.A.C. (Corpus Christi, Tex.), Feb. 7, 1930, box OS1, Idar Papers, NLB.

45. Palomo Acosta and Winegarten, *Las Tejanas,* 85. See also the various studies by Arnoldo De León, particularly, *They Called Them Greasers.*

46. Edna Ochoa, "El periodismo, la mujer y la frontera en Laredo: propuesta de cambio en la obra de Jovita Idar," presented at the Primer Simposio de la Historia del Noreste y Sur de Texas, Archivo Histórico de Reynosa, Reynosa, Tamps., Oct. 2, 2006, 6; "150 Years of Work for Women's Rights," *San Antonio Express News,* July 19, 1998, 6A.

47. Quoted in Ochoa, "El periodismo, la mujer y la frontera," 7.

48. Pérez, *Decolonial Imaginary,* 56.

49. Jovita Idar, undated three-page letter, folder 2, box 1, Idar Papers, NLB.

50. Ochoa, "El periodismo, la mujer y la frontera," 7–8.

51. Ibid., 3.

52. "Esther González Salinas," unpublished biographical essay written by Rosaura Alicia Dávila, AHM. I thank Ms. Dávila for providing me with a copy of this essay.

53. Hart, *Revolutionary Mexico,* 237–43. See also Paul Hart, *Bitter Harvest.*

54. Alejo Francisco, Monterrey, to A. Pedraza, Mexico City, Dec. 3, 1912, caja 10, exp. 10, Departamento del Trabajo, AGN; Hart, *Empire and Revolution,* 24–26.

55. "Extracto de las manifestaciones presentadas por los fabricantes de hilados y tejidos de algodón para el semestre—Enero–Junio 1912," June 1912, caja 5, exp. 4, Departamento del Trabajo, AGN.

56. Antonio de Zamacona, Mexico City, to Departmento del Trabajo, Mexico City, Dec. 18, 1912, caja 3, exp. 12, Departmento del Trabajo, AGN.

57. "Cuestionario para la Estadística de Diferencias y Huelgas," Dec. 1913, caja 5, exp. 1, Departmento del Trabajo, AGN; Gómez Castillo, *Esbozo biográfico del consolidador del Sindicato y Cooperativa del Gremio Unido Alijadores,* 26 (quote).

58. Pozas Horcasitas, "La evolución de la política laboral mexicana," 94.

59. Compañía Industrial de Monterrey, to Adalberto A. Esteva, Mexico City, June 12, 1913, caja 1, exp. 4, Fondo: Fomento, Comercio, y Industria, Asunto: "Algunos industriales del Estado de Puebla, Veracruz, y otros, remiten datos acerca de las huelgas y diferencias registradas en sus fabricas," Departamento del Trabajo, AGN.

60. Ibid.

61. For a history of Monterrey workers during the Mexican Revolution, see Snodgrass, *Deference and Defiance in Monterrey;* Snodgrass, "La lucha sindical," 52; and Cerutti, "Españoles, gran comercio y Brote Fabril en el norte de México," 150, cuadro 15.

62. Departamento del Trabajo, to Cámara de Diputados, Mexico City, Sept. 22, 1911, caja. 1, exp. 1, Departamento del Trabajo, AGN.

63. Ibid.

64. Mayor, Montemorelos, to Governor, Nuevo León, n.d, caja 46, exp. s.n., no. 86, Fondo: Correspondencia de Alcaldes, Sección: Montemorelos, AGENL.

65. Procurador de Justicia, Cd. Victoria, to Síndico Primero del Ayuntamiento en Funciones de Agente de Ministerio Público por Ministerio de Ley, Reynosa, Nov. 17, 1927,

Fondo: Epoca Actual, Sección: Presidencia, Asunto: Reclamaciones entre México y Estados Unidos, AHR; Hernández, "Military Activities," 24–25.

66. Herrera Pérez, *Breve historia de Tamaulipas;* Blanco Caballero, "Problema agrario en Tamaulipas," 247. Sauteña was broken up into several *ejidos.* Río Bravo did not become a *municipio* until 1962. See "Antecedentes," Gobierno Municipal de la Ciudad de Río Bravo, Estado de Tamaulipas, http://www.riobravo.gob.mx/v2002_ esp/riobravo/default.asp; Walsh, *Building the Borderlands,* 70; "Memoria Administrativa del Estado de Tamaulipas," 1892–93, Fondo: Memorias Administrativas del Estado de Tamaulipas, AGET. During the period of Bourbon rule in Mexico, the land was granted in 1781 to Antonio de Urízar, known as El Sauto, and the inhabitants of the region called the place La Sauteña. By 1784 some of the land along the banks of the river had been sold to colonists. While various sources differ slightly on the tenure of the property, we know that the estate had been organized as a hacienda by the late 1840s. By the 1880s, the absentee landowners had sold it to American investors, several of whom had ties to the Texas Company of Mexico. The estate focused on the production of corn, rice, and cotton. The actual corporation of Sauteña, Companía La Sauteña, was so large and economically significant by the late Porfiriato as compared to previous decades that the state treasury actually listed its contributions in a separate column. In the "Contribución de Hacienda del Estado de Tamaulipas" for fiscal year 1891, each district listed its contributions in the form of taxes to the state, and at the bottom of the report three separate columns were reserved, one each for Companía La Sauteña, Patricio Milmo, and Octavio del Conde. Sauteña reported taxes of 2,132.92 pesos, Milmo paid 792.18, and Conde paid 160.02. Given that the Conde family had sold the lands to investors, it is quite possible that some of the land remained in the hands of family members, such as Octavio. Sources also reveal that a family named Sauto had some connection to the estate, given that Policarpo Sauto was acting as general manager of Sauteña as late as 1913. The estate was so immense that, during the agrarian reform debates of the early 1920s, Antonio Díaz Soto y Gama, the intellectual and Mexican senator who represented the Partido Nacional Agrarista and was a PLM supporter, compared La Sauteña to an "octopus with extensive arms." "Transcripción de sesión de la Cámara de Diputados, Jueves 7 de Diciembre de 1922," in caja 1, bis. Serie I, exp. 6, 11–12, Archivo Emilio Portes Gil, AGN; "A última hora, los rebeldes decidieron no atacar Matamoros," *La Prensa* (San Antonio, Tex.), May 15, 1913.

67. Procurador de Justicia, Cd. Victoria, to Síndico Primero del Ayuntamiento en Funciones de Agente de Ministerio Público por Ministerio de Ley, Reynosa, Nov. 17, 1927; Ministerio Público Federal, Nuevo Laredo, to Presidente Municipal, Reynosa, Feb. 20, 1925, both in Fondo: Epoca Actual, Sección: Presidencia, Asunto: Reclamaciones entre México y Estados Unidos, AHR. On the Hacienda Los Borregos land redistribution, see Arizmendi, *Ejido Lucio Blanco, Tamaulipas,* 8. The *ejidatarios* were the following: Florentino Izaguirre, José Izaguirre, Octaviano Govea, Ventura Govea, Apolinar Govea, Ruperto Reyna, Esteban Reyna, Dolores Reyna, Francisco Hernández, Higinio Gamez, and Juan Campos. The lands of other large estates were also distributed among campesinos, including some of the land in Jacobo Martínez's Hacienda Santa Engracia in 1925 in Tamaulipas; see *Corridos Agraristas de Tamaulipas.* When the hacienda lands were distributed among

campesinos, Martínez's descendants, José Castañeda and José Martínez, managed the estate. See the updated website of the Hacienda Santa Engracia, now a hotel, in central Tamaulipas, www.haciendase.com/historia.html.

68. On the Texas Company, see Pratt, *Growth of a Refining Region.*

69. *Liga de Comunidades Agrarias y Sindicatos Campesinos del Estado de Tamaulipas.*

70. El Aguila to Secretaría de Guerra y Marina, May 3, 1919, caja 7, exp. 40, Serie: Quejas y Reclamaciones, Departamento de Petróleo, AGN. See also El Aguila to Secretaría de Guerra y Marina, Feb. 2, 1918, caja 7, exp. 35, Serie: Quejas y Reclamaciones, Departamento de Petróleo, AGN; and Olvera Rivera, "Identity, Culture, and Workers' Autonomy." The previous year, Edward Doheny had also suffered deprivations from Constitutionalist general Miguel M. Acosta and his troops when they occupied the labor camps at Los Naranjos. They took several horses and mules, as well as clothes, belonging to the *petroleros* who were known to support their employers. At Weetman Pearson's El Aguila Oil Company labor camps, company agents made frequent requests for aid from authorities.

71. "Los amigos de los aliados," *El Mundo* (Tampico), June 24, 1968.

72. Menéndez, *El cacique de las Huastecas,* 3–5. The book is based on the historian Gabriel A. Menéndez's interview with Peláez. This interview/biography was reproduced in Menéndez's book *Doheny El Cruel;* see "Los amigos de los aliados," *El Mundo* (Tampico), June 24, 1968.

73. Menéndez, *El cacique de las Huastecas,* 3–5. See also Guerrero Miller, *Cuesta abajo,* 72–93.

74. Menéndez, *El cacique de las Huastecas,* 3–6; Santiago, "Rejecting Progress in Paradise," 174–77. See also Santiago, "Women of the Mexican Oil Fields"; and Santiago, *Ecology of Oil.*

75. On William Salomon's partnership with Edward Doheny, see Hart, *Empire and Revolution,* 99–100.

76. The Huasteco population was more pronounced in the southern part of Tamaulipas and northern Veracruz and Hidalgo. By 1900 there were approximately twenty-five thousand adult *huasteco* speakers in the region. The majority of the population in the Northeast, however, was mestizo. See Santiago, "Rejecting Progress in Paradise," 177. For population statistics, see the chapter on the popular and urban class in Iturriaga, *La estructura social y cultural de México.*

77. "Se encuentra en New Orleans el Jefe Manuel Pelaez," *La República* (El Paso, Tex.), Dec. 23, 1919.

78. Ribb, "La Rinchada," 60, 92–96.

79. Sworn testimony of James R. Clayton, claimant, n.d., Hart Collection.

80. E. P. Nafarrate to Teódulo Ramírez, May 21, 1922, Teódulo Ramírez Papers, NLB.

81. Violence toward Americans also spilled over to the US side of the border. See John A. Pool and Jesse W. Pool, claimants, Agency no. 2336, Sept. 10, 1923, Hart Collection. Several studies have emphasized the Mexican Revolution as a factor contributing to various uprisings; see, for example, Rocha, "Influence of the Mexican Revolution on the Texas-Mexico Border"; Sandos, *Rebellion in the Borderlands;* and Harris and Sadler, *Texas Rangers and the Mexican Revolution.*

82. Nicéforo Zambrano, to Antonio L. Villarreal, Monterrey, May 20, 1914, in "Acta de

la Sesión preliminar por la que quedó instalada a la Comisión Agraria Central de Nuevo León," caja 1893–1915, Fondo: Archivo de la Comisión Agraria, AGENL.

83. Ibid.

84. Bartolo Rodríguez, Tamaulipas, to Francisco I. Madero, Mexico City, Mar. 18, 1912, as quoted in González Salas, *Acercamiento a la historia del movimiento obrero de Tampico,* 74–75. *Gente conocida* refers to a neighbor or neighbors.

85. Quoted in González Salas, *Acercamiento a la historia del movimiento obrero de Tampico,* 75–76. W. M. Hansom was the general manager; see Yankelevich, "Mexico for the Mexicans." The Mexico Land Company from Cleveland, Ohio, owned the Conejo Hacienda and Conejo Land Company.

86. Ribb, "La Rinchada," 60–61, 92. Yankelevich uses "Hansom" instead of Hanson. Ribb, "La Rinchada," spells it "Hanson."

87. Yankelevich, "Mexico for the Mexicans."

88. Ribb, "La Rinchada," 62; Story, "Genesis of Revolution in the Tamaulipas Sierra."

89. Zorilla, *La mujer en Tamaulipas,* 49–51.

90. Quoted in Arzola, *Una historia vivida,* 12–13. Tapia and her family received land in 1922 from Alvaro Obregón and Placido Cedillo.

91. Arzola, *Una historia vivida,* 8. On the origins of the Mexican Revolution in the Huasteca region, see Saka, "Agrarian Rebellion and Clerical Insurrection in Nineteenth-Century Mexico." See also Santiago, *Ecology of Oil.*

92. Mora García, *El General Alberto Carrera Torres,* 145.

93. See the various photographs in the Robert Runyon Photographic Collection, Dolph Briscoe Center for American History, University of Texas at Austin. See also Casasola, *Mexico.*

94. Quoted in Arzola, *Una historia vivida,* 7.

95. For a discussion on sexual violence and war, see Castañeda, "Presidarias y Pobladoras." See also Alonso, *Thread of Blood.*

96. Olivares Arriaga and Tejeda de Tamez, *Mujeres que han dejado testimonio en Tamaulipas,* 319.

97. Walsh, *Building the Borderlands,* 55–57.

98. Hernández, "El alma de la rebelión," 212, 214; Zorilla, *La mujer en Tamaulipas,* 52.

99. Teódulo Ramírez, Matamoros, to Refugia Venabides de Ramírez, Laredo, Aug. 20, 1915, Ramírez Papers, NLB. Refugia was probably Teódulo's first wife. Other documents show Laurencia Martínez Viuda de Ramírez as Teódulo's widow; in a letter dated 1947 Laurencia states that Teódulo had died in 1924. See Laurencia Martínez Viuda de Ramírez to Raúl Gárate, Gobernador Provisional del Estado de Tamaulipas, June 25, 1947, Ramírez Papers, NLB.

100. Paula Serna, Tamaulipas, to Emilio Portes Gil, Mexico City, Sept. 20, 1928, caja 14, exp. 1, Archivo Emilio Portes Gil, AGN.

101. E. P. Nafarrate, Gral C.A de la 5a Div. del C. de E. de Noreste, "Circular no. 6 a los Tamaulipecos," Dec. 29, 1915; E. P. Nafarrate, Gral C.A de la 5a Div. del C. de E. de Noreste, "Circular no. 14 a los Tamaulipecos," Mar. 24, 1916, both in Ramírez Papers, NLB. Teódulo Ramírez served as *coronel de caballería* of the Constitutionalist forces in Tamaulipas.

102. "Sesión ordinaria del 26 de febrero 1921," "Sesión ordinaria del 29 de enero de

1921," "Sesión 10 de febrero del 1921," all in Fondo: Presidencia (Actas de Cabildo, 1920–30), AHM. The municipal government required the signatures of at least twenty residents to make the hiring of a teacher official. See "Sesión ordinaria de 19 de abril del 1921," in ibid.

103. Presidente Municipal to Tesorero Municpal, regarding the case of Sra. Guadalupe Juárez, Sept. 23, 1920, cajas 1–3 (1917), Fondo: Presidencia, AHT.

104. Santiago, "Women of the Mexican Oil Fields," 96; Hernández, "El alma de la rebelión."

CHAPTER FIVE. WOMEN'S LABOR AND ACTIVISM IN THE GREATER MEXICAN BORDERLANDS, 1910–1930

Epigraphs: Jovita Idar, undated three-page letter, folder 2, box 1, Idar Papers, NLB; "Estatutos de la Unión de Obreras 'Fraternidad Femenil,'" Xicotencatl, Tamaulipas, presented to the JCCA, Cd. Victoria, Tamps., by María De la Luz Yzaguirre and María Ynocencia Vega, Aug. 11, 1925, caja 3, exp. 3, no. 20, Fondo Junta Central de Conciliación y Arbitraje, AGET.

1. The historian Emilio Zamora points out that migration in the pre-Revolution period consisted more of a cycle, one in which Mexicans frequently returned to Mexico for periods of time and then headed back to the United States. He argues that "return migrations reinforced a pattern of cultural and political interactions between communities on both sides of the border." Zamora, *World of the Mexican Worker in Texas,* 15.

2. For women in the US Southwest, see Ruiz, *Cannery Women, Cannery Lives.* See also Ruiz, *From Out of the Shadows.* For the Mexican North, see Snodgrass, *Deference and Defiance in Monterrey;* and Olcott, *Revolutionary Women in Postrevolutionary Mexico.* For Mexico City, see Porter, *Working Women in Mexico City.*

3. See the various essays that address this question in Olcott, Vaughan, and Cano, *Sex in Revolution.*

4. Palomo Acosta and Winegarten, *Las Tejanas,* 97.

5. Bacha-Garza and the San Juan Economic Development Corp., *Images of America,* 12–13.

6. Ibid., 100.

7. Ibid., 34.

8. Orozco, "Mexican-American Women," *Handbook of Texas Online.*

9. Zamora, *World of the Mexican Worker in Texas,* 26. See also Zamora, "Mexican Labor Activity in South Texas," 42–44; and Orozco, *No Mexicans, Women, or Dogs Allowed,* 212–14.

10. Zamora, "Mexican Labor Activity in South Texas," 42–44.

11. Bacha-Garza and the San Juan Economic Development Corp., *Images of America,* 22, 44, 52.

12. Zamora, *World of the Mexican Worker in Texas,* 214, table 6; Ledesma, "Texas Newspapers and Chicana Workers' Activism," 312.

13. Quoted Ledesma, "Texas Newspapers and Chicana Workers' Activism," 312.

14. Quoted in ibid., 314.

15. Clemente N. Idar, Laredo, to Margarito Romo, Laredo, Tex., Oct. 10, 1918, folder 3, box 2, Idar Papers, NLB.

16. Clemente Idar, AFL organizer, Laredo, Tex., to Judge B. F. Patterson, San Antonio, Tex., June 24, 1921, folder 3, box 2, Idar Papers, NLB.

17. Ibid.

18. Ibid.

19. See app. 1.

20. Miguel Pavio, Fentress, Tex., to Clemente N. Idar, [no month] 27, 1920, folder 3, box 2, Idar Papers, NLB.

21. See González Quiroga and Cerutti, "Guerra y comercio en torno al Rió Bravo."

22. Miguel Pavio, Fentress, Tex., to Clemente N. Idar, [no month], 27, 1920, folder 3, box 2, Idar Papers, NLB.

23. Pastrano, "Bureaucratic Origins of Migrant Poverty," 688.

24. Ibid., 711–12.

25. Allen, *Labor of Women in the Production of Cotton,* 103; Zamora, *Claiming Rights and Writing Wrongs,* 106. See also Foley, *White Scourge.*

26. Allen, *Labor of Women in the Production of Cotton,* 220.

27. Ibid., 231; Palomo Acosta and Winegarten, *Las Tejanas,* 104. Palomo Acosta and Winegarten also discuss women's agricultural work during the 1930s in chapter 5 of their book.

28. Allen, *Labor of Women in the Production of Cotton,* 233.

29. "Algunos datos de interés general para los Mexicanos que residen en el estado de Texas," in *Album conmemorativo de las Comisiones Honoríficas y Brigada Cruz Azul* (1925), 18, microfilm reel 1, Cepeda Papers, NLB.

30. Ibid.

31. Vargas, "Mexican Migrant Workers in the Midwest."

32. Los Fantasmas del Valle, "Bellos Recuerdos," in *Taquachito Nights: Conjunto Music from South Texas,* recorded live at the 16 de Septiembre Conjunto Festival, Smithsonian Folkways, 1999, compact disc. See also Palomo Acosta and Winegarten, *Las Tejanas,* 106.

33. "Algunos datos de interés general para los Mexicanos," 18.

34. Ibid.

35. Allen, *Labor of Women in the Production of Cotton,* 233. The numbers are based on a sample group of 106 Mexican women.

36. Quoted in Allen, *Labor of Women in the Production of Cotton,* 239.

37. Ledesma, "Texas Newspapers and Chicana Workers' Activism," 310–11.

38. Ibid., 311–12.

39. Ibid., 314.

40. See Johnson, *Revolution in Texas;* Rocha, "Influence of the Mexican Revolution on the Texas-Mexico Border"; Sandos, *Rebellion in the Borderlands;* and Gonzáles, "Mexican Revolution, *Revolución de Texas,* and *Matanza de 1915.*"

41. Ledesma, "Texas Newspapers and Chicana Workers' Activism," 317.

42. Levario, *Militarizing the Border.*

43. "Las trabajadoras mexicanas de lavanderías de El Paso, fueron indignamente engañadas y perjudicadas bajo el pretexto de una unión," *La República* (El Paso, Tex.), Dec.

23, 1919, box OS1, Idar Papers, NLB. For a discussion on the role of media in Mexican women's labor issues, see Ledesma, "Texas Newspapers and Chicana Workers' Activism."

44. Snodgrass, *Deference and Defiance in Monterrey*, 129–33.

45. Ledesma, "Texas Newspapers and Chicana Workers' Activism," 317.

46. Snodgrass, *Deference and Defiance in Monterrey*, 39.

47. Ibid., 171.

48. See various Dictamenes de la Junta de Conciliación y Arbitraje, Cd. Victoria, Tamaulipas (1920–25), Fondo: Junta Central de Conciliación y Arbitraje, AGET.

49. Fowler-Salamini, "De-centering the 1920s," 327.

50. Ibid., 315.

51. Snodgrass, *Deference and Defiance in Monterrey*, 129–33. See also Quintero Ramírez, "La organización laboral en la frontera este de México y Estados Unidos."

52. Ledesma, "Texas Newspapers and Chicana Workers' Activism," 317. See also González, "Carolina Munguía and Emma Tenayuca." See also Carmen Tafolla's poem "La Pasionaria" in the *Frontiers* special issue on gender on the borderlands (2003), as well as other works on Tenayuca by Tafolla.

53. Quoted in Sonia Hernández and Charles Waite, eds., *The Mexican American Experience in Texas: A Primary Source Reader* (Dubuque: Kendall Hunt Publishers, 2009), 109–10.

54. See González, "Carolina Munguía and Emma Tenayuca"; Ruiz, *Cannery Women, Cannery Lives.* See also Ruiz, "Una Mujer sin Fronteras"; and Orozco, *No Mexicans, Women, or Dogs Allowed*, 212–14.

55. "Lo que serán las conferencias obreras en Laredo el próximo 13 de Noviembre: los obreros de los dos países trataran importantes asuntos, un abrazo fraternal, se darán en el Puente, las fiestas se preparan," *Evolución* (Laredo, Tex.), Oct. 26, 1918, box OS1, Idar Papers, NLB.

56. Quoted in Alcayaga Sasso, "Librado Rivera y los Hermanos Rojos," 144.

57. Clemente N. Idar, Torreón, to the Bakery and Confectionery Workers' International Union, Chicago, Apr. 20, 1922, folder 5, box 4, Idar Papers, NLB.

58. Limón, "El Primer Congreso Mexicanista de 1911," 97; Quintero Ramírez, "La organización laboral en la frontera este de México y Estados Unidos," 405–406.

59. Blackwell, *¡Chicana Power!*, 49; Palomo Acosta and Winegarten, *Las Tejanas*, 101, 133.

60. "Estatutos de la Unión de Obreras 'Fraternidad Femenil,'" Xicotencatl, Tamaulipas, presented to the Junta de Conciliación y Arbitraje, Cd. Victoria, Tamps., by María De la Luz Yzaguirre and María Ynocencia Vega, Aug. 11, 1925, caja 3, exp. 3, no. 20, Fondo: Junta Central de Conciliación y Arbitraje, AGET. See app. 3 for selected by-laws of the *unión*.

61. President, Junta Central de Conciliación y Arbitraje, to President, Unión de Obreras "Fraternidad Femenil," Aug. 14, 1925, caja 3, exp. 3, no. 20, Fondo: Junta Central de Conciliación y Arbitraje, AGET.

62. On domestic workers' unionization, see Goldsmith Connelly, "Política, trabajo y género."

63. Santiago, "Women of the Mexican Oil Fields," 101.

64. Olivares Arriaga and Tejeda de Tamez, *Mujeres que han dejado testimonio en Tamaulipas,* 92; Tuñón Pablos, *Women in Mexico,* 101.

65. Tuñón Pablos, *Women in Mexico,* 101. See also Olcott, *Revolutionary Women in Postrevolutionary Mexico,* 111.

66. Olcott, *Revolutionary Women in Postrevolutionary Mexico,* 164.

67. Ibid., 232–35. Women would finally get the vote in 1953; they voted in the presidential election for the first time in 1958.

68. Extensive social networks of support had been entrenched since the turn of the twentieth century. Possibly even prior to that time *mexicanos* from Monterrey adhered to the Círculo de Obreros and received news from their compañeros across the border. When Texas authorities detained and jailed Mexican citizen Gregorio Cortéz for killing a sheriff in self-defense, the Laredo-based Sociedad Obreros Igualdad y Progreso, with the assistance of Monterrey obreros, intervened. Sociedad Obreros Igualdad y Progreso, Laredo, to Governor, Nuevo León, July 30, 1901, Fondo: Trabajo, Asunto: Asociaciones, Organizaciones y Sindicatos, AGENL. See also letter dated Sept. 17, 1901, in ibid.

69. Guadalupe V. de Garza, to Presidente y Socios de la Sociedad Mutualista Melchor Ocampo, June 8, 1936, folder 2, box 1, Sociedad Mutualista Melchor Ocampo Papers, NLB (hereafter, Sociedad Ocampo Papers, NLB). Unfortunately, we do not know if Guadalupe received aid. We do know, based on other documents, that other women who petitioned the organization did receive some form of aid. See, for example, Juana Viuda de Flores to Sociedad M. Melchor Ocampo, Nov. 10, 1936, in ibid.

70. Victoria Ureste to Sociedad M. Melchor Ocampo, n.d., folder 2, box 1, Sociedad Ocampo Papers, NLB. Like the campesinas and campesinos of northeastern Mexico, Mexican immigrants to Texas whose agricultural skills were in demand there negotiated labor conditions through the assistance of public officials, who sometimes received honorary union membership; the naming of honorary union members was a common Mexican cultural practice. The organized farm workers from Central Texas, for instance, extended an invitation to Judge B. F. Patterson to serve as their honorary member and help them negotiate working conditions. See Clemente Idar, AFL organizer, Laredo, to Judge B. F. Patterson, San Antonio, June 24, 1921, folder 3, box 2, Idar Papers, NLB. See also Sociedad Mutualista "Hijos de Hidalgo," San Diego (Texas), to Governor, Nuevo León, n.d.; and Sociedad Unión Fraternal Obreros de Brownsville, to Governor, Nuevo León, Mar. 30, 1892, both in Fondo: Trabajo, Asunto: Asociaciones, Organizaciones y Sindicatos, AGENL.

71. "Atenta Invitación de parte de Sociedad Mutualista Melchor Ocampo," Apr. 14, 1930, folder 2, box 1, Sociedad Ocampo Papers, NLB.

72. Porter, *Working Women in Mexico City,* 187.

73. Ibid., 188–89. For a discussion of divorce and morality in Nuevo León during the Porfiriato, see Calderoni Bonleux, "Haciendo públicos actos de nuestra vida privada."

74. Olcott, Vaughan, and Cano, *Sex in Revolution,* 27–29.

75. Walsh, *Building the Borderlands,* 26.

76. Hernández, "'¡Cooperación de los Sexos para el bien de la Nación!'"

77. Olcott, Vaughan, and Cano, *Sex in Revolution,* 22.

78. Clemente N. Idar[?], to J. M. Plata, Mar. 19, 1920, folder 3, box 2, Idar Papers, NLB.

79. Ibid.

80. "Acta de la sesión inaugural del tercer congreso de delegados de las Comisiones Honoríficas y Brigadas de la Cruz Azul Mexicana, de la Primera Divisón effectuado en la ciudad de San Antonio, Texas, durante los días 12, 14, y 15 de octubre de 1925," *Album Conmemorativo de las Comisiones Honoríficas y Brigadas de la Cruz Azul Mexicana* (1925), microfilm reel 1, Cepeda Papers, NLB.

81. As quoted in Limón, "El Primer Congreso Mexicanista de 1911," 95.

82. Ibid.

83. Blackwelder, *Women of the Depression,* 62. See also Vargas, "Tejana Radical."

84. There were also Mexicans and Mexican Americans who left the country voluntarily.

CHAPTER SIX. CLASS, GENDER, AND POWER IN THE POSTREVOLUTIONARY BORDERLANDS

Epigraphs: Report on María Luisa Corona, Aug. 17, 1937, caja 94, exp. 3; Frente Unico de Trabajadores de Linares to Presidente de la JLCA, July 19, 1937, caja 118, exp. 5, both in Fondo: Trabajo, Asunto Junta Local de Conciliación y Arbitraje, AGENL.

1. Juan G. González, to JLCA, Aug. 31, 1937, caja 121, exp. 7, Fondo: Trabajo, Asunto: Junta Local de Conciliación y Arbitraje, AGENL.

2. Ibid.; Luz María Echavarría Reyes, ed., *Trabajadores y empresarios en Monterrey: catálogo de la Junta Local de Conciliación y Arbitraje 1923–1937* (Monterrey: AGENL, 1999), 286, expediente 121/7; SUOICL to Junta Permanente de Conciliación, Aug. 9, 1937, caja 121, exp. 7, Fondo: Trabajo, Asunto: Junta Local de Conciliación y Arbitraje, AGENL; Snodgrass, *Deference and Defiance in Monterrey,* 38. The Ley Federal de Trabajo stipulated that companies either reinstate workers or offer severance pay equal to three months' wages. Employers often used this measure to their advantage, paying to rid themselves of labor activists. Ibid., 132.

3. For studies on the industrialization of Nuevo León, particularly Monterrey, see Mora-Torres, *Making of the Mexican Border;* Morado Macías, "Empresas mineras y metalúrgicas"; *Nuevo León: imágines de nuestra historia;* Saldaña, *¿Y que hicimos?;* Saragoza, *Monterrey Elite and the Mexican State;* Snodgrass, *Deference and Defiance in Monterrey;* Snodgrass, "La lucha sindical"; Snodgrass, "Contesting Identities"; Vázquez Juárez, "Joseph Andrew Robertson empresario norteamericano"; Vizcaya Canales, *Los orígenes de la industrialización de Monterrey;* Rojas Sandoval, *Monterrey;* Rojas Sandoval, "Minería en Nuevo León"; Olvera Sandoval, *Monterrey y sus caminos de hierro;* Garza Sada, *Ensayos sobre la historia de una industria;* Flores Torres, *Burguesía, militares, y movimiento obrero;* Beato and Sindico, "Beginning of Industrialization in Northeast Mexico."

4. Besse, *Restructuring Patriarchy.*

5. I employ the terms *regiomontano* and *norteño* interchangeably in this chapter. Both refer to people residing in the Mexican North; however, regiomontano is more closely associated with Monterrey inhabitants.

6. See the various essays in Olcott, Vaughan, and Cano, *Sex in Revolution,* particularly those by Heather Fowler-Salamini, Susan M. Gauss, and Jocelyn Olcott. The history of women's labor is intimately tied to the larger issue of women's suffrage.

7. The exception is Snodgrass, who examines women's labor in the Cervecería Cuauhtémoc in *Deference and Defiance in Monterrey,* chap. 1. There are other studies on women workers (particularly agricultural workers), but most focus on the post-1940 period; see, for example, Zebadúa, "Género, política y vida cotidiana"; and the numerous works by Veronika Sieglin. See also the works that analyze masculinity in the Mexican North, including those of Snodgrass; Alonso, *Thread of Blood;* and Misael Hernández, "Estado, cultura y masculinidades en el noreste." There is still some resistance to this type of research; see Frader, "Labor History after the Gender Turn," 24; and Scott, "Gender." See also Camarena Ocampo and Fernández, "Culture and Politics."

8. Viotti da Costa, "Experience versus Structures," 17–18. Studies on the socioeconomic transformations of other parts of the Mexican North in the late nineteenth century have helped to explain similar processes in the Mexican Northeast. See, for example, Tinker Salas, *In the Shadow of the Eagles;* Truett, *Fugitive Landscapes;* Wasserman, *Persistent Oligarchs;* and Wasserman, *Capitalists, Caciques, and Revolution.*

9. Keremitsis, "Latin American Women Workers in Transition," 497.

10. Camacho Morfín, "La historieta, mirilla de la vida cotidiana," 55. On the question of morality, see Porter, *Working Women in Mexico City;* and Farnsworth-Alvear, *Dulcinea in the Factory.*

11. Snodgrass, *Deference and Defiance in Monterrey,* 112, 165–67.

12. Olcott, "Center Cannot Hold," 236–38. See also Olcott, "Miracle Workers." For women's activism in Guadalajara, particularly women affiliated with the CTM, see Fernández Aceves, "Guadalajaran Women and the Construction of National Identity." See also Olcott, *Revolutionary Women in Postrevolutionary Mexico.*

13. At El Buen Tono, the mostly female labor force continued to work in the packaging department. Camacho Morfín and Pichardo Hernández, "La cigarrera 'El Buen Tono,'" 85.

14. See the many cases of labor grievances filed with the Junta Central de Conciliación y Arbitraje and the Junta Local de Conciliación y Arbitraje, AGENL.

15. Sindicato Unico de Obreras de la Industria Cigarrera de Linares versus Arturo Alaníz and La Esmeralda, July–Aug. 1937, caja 118, exp. 5, Fondo: Trabajo, Asunto: Junta Local de Conciliación y Arbitraje, AGENL.

16. Porter, *Working Women in Mexico City,* 25.

17. Snodgrass, *Deference and Defiance in Monterrey,* 39.

18. The first case presented to a labor board by a cigarrera was not until the mid-1930s; Snodgrass points out that the national average of cases won by labor in the 1920s was much higher than the average in Monterrey. Snodgrass, *Deference and Defiance in Monterrey,* 133. More research is needed to determine the percentage of cases won by labor in the entire state as compared to national figures. Moreover, we do not know the exact number of cases presented by obreras statewide. The number of labor cases submitted in the state capital did increase in the 1930s.

19. While *torcedor/a* is a term used to describe workers who rolled cigars, obreras rarely used the term; instead, they used *cigarrera.*

20. Fowler-Salamini, "Gender, Work, and Working-Class Women's Culture in the Veracruz Coffee Export Industry," 117.

21. Federación Regional de Trabajadores Obreros y Campesinos de Tamaulipas (Cd.

Victoria), "Protesta contra actos de la clase patronal de Nuevo León," Compañeros de Artefactos Metálicos, Fábricas Orión, Fábrica de Hilados y Tejidos La Fama, La Industrial Financiera, & Fábrica de Cigarros de Hoja (Cigarrera Linares), Oct. 10, 1936, 2.331.8 (16), caja 32-A, exp. 76, Dirección General de Gobierno, Serie: Sindicatos y Agrupaciones, AGN; Juan G. González to JLCA, Aug. 31, 1937, caja 121, exp. 7, Fondo: Trabajo, Asunto: Junta Local de Conciliación y Arbitraje, AGENL.

22. Juan G. González, to JLCA, Aug. 31, 1937, caja 121, exp. 7, Fondo: Trabajo, Asunto: Junta Local de Conciliación y Arbitraje, AGENL.

23. The number of women in the Nuevo León workforce during this period has been estimated at three thousand, but the actual figure is probably higher because of unknown numbers of people working from home. Snodgrass, *Deference and Defiance in Monterrey,* 143.

24. Snodgrass, *Deference and Defiance in Monterrey,* 171. The company unions were organized as the "Independent Unions of Nuevo León."

25. It was in the Cigarrera La Moderna factory that the red union Sindicato de Trabajadores de la Cía Cigarrera "La Moderna" triumphed over the independent Unión de Obreros de la Cía Cigarrera "La Moderna" during the 1930s. See "Caso del Sindicato de Trabajadores de la Cía Cigarrera 'La Moderna,'" 1936–37, caja 90, exp. 7, Fondo: Trabajo, Asunto: Junta Local de Conciliación y Arbitraje, AGENL. However, the victory was a limited one given that La Moderna adopted company paternalism, resembling that of Cervecería Cuauhtémoc; at Vidriera Monterrey (Monterrey Glassworks), only 2 women (out of 100) from the decorating department chose to join the red union in 1936. Snodgrass argues that relations between the obreras and their supervisors were harmonious and that the company "did not require its female operatives to retire upon marriage." Snodgrass, *Deference and Defiance in Monterrey,* 208. One of the few factories that incorporated modern technology, Cigarrera La Moderna was not established until 1934, much later than the smaller shops that had been operating since the early 1900s. With machinery that produced up to 1,000 cigarettes (unlike the larger, hand-rolled cigars) per minute, the 350-worker labor force produced up to 8 million cigarettes per day, sold under six brand names, for between five and twenty centavos per pack. Dicken, "Monterrey and Northeastern Mexico," 150. José P. Saldaña notes that the factory of La Moderna was established in 1936. Saldaña, *¿Y que hicimos?,* 83.

26. Canning, "Gender and the Politics of Class Formation," 745; Farnsworth-Alvear, introduction to *Dulcinea in the Factory.*

27. Hernández, "*Las Obreras de Monterrey.*"

28. Each standard *tarea* consisted of twenty boxes containing sixty rolled cigars.

29. Sindicato Unico de Obreras de la Industria Cigarrera de Linares versus Arturo Alaníz, owner of La Esmeralda, July–Aug. 1937, caja 118, exp. 5, Fondo: Trabajo, Asunto: Junta Local de Conciliación y Arbitraje, AGENL.

30. Ibid. Although María Díaz was not part of the SUOICL, the union members helped her with the case since the other obreras at La Esmeralda were part of the union. For a discussion on female domestic workers and their use of the labor boards in Tampico, see Goldsmith Connelly, "Política, trabajo y género."

31. Porter, *Working Women in Mexico City,* 48.

32. Frente Unico de Trabajadores de Linares, to Presidente de la JLCA, July 19, 1937, caja 118, exp. 5, Fondo: Trabajo, Asunto: Junta Local de Conciliación y Arbitraje, AGENL. For a discussion of the women's rights movement in Mexico, see Olcott, "Center Cannot Hold"; and Olcott, *Revolutionary Women in Postrevolutionary Mexico.*

33. Sindicato Unico de Obreras de la Industria Cigarrera de Linares, report on La Esmeralda presented to JLCA, July 19, 1937, caja 118, exp. 5, Fondo: Trabajo, Asunto: Junta Local de Conciliación y Arbitraje, AGENL; Snodgrass, *Deference and Defiance in Monterrey,* 77.

34. Consuelo Flores, complaint against Manuel González Garza, Dec. 2, 1936, caja 91, exp. 3, Fondo: Trabajo, Asunto: Junta Local de Conciliación y Arbitraje, AGENL.

35. Dictamen de la JCCA, caso de Consuelo Flores, July 22, 1937; Manuel González Garza to JLCA, Mar. 14, 1937, both in caja 91, no. 3, Fondo: Trabajo, Asunto: Junta Central de Conciliación y Arbitraje, AGENL.

36. Ibid. (both cases). See also Echavarría Reyes, *Trabajadores y empresarios en Monterrey,* 206; and Juan G. González, to JLCA, Aug. 31, 1937, caja 121, exp. 7, Fondo: Trabajo, Asunto: Junta Local de Conciliación y Arbitraje, AGENL.

37. Echavarría Reyes, *Trabajadores y empresarios en Monterrey,* 301, exp. 128/8.

38. Sindicato de Obreras de la Fábrica "La Violeta," to Lázaro Cárdenas, Mexico City, May 25, 1937, caja 32-A, exp. 77, Serie: Sindicatos y Agrupaciones, Dirección General de Gobierno, AGN.

39. Sindicato de Obreras "La Esmeralda," Linares, to Presidente Lázaro Cárdenas, July 1, 1937, caja 32-A, exp. 17, Serie: Sindicatos y Agrupaciones, 2331.8 (16), Dirección General de Gobierno, AGN.

40. Klubock, *Contested Communities,* 243.

41. El Sindicato de Empleados, Obreros, y Obreras de la "Industrial" Fábrica de Galletas y Pastas, S.A., Monterrey, to Lázaro Cárdenas, Mexico City, Oct. 1, 1936; Sindicato de Panaderos y Empleados de "La Superior" Monterrey to Lázaro Cárdenas, Mexico City, Oct. 2, 1936, both in caja 32-A, exp. 77, Serie: Sindicatos y Agrupaciones, Dirección General de Gobierno, AGN.

42. Scott, "Gender," 1054–55.

43. Soledad González, SUOCIL, to JLCA Linares, Aug. 19, 1937; Sindicato Unico de Obreras de la Industria Cigarrera de Linares La Esmeralda, Report on La Esmeralda, to JLCA, July 19, 1937, caja 118, exp. 5; Juan G. González to JLCA, Aug. 31, 1937, caja 12, exp. 7, all in Fondo: Trabajo, Asunto: Junta Local de Conciliación y Arbitraje, AGENL.

44. Canning, "Gender and the Politics of Class Formation," 746.

45. See Fowler-Salamini, "Gender, Work, and Working-Class Women's Culture in the Veracruz Coffee Export Industry," 117.

46. Report on María Luisa Corona, Aug. 17, 1937, caja 94, exp. 3, Fondo: Trabajo, Asunto: Junta Local de Conciliación y Arbitraje, AGENL.

47. Ibid. Hutchison, *Labors Appropriate to Their Sex,* 51. For women's morality and industrialization, see Porter, *Working Women in Mexico City.*

48. Testimony of Francisca Prieto in the case of Rafaela Hernández before the JLCA, Aug. 31, 1937, caja 121, exp. 7, Fondo: Trabajo, Asunto: Junta Local de Conciliación y Arbitraje, AGENL.

49. Sindicato Unico de Obreras de la Industria Cigarrera de Linares, Report on La Esmeralda, to JLCA, July 19, 1937, caja 118, exp. 5, Fondo: Trabajo, Asunto: Junta Local de Conciliación y Arbitraje, AGENL; Vizcaya Canales, *Los orígenes de la industrialización de Monterrey*, 96–97.

50. Leal Ríos, *Linares: capital de Nuevo León*, 87. See Snodgrass, *Deference and Defiance in Monterrey;* and Rojas Sandoval, *Monterrey*, for labor union activity in Nuevo León; Juan G. González to JLCA, Aug. 31, 1937, caja 121, exp. 7, Fondo: Trabajo, Asunto: Junta Local de Conciliación y Arbitraje, AGENL. See also James, *Doña María's Story;* and James, "'Tales Told Out on the Borderlands.'"

51. Alfonso Santos Palomo, to JLCA, July 31, 1937, caja 118, exp. 5, Fondo: Trabajo, Asunto: Junta Local de Conciliación y Arbitraje, AGENL.

52. Nemesio Dueñas to JLCA, Aug. 9, 1937, caja 118, exp. 5, Fondo: Trabajo, Asunto: Junta Local de Conciliación y Arbitraje, AGENL.

53. Ibid.; Hutchison, *Labors Appropriate to Their Sex*, 51.

54. See Fowler-Salamini, "Gender, Work, and Working-Class Women's Culture in the Veracruz Coffee Export Industry"; and Carmen Ramos Escandón, "Gender, Labor, and Class Consciousness in the Mexican Textile Industry."

55. Hutchison, *Labors Appropriate to Their Sex*, 49.

56. Farnsworth-Alvear, *Dulcinea in the Factory*, 33. *Trabajadoras de confianza* (also known as *empleadas de confianza*, particularly in Heather Fowler-Salamini's work) in tabacaleras were different from the empleados de confianza in the cement industry referenced by Michael Snodgrass in *Deference and Defiance in Monterrey*. The trabajadoras de confianza in tabacaleras were not office or salaried employees; they, too, were obreras who rolled and packaged cigars but who had earned a confianza position due to their experience.

57. Hutchison, *Labors Appropriate to Their Sex*, 49.

58. Alfonso Santos Palomo, to JLCA, July 31, 1937, caja 118, exp. 5, Fondo: Trabajo, Asunto: Junta Local de Conciliación y Arbitraje, AGENL. See Porter, *Working Women in Mexico City*, for national figures.

59. For an example of a case involving trabajadoras de confianza, see Vicente J. Abdo to JLCA, Dec. 14, 1936, caja 9, exp. 9, Fondo: Trabajo, Asunto: Junta Local de Conciliación y Arbitraje, AGENL.

60. Alfonso Santos Palomo, to JLCA, July 31, 1937, caja 118, exp. 5, Fondo: Trabajo, Asunto: Junta Local de Conciliación y Arbitraje, AGENL.

61. Fowler-Salamini, "Gender, Work, Trade Unionism, and Working-Class Women's Culture in Post-Revolutionary Veracruz," 167. See also Winn, *Weavers of Revolution*, 34–35. There is no indication that cigarrera unions in the North chose their own trabajadoras de confianza.

62. Soledad González, representing María Luisa Corona, to Representantes que integran el grupo no. 2 de JLCA, Feb. 26, 1937, caja 94, exp. 3, Fondo: Trabajo, Asunto: Junta Local de Conciliación y Arbitraje, AGENL.

63. Ibid.

64. Echavarría Reyes, *Trabajadores y empresarios en Monterrey*, 253, exp. 214/4.

65. Interviews with María Luisa Corona and Eusebio Ramírez, Aug. 17, 1937, caja 94,

exp. 3, Fondo: Trabajo, Asunto: Junta Local de Conciliación y Arbitraje, AGENL. Citing a report from the El Imparcial factory, "Población según ocupación principal," Memorias de Bernardo Reyes, 1900–1906, AGENL, Thelma Camacho Morfín and Hugo Pichardo Hernández argue that the practice of keeping women workers silent was uncommon by 1908. Camacho Morfín and Pichardo Hernández, "La cigarrera 'El Buen Tono,'" 89.

66. See, for example, Juan G. González, to JLCA, Aug. 31, 1937, caja 121, exp. 7, Fondo: Trabajo, Asunto: Junta Local de Conciliación y Arbitraje, AGENL. On empleadas/os, see Snodgrass, "Contesting Identities," 9.

67. Echavarría Reyes, *Trabajadores y empresarios en Monterrey*, 283–84, exp. 230/4.

68. Hernández, "*Las Obreras de Monterrey.*"

69. Kessler-Harris, "Wages of Patriarchy," 9.

70. Fowler-Salamini, "Gender, Work, Trade Unionism," 162–63.

71. Snodgrass, *Deference and Defiance in Monterrey*, 305.

72. Ibid., 174–78. The independent unions of Nuevo León were unable to appoint their own delegates to the labor arbitration boards when workers from the Fundidora de Fierro y Acero joined the miners and metalworkers union.

73. Fowler-Salamini, "Gender, Work, Trade Unionism," 162–63. On President Cárdenas's abandonment of progressive policies toward obreras, see Olcott, "Miracle Workers," 45–62. See also similar findings in Santiago, "Women of the Mexican Oil Fields," 89.

74. Gauss, "Working-Class Masculinity and the Rationalized Sex," 183. On women's labor in Cervecería Cuauhtémoc, see Snodgrass, *Deference and Defiance in Monterrey*, 76; and on female tortilla workers in Guadalajara and the shift to mechanization in the tortilla industry, see Fernández Aceves, "Guadalajaran Women and the Construction of National Identity," 152–53.

EPILOGUE

Epigraphs: Jovita Idar, "Debemos trabajar" (We must work), *La Crónica* (Laredo, Tex.), n.d., 1911, as quoted in Edna Ochoa, "El periodismo, la mujer y la frontera en Laredo: propuesta de cambio en la obra de Jovita Idar," 6, presented at the Primer Simposio de la Historia del Noreste y Sur de Texas, Archivo Histórico de Reynosa, Reynosa, Tampaulipas, Oct. 2, 2006; *El Surco* (Victoria, Tamps.), tomo I, no. 11, Oct. 1, 1925; testimony of Rafaela Hernández in Juan G. González to JLCA, Aug. 31, 1937, caja 121, exp. 7, Fondo: Trabajo, Asunto: Junta Local de Conciliación y Arbitraje, AGENL.

1. Gutiérrez and Young, "Transnationalizing Borderlands History," 28–29.

2. See, for example, Emilio Pena, to JCCA, July 1, 1918, exp. 26, Fondo: Junta Central de Conciliación y Arbitraje, AGET. See also Caso del Sindicato de Obreras de la Fábrica de Camisas "La Palma," Nov. 12, 1934, caja 34, exp. 8, Fondo: Trabajo, Asunto: Junta Local de Conciliación y Arbitraje, AGENL; Hernández, "*Las Obreras de Monterrey.*"

3. Fowler-Salamini, "De-Centering the 1920s," 293.

4. Sieglin, "Agua, acumulación de capital, y burguesía," 45 and footnote 85. Sieglin notes the numerous accusations of theft by unscrupulous landowners in southern Nuevo León.

5. Zebadúa, "La lucha por la tierra en la región citrícola" 187–88; Sieglin, "Agua,

acumulación de capital, y burguesía," 55. See also the case of the permanent worker and *terciero* (sharecropper) Jesús Alaníz, who explains that he knew that nearby haciendas provided "*el arado* [plow], seeds, hoes," even if through a rental system, but when the foreman of Hacienda La Clementina failed to provide such basic resources, Jesús submitted his grievance. While the hacienda management argued that "the company was not required to purchase shoddy harvests," the board ultimately declared in favor of the campesino. Case of Jesús Alaníz versus La Clementina, Dec. 12, 1925, caja 3, exp. 75, 78, Fondo: Junta Central de Conciliación y Arbitraje, AGET.

6. Sieglin, "Agua, acumulación de capital, y burguesía," 45; Tuñón Pablos, *Women in Mexico,* 104.

7. See Momen, "Redefining Patriarchy," 83–87; Tiano, *Patriarchy on the Line;* and Ruiz and Tiano, *Women on the U.S.–Mexico Border.* The secondary literature on women's work in *maquiladoras* has grown significantly in the past several decades. Oscar Misael Hernández, "Procesos de cambio, género y reorganización."

Bibliography

ARCHIVAL MATERIAL

Mexico

National

Archivo General de la Nación, Mexico City (AGN)
Archivo Histórico Particular de Emilio Portes Gil
Departamento de Petróleo
    Serie: Quejas y Reclamaciones
Departamento del Trabajo
    Fondo: Secretaría de Fomento, Colonización, e Industria
Dirección General de Gobierno
    Serie: Estadísticas
    Serie: Fomento
    Serie: Petroleros Transitorios
    Serie: Sindicatos y Agrupaciones
Instituto Nacional de Estudios Históricos sobre la Revolución Mexicana Biblioteca, Mexico City (INEHRM)
Universidad Nacional Autónoma de México, Mexico City (UNAM)
    Hemeroteca y Biblioteca Nacional

State

Nuevo León

Archivo General del Estado de Nuevo León, Monterrey (AGENL)
  Fondo: Archivo de la Comisión Agraria (Secretaría de la Comisión Agraria)
Fondo: Comunicaciones
    Asunto: Locales, Ferrocarriles y Tranvías
Fondo: Correspondencia de Alcaldes
    Sección: Monterrey
    Sección: Montemorelos
Fondo: Justicia
    Sección: Justicia

Asunto: Falta a la Moral
Asunto: Abuso de Confianza
Asunto: Falta de Respeto a la Autoridad
Fondo: Secretaría General de Gobierno
Serie: Estadísticas
Asunto: Monterrey (y otros municipios)
Fondo: Trabajo
Asunto: Asociaciones, Organizaciones y Sindicatos
Asunto: Junta Central de Conciliación y Arbitraje
Asunto: Junta Local de Conciliación y Arbitraje
Asunto: Sirvientes
Fondo: Secretaría de Industria, Comercio y Trabajo
AGENL, Biblioteca Ricardo Covarrubias
AGENL, Memorias de Bernardo Reyes
AGENL, Memorias de Pedro Benítez Leal
Archivo de Juzgado del Primer Distrito con sede en Monterrey
Sección: Poder Judicial
Asunto: Juicios de Amparo
Biblioteca Fray Servando Teresa de Mier, Monterrey
Casa de la Cultura: Estación Antigua del Monterrey al Golfo, Monterrey
Centro de Investigaciones y Estudios Superiores en Antropología Social, Monterrey
Colegio de la Frontera Norte, Monterrey
Universidad Autónoma de Nuevo León, Monterrey (UANL)
Librería de la Facultad de Letras y Humanidades
Biblioteca Rangel Frías
Fondo: Santiago Roel
Vidriera Monterrey: Museo del Vidrio, Monterrey
Exhibiciones y Archivo Fotográfico

Tamaulipas

Archivo General del Estado de Tamaulipas, Ciudad Victoria (AGET)
Fondo: Anuarios Estadísticos del Estado de Tamaulipas
Fondo: Memorias Administrativas del Estado de Tamaulipas
Fondo: Junta Central de Conciliación y Arbitraje
Sección: Demandas
Sección: Datos Estadísticos
Fondo: Junta Local de Conciliación y Arbitraje
Biblioteca Marte R. Gómez, Ciudad Victoria
Fondo: Gabriel Saldivar
Fondo: Tamaulipas
Instituto de Investigaciones Históricas–Archivo Histórico, Universidad Autónoma de Tamaulipas, Ciudad Victoria (IIH-UAT)
Fondo: Esteban Méndez
Hemeroteca Histórica
Biblioteca

Municipal

Archivo Histórico de Matamoros (AHM)
Fondo: Presidencia (Actas de Cabildo, 1920–30)
Archivo Histórico de Reynosa (AHR)
Fondo: Epoca Actual
Sección: Presidencia, Tesorería, Judicial
Asunto: Reclamaciones entre México y Estados Unidos
Sección: Juzgado Penal
Asunto: Sindicatos, Sociedades, y Agrupaciones
Archivo Histórico de Tampico Carlos González Salas, Tampico (AHT)
Fondo: Presidencia
Fondo: Tesorería
Casco Antiguo de la Hacienda Sauteña, Casa de la Cultura, Río Bravo

United States

Dolph Briscoe Center for American History, University of Texas at Austin
Robert Runyon Photographic Collection
Geology Library, University of Texas at Austin
Hart Collection, Houston, Tex.
Private collection of files on Tamaulipas, Nuevo León, and San Luis Potosí
Hispanic Recovery Project, University of Houston, Houston, Tex.
Institute of Texan Cultures, University of Texas at San Antonio Libraries, San Antonio, Tex.
Rare Books and Photographs
Library of Congress, Washington, D.C.
M. D. Anderson Library, University of Houston, Houston, Tex. (MDA)
Consular Dispatches, United States. Records Relating to the Internal Affairs of Mexico
(Record Group 812), Monterrey, Tampico, and Matamoros
Mary Norton Clapp Library, Occidental College, Los Angeles, Calif. (OC)
E. L. Doheny Research Foundation Collection
Nettie Lee Benson Latin American Collection, University of Texas at Austin (NLB)
American-Mexican Claims Commission
Cepeda, Eustacio. Papers
Idar, Clemente N. Papers
Prieto, Alejandro. Papers
Ramírez, Teódulo. Papers
Sociedad Mutualista Melchor Ocampo. Papers
Special Collections, Lower Rio Grande Valley, University of Texas–Pan American Library, Edinburg, Tex. (LRGV)
Rare Books and Maps
US National Archives, College Park, Md.
Woodson Research Center, Fondren Library, Rice University, Houston, Tex.

NEWSPAPERS

Avante (Doña Cecilia, Tamps.), Hemeroteca del Fondo Esteban Méndez, IIH-UAT
El Cauterio (Tamaulipas), Hemeroteca, IIH-UAT
El Mundo (Tampico, Tamps.), Hemeroteca, UNAM
El Norte (Nuevo León), AGENL
El Progresista (Victoria, Tamps.), Hemeroteca, IIH-UAT
El Surco (Tamaulipas, published by the Escuela de Agricultura de Tamaulipas), NLB
El Tulteco (Tula, Tamps.), Hemeroteca, IIH-UAT
La Prensa (San Antonio, Tex.), NLB
La República (El Paso, Tex.), NLB
La Voz de Nuevo León (Nuevo León), AGENL
Revista Ferronales (Tamaulipas), NLB
Revista Tamaulipas (Tamaulipas), LRVG
Sagitario (Doña Cecilia, Tamps.), Hemeroteca del Fondo Esteban Méndez, IIH-UAT
San Antonio Express-News (Texas), NLB

MEMOIRS, DIARIES, AND RARE BOOKS

Alanis de Salazar, Antonia. *En el Tampico aquel: relatos.* Tampico, 1981.
McGary, Elizabeth Visère. *An American Girl in Mexico.* New York: Knopf, 1903.
Mrs. Herbert's Scientific System of Dress-Cutting, for Self-Instruction. New York: Dress Maker's Tradeschool, 1897.
Primer Congreso Pedagógico de Tamaulipas. Ciudad Victoria, Tamps., ca. 1880.
Ruiz, Francisco. *La Sociedad Mutualista "Alianza Obrera Progresista" de Ciudad Victoria, Tamaulipas.* Book 1, Edición del Comité de los Festejos del Cincuentenario de la Agrupación. Mexico City: Imprenta Mexicana, S.de R.L.y C.V., 1951.
Traffic and Industrial Departments of the National Railways of Mexico. *Facts and Figures about Mexico and Its Great Railway System, the National Railways of Mexico.* [Mexico City], 1911.

BOOKS, ARTICLES, THESES, AND DISSERTATIONS

Adelman, Jeremy, and Stephen Aron. "From Borderlands to Border: Empires, Nation-States, and the Peoples in between in North American History." *American Historical Review* 104, no. 3 (June 1999): 814–41.
Adelson, S. Leif. "The Cultural Roots of the Oil Workers' Unions in Tampico, 1910–1925." In *The Mexican Petroleum Industry in the Twentieth Century,* edited by Jonathan C. Brown and Alan Knight, 36–57. Austin: University of Texas Press, 1992.
———. "Historia social de los obreros industriales de Tampico, 1906–1919." PhD dissertation, El Colegio de México, 1982.
Aguayo, Fernando. *Estampas ferrocarrileras: fotografía y grabado, 1860–1890.* Mexico City: Instituto de Investigaciones José María Luis Mora, 2003.
Aguilar Belden de Garza, Sara. *Una ciudad y dos familias.* Mexico City: Editorial Jus, 1970.
Aguilar Camín, Hector, and Lorenzo Meyer. *In the Shadow of the Mexican Revolution:*

Contemporary Mexican History, 1910–1989. Translated by Luis Alberto Fierro. Austin: University of Texas Press, 1993.

Alarcón Cantú, Eduardo. *Evolución y dependencia en el Noreste: las ciudades fronterizas de Tamaulipas*. Tijuana: El Colegio de la Frontera Norte, 1990.

———. "Nuevo Laredo, Tamaulipas: cincuenta años de crecimiento urbano, 1940–1990." *Río Bravo* 2, no. 2 (spring 1993).

Alcayaga Sasso, Aurora Mónica. "Librado Rivera y los Hermanos Rojos en el movimiento social y cultural anarquista en Villa Cecilia y Tampico, Tamaulipas, 1915–1931." Doctoral thesis, Universidad Iberoamericana, 2006.

Aldape Barrera, Fernando. *Petroleros ¡Ánimo . . . Ánimo!* 6th ed. Tampico: Editora Tamaulipas del Golfo, S.A., 1984.

Allen, Ruth. *The Labor of Women in the Production of Cotton*. Bureau of Research in the Social Sciences Study no. 3, Bulletin no. 3134. Austin: University of Texas, 1931.

Allhands, J. L. *Gringo Builders*. N.p.: Privately printed, 1931.

Alonso, Ana María. *Thread of Blood: Colonialism, Revolution, and Gender on Mexico's Northern Frontier*. Tucson: University of Arizona Press, 1995.

Alston, Lee J., Shannan Mattiace, and Thomas Nonnenmacher. "Coercion, Culture, and Contracts: Labor and Debt on Henequen Haciendas in Yucatan, Mexico 1870–1915." *Journal of Economic History* 69, no. 1 (March 2009): 104–107.

Alvarado Mendoza, Arturo. *Tamaulipas: sociedad, economía política y cultura*. Mexico City: UNAM, 2004.

Anderson, Rodney. *Outcasts in Their Own Lands: Mexican Industrial Workers, 1906–1911*. DeKalb: Northern Illinois University Press, 1976.

Ansell, Martin R. *Oil Baron of the Southwest: Edward L. Doheny and the Development of the Petroleum Industry in California and Mexico*. Columbus: Ohio State University Press, 1988.

Anuario Estadístico de Tamaulipas. Mexico City: Instituto Nacional de Estadísticas, Geografía, e Informática, 1988.

Anzaldúa, Gloria. *Borderlands/La Frontera: The New Mestiza*. 2nd ed. San Francisco: Aunt Lute Books, 1987, 1999.

Arenal, Sandra. *Mujeres de tierra y libertad*. Monterrey: Fondo Estatal para la Cultura y las Artes de Nuevo León, 1999.

Arguelles, Adalberto. *Reseña del estado de Tamaulipas*. Victoria, Tamps.: Oficina Tipográfica del Gobierno del Estado, 1910.

Arizmendi, Alberto. *Ejido Lucio Blanco, Tamaulipas*. Mexico City: Procuraduría Agraria Crónica, n.d.

Arnold, Linda. "Vulgar and Elegant: Politics and Procedure in Early National Mexico." *The Americas* 4 (April 1994): 481–500.

Arzola, Jesús. *Una historia vivida: según el testimonio de Ursula Tapia*. Victoria: Instituto Tamaulipeco de Cultura, 1991.

Bacha-Garza, Roseann, and the San Juan Economic Development Corp. *Images of America: San Juan*. Charleston, S. Car.: Arcadia Publishing, 2010.

Baker, Richard D. *Judicial Review in Mexico: A Study of the Amparo Suit*. Austin: University of Texas Press, 1971.

Bannon, John Francis, ed. *Bolton and the Spanish Borderlands.* Norman: University of Oklahoma, 1964.

———. *Greater America: Essays in Honor of Herbert Eugene Bolton.* Freeport, N.Y.: Books for Libraries Press, 1945, 1968.

Barrera, Cordelia. "Border Places, Frontier Spaces: Deconstructing Ideologies of the Southwest." PhD dissertation, University of Texas at San Antonio, 2009.

Basols Batalla, Angel. "Ciclos Económicos Regionales en la Huasteca." In *Las Huastecas,* edited by Angel Basols Batalla. Mexico City: Editorial Trillas, 1977.

———, and Santiago Rentería Romero et al. *Las Huastecas en el desarrollo regional de Mexico.* Mexico City: Editorial Trillas, 1977.

Baud, Michiel, and Willem van Schendel. "Toward a Comparative History of the Borderlands." *Journal of World History* 8, no. 2 (fall 1997): 211–42.

Beato, Guillermo, and Domenico Sindico. "The Beginning of Industrialization in Northeast Mexico." *The Americas* 39 (April 1983): 499–518.

Besse, Susan K. *Restructuring Patriarchy: The Modernization of Gender Inequality in Brazil, 1914–1940.* Chapel Hill: University of North Carolina Press, 1996.

Blackwelder, Julia Kirk. *Women of the Depression: Caste and Culture in San Antonio, 1929–1939.* College Station: Texas A&M University Press, 1984.

Blackwell, Maylei. *¡Chicana Power! Contested Histories of Feminism in the Chicano Movement.* Austin: University of Texas Press, 2011.

Blanco Caballero, Feliciano. "Problema agrario en Tamaulipas: región norte." Thesis, Universidad Nacional Autónoma de México, 1957.

Bolton, Herbert Eugene, and Thomas Maitland Marshall. *The Colonization of North America, 1492–1783.* New York: Macmillan, 1920.

Bose, Christine E., and Edna Acosta-Belén. *Women in the Latin American Development Process.* Philadelphia: Temple University Press, 1994.

Calderón, Roberto R. *Mexican Coal Mining Labor in Texas and Coahuila, 1880–1930.* College Station: Texas A&M University Press, 2000.

Calderoni Bonleux, Sonia. "Haciendo públicos actos de nuestra vida privada: el divorcio en Nuevo León, 1890–1910." In *Historia de la vida cotidiana en México.* Book 4, *Bienes y vivencias, el siglo XIX,* coordinated by Anne Staples, 463–98. Mexico City: Colegio de México, Fondo de Cultura Económica, 2005.

Camacho Morfín, Thelma. "La historieta, mirilla de la vida cotidiana en la Ciudad de México (1904–1940)." In *Historia de la vida cotidiana en México.* Book 5, volume 2, *Siglo XX: la imagen, espejo de la vida?,* coordinated by Aurelio de los Reyes. Mexico City: Colegio de México/Fondo de Cultura Económica, 2006.

———, and Hugo Pichardo Hernández. "La cigarrera 'El Buen Tono' (1889–1929)." In *Poder* público y poder privado: *gobiernos, empresarios, y empresas, 1880–1980,* edited by Romero Ibarra María Eugenia, Mario Contreras, and Jesús Méndez Reyes, 83–106. Mexico City: UNAM Facultad de Economía, 2006.

Camarena Ocampo, Mario, and Susana A. Fernández. "Culture and Politics: Mexican Textile Workers in the Second Half of the Nineteenth Century." In *Border Crossings: Mexican and Mexican American Workers,* edited by John M. Hart. Wilmington, Del.: Scholarly Resources, 1998.

Canning, Kathleen. "Gender and the Politics of Class Formation: Rethinking German Labor History." *American Historical Review* 97, no. 3 (June 1992): 736–68.

Canseco, José Raul. *Historia de Matamoros.* Victoria: Universidad Autónoma de Tamaulipas, 1980.

Casasola, Agustín V. *Mexico: The Revolution and Beyond.* New York: Aperture, 2003.

Castañeda, Antonia I. "Presidarias y Pobladoras: Spanish Mexican Women in Frontier Monterrey, Alta California, 1770–1821." PhD dissertation, Stanford University, 1990.

Cavazos Garza, Israel. "Jeronimo Treviño." In *El Gobernador Bernardo Reyes y sus homólogos en la frontera norte,* edited by David Piñera Ramírez. Monterrey: Fondo Editorial Nuevo León, 1991.

Ceballos Ramírez, Manuel, coord. *Encuentro en la frontera: mexicanos y norteamericanos en un espacio común.* Mexico City: Colegio de México, Colegio de la Frontera Norte, UAT, 2001.

Cerutti, Mario, ed. *Agua, tierra, y capital en el Noreste de México: la región citrícola de Nuevo León, 1850–1940.* Monterrey: Universidad Autónoma de Nuevo León, 1991.

———. *Burguesía, capitales e industria en el norte de México: Monterrey y su ámbito regional, 1850–1910.* Monterrey: Alianza Editorial, 1992.

———. *Economía de guerra y poder regional en el siglo XIX: gastos militares, aduanas, y comerciantes en los años de Vidaurri, 1855–1864.* Monterrey: Archivo General del Estado de Nuevo León, 1983.

———. "Españoles, gran comercio y Brote Fabril en el norte de México: 1850–1910." *Siglo XIX* 1, no. 2 (February 1992).

———. "Monterrey and Its Ambito Regional, 1850–1910: Historical Context and Methodological Recommendations." In *Mexico's Regions: Comparative History and Development,* edited by Eric Van Young, 145–65. La Jolla: Center for US-Mexican Studies, University of California, San Diego, 1992.

———, and Oscar Flores Torres. *Españoles en el norte de México.* Monterrey: Universidad Autónoma de Nuevo León, 1997.

Chapa, Juan Bautista. *Texas and Northeastern Mexico, 1630–1690.* Edited and introduced by William C. Foster. Translated by Ned F. Bierly. Austin: University of Texas Press, 1997.

Chassen López, Francie. "'Cheaper Than Machines': Women and Agriculture in Porfirian Oaxaca, 1880–1911." In *Women of the Mexican Countryside, 1850–1990: Creating Spaces, Shaping Transitions,* edited by Heather Fowler-Salamini and Mary Kay Vaughan, 27–50. Tucson: University of Arizona Press, 1994.

———. "Más barratas que las máquinas: mujeres y agricultura en Oaxaca, 1880–1911." *Siglo XIX: Cuadernos de Historia* 5, no. 14 (January–April 1996).

Chevalier, François. *Land and Society in Colonial Mexico: The Great Hacienda.* Translated by Alvin Eustis. Berkeley: University of California Press, 1963.

Coatsworth, John. *Growth against Development: The Economic Impact of Railroads in Porfirian Mexico.* DeKalb: Northern Illinois University Press, 1981.

Corridos Agraristas de Tamaulipas. Victoria: Ciudad Victoria, 1996.

Cronon, William. *Nature's Metropolis: Chicago and the Great West.* New York: Norton, 1992.

Cuaderno Estadístico Municipal, Estado de Tamaulipas. Aguascalientes: Instituto Nacional de Estadística, Geografía e Informática, 1995.

Cuellar, Andrés F. "Las mujeres y la vida nocturna de Matamoros." Unpublished essay, 2000.

———. "La recreación en Matamoros." Unpublished essay, 2000.

Cuellar, Margarito. *Cárdenas en Monterrey: Febrero 1936*. Monterrey: UANL, n.d.

Cuello, José. *El norte, el noreste y Saltillo en la historia colonial de México.* Saltillo: Archivo Histórico Municipal, 1990.

Cumberland, Charles C. *The Mexican Revolution: Genesis under Madero.* Austin: University of Texas Press, 1952.

Deans-Smith, Susan. *Bureaucrats, Planters, and Workers: The Making of the Tobacco Monopoly in Bourbon Mexico.* Austin: University of Texas Press, 1992.

Deere, Carmen Diana, and Magdalena León, eds. *Rural Women and State Policy: Feminine Perspectives on Latina American Agricultural Development.* Boulder, Colo.: Westview Press, 1987.

De León, Arnoldo. *They Called Them Greasers: Anglo Attitudes toward Mexicans, 1821–1900*. Austin: University of Texas Press, 1983.

———, ed. *War along the Border: The Mexican Revolution and Tejano Communities.* College Station: Texas A&M University Press, 2011.

Dicken, Samuel N. "Monterrey and Northeastern Mexico." *Annals of the Association of American Geographers* 29, no. 2 (June 1939): 127–58.

Dillman, Charles. "Functions of Brownsville, Texas and Matamoros, Tamaulipas: Twin Cities of the Lower Rio Grande Valley." PhD dissertation, University of Michigan, 1968.

Donnan, Hastings, and Thomas M. Wilson. *Borders: Frontiers of Identity, Nation and State.* Oxford: Berg, 2001.

Echavarría Reyes, Luz María, ed. *Trabajadores y empresarios en Monterrey: catálogo de la Junta Local de Conciliación y Arbitraje 1923–1937*. Monterrey: AGENL, 1999.

Elizondo Elizondo, Ricardo. "Bajo la mirada de la sospecha: cuatro vidas en Monterrey, 1868–1870." In *Historia de la vida cotidiana en México.* Volume 4, *Bienes y vivencias, el siglo XIX,* edited by Anne Staples, 119–46. Mexico City: Colegio de México, Fondo de Cultura Económica, 2005.

Evans, Sterling. *Bound in Twine: The History and Ecology of the Henequen-Wheat Complex for Mexico and the American and Canadian Plains, 1880–1950*. College Station: Texas A&M University Press, 2007.

Falcón, Romana, coord. *Culturas de pobreza y resistencia: estudios de marginados, proscritos y descontentos, México, 1804–1910*. Mexico City: Colegio de México, Universidad Aútonoma de Querétaro, 2005.

Farnsworth-Alvear, Ann. *Dulcinea in the Factory: Myths, Morals, Men, and Women in Colombia's Industrial Experiment, 1905–1960*. Durham: Duke University Press, 2000.

Fernández Aceves, María Teresa. "Guadalajaran Women and the Construction of National Identity." In *The Eagle and the Virgin: Nation and Cultural Revolution in Mexico, 1920–1940,* edited by Mary Kay Vaughan and Stephen E. Lewis, 297–313. Durham: Duke University Press, 2006.

———. "Once We Were Corn Grinders: Women and Labor in the Tortilla Industry of

Guadalajara, 1920–1940." *International Labor and Working-Class History* 63 (April 2003).

———, Carmen Ramos Escandón, and Susie Porter, coords. *Orden social e identidad de género: México, siglos XIX y XX*. Guadalajara: Universidad de Guadalajara, 2006.

Fernández-Kelly, María Patricia. *For We Are Sold, I and My People: Women and Industry in Mexico's Frontier.* Albany: State University of New York Press, 1983.

Flores, Anselmo Marino. "Los problemas sociales de México en 1900 y 1950." *Journal of Inter-American Studies* 4, no. 2 (April 1962).

Flores Torres, Oscar. *Burguesía, militares, y movimiento obrero en Monterrey.* Monterrey: Facultad de Filosofía y Letras de la Universidad Autónoma de Nuevo León, 1991.

Foley, Neil. *The White Scourge: Mexicans, Blacks, and Poor Whites in Texas Cotton Culture.* Berkeley: University of California Press, 1999.

Fowler-Salamini, Heather. "De-centering the 1920s: Socialismo a la Tamaulipeca." *Estudios Mexicanos* 14, no. 2 (summer 1998): 287–313.

———. "Gender, Work, and Working-Class Women's Culture in the Veracruz Coffee Export Industry, 1920–1945." *International Labor and Working-Class History* 63 (spring 2003): 102–21.

———. "Gender, Work, Trade Unionism, and Working-Class Women's Culture in Post-Revolutionary Veracruz." In *Sex in Revolution: Gender, Politics, and Power in Modern Mexico,* edited by Jocelyn Olcott, Mary Kay Vaughan, and Gabriela Cano, 162–80. Durham: Duke University Press, 2006.

———. "Tamaulipas: Land Reform and the State." In *Provinces of the Mexican Revolution: Essays on Regional Mexican History, 1910–1929,* edited by Thomas Benjamin and Mark Wasserman. Albuquerque: University of New Mexico Press, 1990.

———, and Mary Kay Vaughan, eds. *Women in the Mexican Countryside, 1850–1990.* Tucson: University of Arizona Press, 1994.

Frader, Laura L. "Labor History after the Gender Turn: Transatlantic Cross Currents and Research Agendas." *International Labor and Working-Class History* 63 (spring 2003): 21–31.

———. "Women, Gender, and Unions in France in the Interwar Years." Working paper, Northeastern University, Boston, 1991.

———, and Sonya E. Rose, eds. *Gender and Class in Modern Europe* Ithaca: Cornell University Press, 1996.

French, John D., and Daniel James, eds. *The Gendered Worlds of Latin American Women Workers: From Household and Factory to the Union Hall and Ballot Box.* Durham: Duke University Press, 1997.

French, William. *A Peaceful and Working People: Manners, Morals, and Class Formation in Northern Mexico.* Albuquerque: University of New Mexico Press, 1996.

Gamboa, Leticia. "Los momentos de la actividad textil." In *La industria textil en México,* edited by Aurora Gómez-Galvarriato. Mexico City: Instituto de Investigaciones José María Luís Mora, 1999.

García Martínez, Bernardo. "El espacio del (des)encuentro." In *Encuentro en la frontera: mexicanos y norteamericanos en un espacio común,* edited by Manuel Ceballos

Ramírez, 19–51. Mexico City: Colegio de México, Colegio de la Frontera Norte, UAT, 2001.

Garza Sada, Roberto. *Ensayos sobre la historia de una industria.* Monterrey: Talleres de Litográfica Monterrey, S.A., 1981.

Gauss, Susan M. "Working-Class Masculinity and the Rationalized Sex: Gender and Industrial Modernization in the Textile Industry in Post-Revolutionary Puebla." In *Sex in Revolution: Gender, Politics, and Power in Modern Mexico,* edited by Jocelyn Olcott, Mary Kay Vaughan, and Gabriela Cano, 181–98. Durham: Duke University Press, 2006.

Goldsmith, Mary R. "Sindicato de trabajadoras domésticas en México, 1920–1950." *Política y Cultura* (Universidad Autónoma Metropolitana–Xochimilco), no. 1 (fall 1992).

Goldsmith Connelly, Mary. "Política, trabajo y género: la sindicalización de las y los trabajadores domésticos y el estado mexicano." In *Orden social e identidad de género: México, siglos XIX y XX,* coordinated by María Teresa Fernández Aceves, Carmen Ramos Escandón, and Susie Porter, 215–44. Guadalajara: Universidad de Guadalajara, 2006.

Gómez Castillo, Gerardo. *Esbozo biográfico del consolidador del Sindicato y Cooperativa del Gremio Unido Alijadores, S.C. de R.L.* Mexico City: Edición patrocinada por el Gremio Unidode Alijadores, S.C. de R.L., n.d.

Gómez-Quiñones, Juan. *Sembradores, Ricardo Flores Magón y el Partido Liberal Mexicano: A Eulogy and Critique.* Los Angeles: Aztlán Publications, 1973.

Gonzáles, Trinidad. "The Mexican Revolution, *Revolución de Texas,* and *Matanza de 1915.*" In *War along the Border: The Mexican Revolution and Tejano Communities,* edited by Arnoldo De León, 107–33. College Station: Texas A&M University Press, 2012.

———. "The World of Mexico Texanos, Mexicanos and Mexico Americanos: Transnational and National Identities in the Lower Rio Grande Valley during the Last Phase of United States Colonization, 1900 to 1930." PhD dissertation, University of Houston, 2008.

González, Deena. "Gender in the Borderlands: Re-Textualizing the Classics." *Frontiers: A Journal of Women Studies* 24 (2003).

———. *Refusing the Favor: The Spanish-Mexican Women of Santa Fe, 1820–1880.* Oxford: Oxford University Press, 1999.

González, Gabriela. "Carolina Munguía and Emma Tenayuca: The Politics of Benevolence and Radical Reform." *Frontiers: A Journal of Women Studies* 24, no. 2–3, (2003): 200–29.

González, Gilbert G. *American Writers, Mexico, and Mexican Immigrants, 1880–1930.* Austin: University of Texas Press, 2003.

González Filizola, Enrique Martín. *Una victoria perdida: relatos de este lado del tablero.* Victoria, Tamps.: IIH-UAT, 1994.

González Quiroga, Miguel Angel. "Mexicanos in Texas during the Civil War." In *Mexican Americans in Texas History,* edited by Emilio Zamora, Cynthia Orozco, and Rodolfo Rocha. Austin: Texas State Historical Association, 2000.

———, and Mario Cerutti. "Guerra y comercio en torno al Rió Bravo (1855–1867), línea fronteriza, espacio económico común." *Historia Mexicana* 40, no. 2 (October–December 1990): 217–97.

———. *Texas y el norte de México (1848–1880): comercio, capitales y trabajadores en una economía de frontera.* Mexico City: Instituto Mora, 1999.

González Salas, Carlos. *Acercamiento a la historia del movimiento obrero de Tampico: 1887–1983.* Victoria: UAT, 1987.

———. *El casino tampiqueño: 1890–1990.* Tampico: Publicaciones Mar Adentro, 1994.

González Sánchez, Juan Manuel. *Vallecillo, Nuevo León: los caminos de su historia.* Monterrey: Grafo Editores, 1993.

González Sierra, José. *El monopolio del humo.* Xalapa: Universidad Veracruzana, Centro de Investigaciones Históricas, Colección Historias Veracruzanas, 1987.

Graf, Leroy. "The Economic History of the Lower Rio Grande Valley, 1820–1875." PhD dissertation, Harvard University, 1942.

Greater America: Essays in Honor of Herbert Eugene Bolton. Freeport, N.Y.: Books for Libraries Press, 1945, 1968.

Gresham Chapman, John. *La construcción del Ferrocarril Mexicano: 1837–1880.* Translated by Roberto Gómez Ciriza. Mexico City: Sep Setentas, 1975.

Guerrero Miller, Alma Yolanda. *Cuesta abajo: delinación de tres caciques Huastecos revolucionarios; Cedillo, Santos y Peláez.* Mexico City: Editorial Miguel Ángel Porrua, 1991.

———, and César Leonel Ayala. *Por eso! Historia de el Sindicato de Jornaleros y Obreros Industriales de Matamoros, Tamaulipas.* Mexico City: Centro de Investigación Multidisciplinaria de Tamaulipas, 1993.

Gutiérrez, Ramón. *When Jesus Came, the Corn Mothers Went Away: Marriage, Sexuality, and Power in New Mexico, 1500–1846.* Stanford: Stanford University Press, 1992.

———, and Elliott Young. "Transnationalizing Borderlands History." *Western Historical Quarterly* 41 (spring 2010): 27–53.

Guttman, Herbert G. *Work, Culture, and Society in Industrializing America: Essays in American Working-Class and Social History.* New York: Vintage Books, 1977.

Guy, Donna J. *Sex and Danger in Buenos Aires: Prostitution, Family, and the Nation.* Lincoln: University of Nebraska Press, 1991.

Hahner, June E., ed. *Women through Women's Eyes: Latin American Women in Nineteenth-Century Travel Accounts.* Wilmington, Del.: Scholarly Resources, 1998.

Harris III, Charles H., and Louis R. Sadler. *The Texas Rangers and the Mexican Revolution: The Bloodiest Decade, 1910–1920.* Albuquerque: University of New Mexico Press, 2006.

Hart, John Mason. "Agrarian Precursors of the Mexican Revolution: The Development of an Ideology," *The Americas* 29 (1973): 131–50.

———. *Anarchism and the Mexican Working Class, 1860–1931.* 2nd ed. Austin: University of Texas Press, 1987.

———. *Empire and Revolution: The Americans in Mexico since the Civil War.* Berkeley: University of California Press, 2002.

———. "The Evolution of the Mexican and Mexican-American Working Classes." In *Border Crossings: Mexican and Mexican American Workers,* edited by John M. Hart, 1–26. Wilmington, Del.: Scholarly Resources, 1998.

———. "Nineteenth-Century Urban Labor Precursors of the Mexican Revolution: The Development of an Ideology." *The Americas* 30 (July 1973–74).

———. *Revolutionary Mexico: The Coming and Process of the Mexican Revolution.* Berkeley: University of California Press, 1987.

Hart, Paul. *Bitter Harvest: The Social Transformation of Morelos, Mexico, and the Origins of the Zapatista Revolution, 1840–1910.* Albuquerque: New Mexico University Press, 2003.

Heath, John R. "Enhancing the Contribution of Land Reform to Mexican Agricultural Development." World Bank Working Paper no. 285, February 1990.

Hernández, José Angel. *Mexican American Colonization during the Nineteenth Century.* New York: Cambridge University Press, 2012.

Hernández, Kelly Lytle. "Borderlands and the Future History of the American West." *Western Historical Quarterly* 42 (autumn 2011): 325–30.

Hernández, Sonia. "'¡Cooperación de los Sexos para el bien de la Nación!' Relaciones de género en el Tamaulipas pos revolucionario, 1920–1930." *Revista Internacional de Ciencias Sociales y Humanidades* 20, no. 1 (January–June 2010): 85–105.

———. "El alma de la rebelión: mujeres, género y revolución en Tamaulipas." In *Tamaulipas en el espejo de su historia.* Book 2, *La revolución,* edited by Jesús Hernández Jaimes. Victoria: Gobierno de Tamaulipas, 2010.

———. "Military Activities in Matamoros during the Mexican Revolution." MA thesis, University of Texas–Pan American, 2001.

Herrera Pérez, Octavio. *Breve historia de Tamaulipas.* Mexico City: Fondo de Cultura Económica, 1999.

———. "El ixtle en Tamaulipas en el Cuarto Distrito 1850–1913." In *Siglo XIX: cuadernos de historia* 10 (1994).

———. *Historia gráfica de Tamaulipas.* Victoria, Tamps.: Instituto de Investigaciones Históricas, UAT, 1989.

———. *Tamaulipas: textos de su historia.* Victoria, Tamps.: Instituto de Investigaciones Históricas, UAT, 1990.

Historia del noreste mexicano: tierra de guerra viva, nómadas y civilizados en el *noreste mexicano, 1800–1885.* Monterrey: Anuario del Archivo General del Estado de Nuevo León, 2003.

Hurtado, Albert L. *Herbert Eugene Bolton: Historian of the American Borderlands.* Berkeley: University of California Press, 2012.

Hutchison, Elizabeth Quay. *Labors Appropriate to Their Sex: Gender, Labor, and Politics in Urban Chile, 1900–1930.* Durham: Duke University Press, 2001.

Iturriaga, José E. *La estructura social y cultural de México.* Mexico City: Instituto Nacional de Estudios Históricos de la Revolución Mexicana, 2003.

James, Daniel. *Doña María's Story: Life History, Memory, and Political Identity.* Durham: Duke University Press, 2001.

———. "'Tales Told Out on the Borderlands': Doña María's Story, Oral History, and Issues of Gender." In *The Gendered Worlds of Latin American Women Workers: From the Household and Factory to the Union Hall and Ballot Box,* edited by John D. French and Daniel James, 31–52. Durham: Duke University Press, 1997.

Jiménez, Alfredo. "El Lejano Norte español: cómo escapar del *American West* y de las *Spanish Borderlands.*" *Colonial Latin American Historical Review* 5, no. 4 (fall 1996): 381–412.

Jiménez, Christina M. "Popular Organizing for Public Services: Residents Modernize Morelia, Mexico, 1880–1920." *Journal of Urban History* 30, no. 4 (2004): 495–518.

Johnson, Benjamin H. *Revolution in Texas: How a Forgotten Rebellion and Its Bloody Suppression Turned Mexicans into Americans.* New Haven: Yale University Press, 2003.

Joseph, Gil. *Revolution from Without: Yucatan, Mexico, and the United States, 1880–1924.* Durham: Duke University Press, 2003.

Kanter, Deborah E. "Native Female Land Tenure and Its Decline in Mexico, 1750–1900." *Ethnohistory* 42, no. 4 (1995): 607–16.

Katz, Friedrich. "Labor Conditions on Haciendas in Porfirian Mexico: Some Trends and Tendencies." *Hispanic American Historical Review* 54, no. 1 (February 1974): 1–47.

———. *The Secret War in Mexico: Europe, the United States, and the Mexican Revolution.* Chicago: University of Chicago Press, 1981.

Kearney, Milo, and Anthony Knopp. *Border Cuates: A History of the U.S.-Mexican Twin Cities.* Austin, Tex.: Eakin Press, 1995.

Kearney, Milo, Anthony Knopp, and Antonio Zavaleta, eds. *Studies in Matamoros and Cameron County History.* Brownsville: University of Texas at Brownsville, 1997.

Kellogg, Susan. *Weaving the Past: A History of Latin America's Indigenous Women from the Prehispanic Period to the Present.* New York: Oxford University Press, 2005.

Keremitsis, Dawn. *La industria textil mexicana en el siglo XIX.* Mexico City: Secretaríade Educación Pública, 1973.

———. "Latin American Women Workers in Transition: Sexual Division of the Labor Force in Mexico and Colombia in the Textile Industry." *The Americas* 40, no. 4 (April 1984): 491–504.

Kessler-Harris, Alice. "The Wages of Patriarchy: Some Thoughts about the Continuing Relevance of Class and Gender." *Labor: Studies in Working-Class History of the Americas,* 3, no. 3 (fall 2006): 7–21.

Klubock, Thomas Miller. *Contested Communities: Class, Gender, and Politics in Chile's El Teniente Copper Mine, 1904–1951.* Durham: Duke University Press, 1998.

Knopp, Anthony. *Boom and Bust: The Historical Cycles of Brownsville and Matamoros.* Austin, Tex.: Eakin Press, 1991.

Kuecker, Glen David. "Alejandro Prieto: Científico from the Provinces." In *The Human Tradition in Mexico,* edited by Jeffrey Pilcher, 91–102. Wilmington, Del.: Scholarly Resources, 2003.

———. "A Desert in the Tropical Wilderness: Limits to the Porfirian Project in Northeastern Veracruz, 1870–1910." PhD dissertation, Rutgers University, 1998.

Kuntz Ficker, Sandra. "La mayor empresa privada del Porfiriato: el Ferrocarril Central Mexicano (1880–1907)." In *Historia de las grandes empresas en México, 1850–1930,* edited by Carlos Marichal and Mario Cerutti. Monterrey: UANL and Fondo de Cultura Económica, 1997.

Las mujeres en la revolución mexicana: biografía de mujeres revolucionarias. Mexico City: INEHRM, 1992.

Lavrin, Asuncion. "Women in Latin American History." *History Teacher* 14, no. 3 (May 1981): 387–99.

Lawhn, Juanita Luna. "The Mexican Revolution and the Women of *México de Afuera*, the Pan American Round Table, and the *Cruz Azul Mexicana*." In *War along the Border: The Mexican Revolution and Tejano Communities*, edited by Arnoldo De León, 156–75. College Station: Texas A&M University Press, 2011.

Leal Ríos, Armando. *Linares: capital de Nuevo León*. Monterrey: UANL, 2001.

———. *Linares: visión del siglo XX*. Monterrey: UANL, 2000.

Ledesma, Irene. "Texas Newspapers and Chicana Workers' Activism, 1919–1974." *Western Historical Quarterly* 26, no. 3 (Autumn 1995): 309–31.

Levario, Miguel Antonio. *Militarizing the Border: When Mexicans Became the Enemy*. College Station: Texas A&M University Press, 2012.

Liga de Comunidades Agrarias y Sindicatos Campesinos del Estado de Tamaulipas, 70 Años, Conmemorativo. Victoria: Liga de Comunidades Agrarias y Sindicatos Campesinos del Estado de Tamaulipas, 1996.

Limón, José E. "El Primer Congreso Mexicanista de 1911: A Precursor to Contemporary Chicanismo." *Aztlán* 5, no. 1–2 (1974): 85–117.

Lomas, Clara. "The Articulation of Gender in the Mexican Borderlands, 1900–1915." In *Recovering the U.S. Hispanic Literary Heritage*, edited by Ramón Gutiérrez and Genaro Padilla. Houston: Arte Público Press, 1993.

———. "Transborder Discourse: The Articulation of Gender in the Borderlands in the Early Twentieth Century." *Frontiers: A Journal of Women Studies* 24, no. 2–3 (2003): 51–74.

Lópes, María-Aparecida de S. "Crisis económica y desorden social en Chihuahua en vísperas de la revolución." In *Culturas de pobreza y resistencia: estudios de marginados, proscritos y descontentos, México, 1804–1910*, edited by Romana Falcón, 329–49. Mexico City: Colegio de México, Universidad Autónoma de Querétaro, 2005.

———. "Del taller a la fábrica: los trabajadores chihuahuenses en la primera mitad del siglo XX." In *Historia de la vida cotidiana en México*. Book 5, volume 1, *Siglo XX, campo y ciudad*, edited by Pilar Gonzalbo Aizpuru and Aurelio de los Reyes. Mexico City: Colegio de México, Fondo de Cultura Económica, 2006.

López Olivares, Reynaldo. *Presidentes municipales de Reynosa, 1895–2005: raices políticas*. Reynosa, 2004.

Lorey, David. *US-Mexican Border Statistics since 1900*. Los Angeles: University of California, 1990.

Loria, Francisco. *La política ferrocarrilera de México*. Mexico City: Tipografía Económica, 1914.

Los pobres de Monterrey: estudio socio-económico. Monterrey: UANL Facultad de Economía Centro de Estudios Económicos, 1965.

Macías, Anna. *Against All Odds: The Feminist Movement in Mexico to 1940*. Westport, Conn.: Greenwood Press, 1982.

MacLachlan, Colin, and Jaime Rodríguez O. *The Forging of the Cosmic Race: A Reinterpretation of Colonial Mexico*. Berkeley: University of California Press, 1980.

Maíz, Rocío G., and Antonio Olvera, eds. *La nueva historia de Nuevo León.* Monterrey: Ediciones Castillo, 1995.

Mallon, Florencia. *The Defense of Community in Peru's Central Highlands: Peasant Struggle and Capitalist Transition, 1860–1940.* Princeton: Princeton University Press, 1983.

———. "Exploring the Origins of Democratic Patriarchy in Mexico: Gender and Popular Resistance in the Puebla Highlands, 1850–1876." In *Women of the Mexican Countryside, 1850–1990: Creating Spaces, Shaping Transitions,* edited by Heather Fowler-Salamini and Mary Kay Vaughan, 3–26. Tucson: University of Arizona Press, 1994.

Marín, Mariano B. *La rebelión de la huertista en Tamaulipas.* 3rd ed. Victoria: Universidad Autónoma de Tamaulipas: Instituto de Investigaciones Históricas, 1977.

———. *Recuerdos de la la Revolución Constitucionalista.* 2nd ed. Victoria: Universidad Autónoma de Tamaulipas: Instituto de Investigaciones Históricas, 1977.

Martin, Cheryl. *Governance and Society in Colonial Mexico: Chihuahua in the Eighteenth Century.* Stanford: Stanford University Press, 1996.

Martínez, Camilo Amado. "The Mexican and Mexican American Laborers in the Lower Rio Grande Valley of Texas, 1870–1930," PhD dissertation, Texas A&M University, 1987.

Melero, Pilar. "Sara Estela Ramírez and Andrea Villarreal González: Revolutionary Voices?" In *Recovering the U.S. Hispanic Literary Heritage,* volume 6, edited by Antonia I. Castañeda and A. Gabriel Meléndez, 182–98. Houston: Arte Público Press, 2006.

Mendieta Alatorre, Angeles. *La mujer en la revolución mexicana.* Mexico City: Biblioteca del Instituto Nacional de Estudios Históricos de la Revolución Mexicana, 1961.

Menéndez, Gabriel A. *El cacique de las Huastecas.* Mexico City: SEP Cuadernos Mexicanos, n.d.

Meyer, Michael C., and William H. Beezley, eds. *The Oxford History of Mexico.* New York: Oxford University Press, 2000.

Middlebrook, Kevin J., and Cirila Quintero Ramirez. "Conflict Resolution in the Mexican Labor Courts: An Examination of Local Conciliation and Arbitration Boards in Chihuahua and Tamaulipas." Bureau of International Labor Affairs, US Department of Labor, October 20, 2005. www.dol.gov/ilab/media/reports/nao/conflictresolution.htm.

Milkman, Ruth. "Redefining Women's Work: The Sexual Division of Labor in the Auto Industry during World War II." *Feminist Studies* 8, no. 2 (1982): 337–72.

Miller, Barbara Ann. "The Role of Women in the Mexican Cristero Rebellion: Las Señoras y las Religiosas." *The Americas* 40, no. 3 (1984): 303–23.

Misael Hernández, Oscar. "Estado, cultura y masculinidades en el noreste de México en la posrevolución." *Gazeta de Antropología* 25, no. 2 (2009).

———. "Procesos de cambio, género y reorganización familiar en una ciudad del noreste de México." *Gazeta de Antropología* 24, no. 1 (2008).

Momen, Mehnaaz. "Redefining Patriarchy: Women, the State and Globalization." In *Río Bravo: A Journal of the Borderlands* 1, no. 1 (Spring 2008).

Monday, Jane Clements, and Frances Brannen Vick. *Petra's Legacy: The South Texas Ranching Empire of Petra Vela and Mifflin Kenedy.* College Station: Texas A&M University Press, 2007.

Montejano, David. *Anglos and Mexicans in the Making of Texas, 1836–1936.* Austin: University of Texas Press, 1987.

Morado Macías, César. "Empresas mineras y metalúrgicas en Monterrey, México, 1890–1908." *Ingenierías* 6, no. 20 (July–September 2003).

———, coord. *Nuevo León en el siglo XX: la transición al mundo moderno.* Volume 1, *Del reyismo a la reconstrucción, 1885–1939.* Monterrey: Fondo Editorial de Nuevo León, 2007.

Mora García, José Carlos. *El General Alberto Carrera Torres y la revolución mexicana en Tamaulipas 1910–1917.* Victoria, Tamps.: n.p., 2007.

Mora-Torres, Juan. *The Making of the Mexican Border: The State, Capitalism, and Society in Nuevo León, 1848–1910.* Austin: University of Texas Press, 2001.

Muir, John M. *Geology of the Tampico Region, Mexico.* Tulsa, Okla.: American Association of Petroleum Geologists; London: Thomas Murby and Company, 1936.

Nuevo León: imágines de nuestra historia. Monterrey: CONARTE, 2003.

O'Brien, Thomas F. *The Revolutionary Mission: American Enterprise in Latin America, 1900–1945.* Cambridge: Cambridge University Press, 1996.

Ocasio Meléndez, Marcial E. *Capitalism and Development: Tampico, Mexico, 1876–1924.* New York: Peter Lang, 1998.

Ochoa, Edna. "El periodismo, la mujer y la frontera en Laredo: propuesta de cambio en la obra de Jovita Idar." Presented at the Primer Simposio de la Historia del Noreste y Sur de Texas, Archivo Histórico de Reynosa, Reynosa, Tamps., October 2, 2006.

Olcott, Jocelyn. "The Center Cannot Hold: Women on Mexico's Popular Front." In *Sex in Revolution: Gender, Politics, and Power in Modern Mexico,* edited by Jocelyn Olcott, Mary Kay Vaughan, and Gabriela Cano, 223–41. Durham: Duke University Press, 2006.

———. "Miracle Workers: Gender and State Mediation among Textile and Garment Workers in Mexico's Transition to Industrial Development." *International Labor and Working-Class History* 63 (December 2003): 45–62.

———. *Revolutionary Women in Postrevolutionary Mexico.* Durham: Duke University Press, 2005.

———, Mary Kay Vaughan, and Gabriela Cano, eds. *Sex in Revolution: Gender, Politics, and Power in Modern Mexico.* Durham: Duke University Press, 2006.

Olivares Arriaga, Ma. Del Carmen, and Altair Tejeda de Tamez. *Mujeres que han dejado testimonio en Tamaulipas.* Victoria: Universidad Autónoma de Tamaulipas, 1989.

Olvera Guerrero, Nereo. *Reseña histórica del municipio de Ocampo, Tamaulipas.* 2nd ed. Victoria, Tamps.: IIH, UAT, 1987.

Olvera Rivera, Alberto. "Identity, Culture, and Workers' Autonomy: The Petroleum Workers of Poza Rica in the 1930s." In *Border Crossings: Mexican and Mexican-American Workers,* edited by John Mason Hart, 117–38. Wilmington, Del.: Scholarly Resources, 1998.

Olvera Sandoval, José Antonio. *Monterrey y sus caminos de hierro.* Monterrey: Consejo para la Cultura de Nuevo León, 1998.

———. "La citricultura en Montemorelos: sus inicios (1890–1910)." In *Monterrey, Nuevo León, el Noreste: siete estudios históricos,* edited by Mario Cerutti. Monterrey: Universidad Autónoma de Nuevo León, 1987.

Orozco, Cynthia. *No Mexicans, Women, or Dogs Allowed: The Rise of the Mexican American Civil Rights Movement.* Austin: University of Texas Press, 2010.

Palomo Acosta, Teresa, and Ruthe Winegarten. *Las Tejanas: 300 Years of History.* Austin: University of Texas Press, 2003.

Pan American Petroleum & Transport Company. *Mexican Petroleum.* New York: Pan American Petroleum & Transport Company, 1922.

Parkes, Henry Bamford. *A History of Mexico.* Boston: Houghton Mifflin, 1938.

Parlee, Lorena. "Impact of United States Railroad Unions on Organized Labor and Government Policy in Mexico, 1880–1911." *Hispanic American Historical Review* 64, no. 3 (August 1984): 443–75.

Pastrano, José Guillermo. "The Bureaucratic Origins of Migrant Poverty: The Texas Cotton Industry, 1910–1930." *Journal of Peasant Studies* 35, no. 4 (October 2008): 688–719.

Perales, Xavier C. *Testimonios de los veteranos de la revolución mexicana I: los tamaulipecos.* N.p., n.d.

Pérez, Emma. *The Decolonial Imaginary: Writing Chicanas into History.* Bloomington: Indiana University Press, 1999.

Pérez-Maldonado, Carlos. *El Casino de Monterrey: bosquejo histórico de la Sociedad Regiomontana.* Monterrey: Impresora Monterrey, S.A., 1950.

Permisos y concesiones 1890–1912. Monterrey: Archivo General del Estado de Nuevo León, [1979?].

Piñera Ramírez, David, ed. *El Gobernador Bernardo Reyes y sus homólogos en la frontera norte.* Monterrey: Fondo Editorial Nuevo León, 1991.

Porter, Susie. "'And That It Is Custom Makes It Law': Class Conflict and Gender Ideology in the Public Sphere, Mexico City, 1880–1910." *Social Science History* 24, no. 1 (spring 2000): 111–48.

———. *Working Women in Mexico City: Public Discourses and Material Conditions, 1879–1931.* Tucson: University of Arizona Press, 2003.

Pozas Horcasitas, Ricardo. "La evolución de la política laboral mexicana, 1857–1920." *Revista Mexicana de Sociología* 38, no. 1 (January–March 1976): 85–109.

Pratt, Joseph A. *The Growth of a Refining Region.* Greenwich, Conn.: Jai Press, 1980.

Pratt, Mary Louise. *Imperial Eyes: Travel Writing and Transculturation.* New York: Routledge, 1992.

Primera convención de la Liga de Comunidades Agrarias y Sindicatos Campesinos del Estado de Tamaulipas. Mexico City: n.p, 1926.

Quintero Ramírez, Cirila. "La organización laboral en la frontera este de México y Estados Unidos (1900–1940)." In *Encuentro en la frontera: mexicanos y norteamericanos en un espacio común,* edited by Manuel Ceballos Ramírez, 378–408. Mexico City: Colegio de México, Colegio de la Frontera Norte, UAT, 2001.

Radding, Cynthia. *Wandering Peoples: Colonialism, Ethnic Spaces, and Ecological Frontiers in Northwestern Mexico, 1700–1850.* Durham: Duke University Press, 1997.

Ramos Aguirre, Francisco. *Mujeres de armas tomar: canciones y soldaderas de la Revolución Mexicana.* Victoria: Comisión Organizadora para la Conmemoración en

Tamaulipas del Bicentenario de la Independencia y Centenario de la Revolución Mexicana, 2010.

Ramos Escandón, Carmen. "Gender, Labor, and Class Consciousness in the Mexican Textile Industry." In *Border Crossings: Mexican and Mexican American Workers*, edited by John M. Hart, 71–92. Wilmington, Del.: Scholarly Resources, 1998.

———, ed. *Presencia y transparencia: la mujer en la historia de México.* 2nd ed. Mexico City: El Colegio de México, 2006.

———. "Señoritas porfirianas: mujer e ideología en el México progresista, 1880–1910." In *Presencia y transparencia: la mujer en la historia de México*, edited by Carmen Ramos Escandón. 2nd ed. Mexico City: El Colegio de México, 2006.

———, and Ana Lau. *Mujeres y revolución, 1900–1917.* Mexico City: Instituto Nacional de Estudios Históricos de la Revolución Mexicana, 1993.

Rangel, Angela. "Participación de las mujeres marginadas." In *Nuevo León, hoy: diez estudios sociopolíticos*, coordinated by Luis Lauro Garza, 109–21. Monterrey: Universidad Autónoma de Nuevo León, La Jornada Ediciones, 1998.

Rangel Frías, Raúl. "Años de Caudillo." In *El Gobernador Bernardo Reyes y sus homólogos en la frontera norte*, edited by David Piñera Ramírez. Monterrey: Fondo Editorial Nuevo León, 1991.

Reséndez Fuentes, Andres. "Battleground Women: Soldaderas and Female Soldiers in the Mexican Revolution." *The Americas* 51, no. 4 (April 1995): 525–53.

Ribb, Richard. "La Rinchada: Revolution, Revenge, and the Rangers: 1910–1920." In *War along the Border: The Mexican Revolution and Tejano Communities*, edited by Arnoldo De León, 56–106. College Station: Texas A&M University Press, 2011.

Rivera Estrada, Araceli, and Tehua Osnaya Rodríguez. "Repercusiones del asentamiento colonial en el valle de la Mota evidencia material de Trapiches." In *Espacios, poblamiento y conflicto en el Noreste Mexicano y Texas / People, Places, and Conflicts in Northeastern Mexico and Texas*, coordinated by Ruth E. Arbolyeda et al., 486–87. Mexico City: INAH; Brownsville: UTB-TSC; Victoria, Tamps.: UAT, 2009.

Rocha, Rodolfo. "The Influence of the Mexican Revolution on the Texas-Mexico Border." PhD dissertation, Texas Tech University, 1981.

Roel Melo, Santiago. *Apuntes históricos de Nuevo León.* Monterrey, 1969.

Rojas Coria, Rosendo. *Tratado del cooperativismo en México.* 2nd ed. Mexico City: Fondo de Cultura Económica, 1982.

Rojas Sandoval, Javier. *El patrimonio industrial histórico de Nuevo León: las fábricas pioneras de la segunda generación.* Monterrey: UANL, 2009.

———. "Minería en Nuevo León: antecedentes de la industria de fundición." *Ingenierías* 1, no. 2 (July–December 1998).

———. *Monterrey: poder político, obreros, y empresarios en la coyuntura revolucionaria.* Monterrey: Facultad de Filosofía y Letras de la Universidad Autónoma de Nuevo León, 1992.

———. *Historia de las relaciones laborales en la cultura industrial de Nuevo León: (de los tiempos del mutualismo a los años revolucionarios).* Monterrey: UANL, 2008.

Roseberry, William. *Anthropologies and Histories: Essays in Culture, History, and Political Economy.* New Brunswick: Rutgers University Press, 1989.

Ruiz, Ramón. *On the Rim of Mexico: Encounters of the Rich and Poor.* Boulder, Colo.: Westview Press, 1998.

Ruiz, Vicki L. *Cannery Women, Cannery Lives: Mexican Women, Unionization, and the California Food Processing Industry, 1930–1950.* Albuquerque: University of New Mexico Press, 1987.

———. *From Out of the Shadows: Mexican Women in Twentieth-Century America.* New York: Oxford University Press, 1998.

———. "Una Mujer sin Fronteras: Luisa Moreno and Latina Labor Activism." *Pacific Historical Review* 73, no.1 (February 2004): 1–20.

———, and Susan Tiano, eds. *Women on the U.S.–Mexico Border: Responses to Change.* Boston: Allen and Unwin, 1987.

Sahlins, Peter. *Boundaries: The Making of France and Spain in the Pyrenees.* Berkeley: University of California Press, 1991.

Saka, Mark Saad. "Agrarian Rebellion and Clerical Insurrection in Nineteenth-Century Mexico: The Siege of Mezcala, 1811–1816." PhD dissertation, University of Houston, 1990.

Salas, Elizabeth. "The Soldadera in the Mexican Revolution: War and Men's Illusions." In *Women of the Mexican Countryside, 1850–1990,* edited by Heather Fowler-Salamini and Mary Kay Vaughan, 93–105. Tucson: University of Arizona Press, 1994.

Saldaña, José P. *¿Y que hicimos? Monterrey en el siglo XX.* Monterrey: Producciones al Voleo–El Troquel, S.A., 1988.

Saldivar, Gabriel. *Historia Compendiada de Tamaulipas.* Mexico City: Editorial Beatriz de Silva, 1945.

Salmon, Roberto Mario. "Mexican American Simpatía during the Mexican Revolution." *Borderlands Journal* 4, no. 2 (spring 1981): 215–40.

Sánchez Mejorada, Carlos. "The Writ of Amparo: Mexican Procedure to Protect Human Rights." *Annals of the American Academy of Political and Social Science* 243 (January 1946): 107–11.

Sandos, James. *Rebellion in the Borderlands: Anarchism and the Plan of San Diego, 1904–1923.* Norman: University of Oklahoma Press, 1992.

Santiago, Myrna. *The Ecology of Oil: Environment, Labor, and the Mexican Revolution, 1900–1938.* New York: Cambridge University Press, 2006.

———. "Rejecting Progress in Paradise: Natives, Oil, and the Environment in Veracruz." *Environmental History* 3, no. 2 (April 1998): 169–88.

———. "Women of the Mexican Oil Fields: Class, Nationality, Economy, Culture, 1900–1938." *Journal of Women's History* 21, no. 1 (spring 2009): 87–110.

Saragoza, Alex M. *The Monterrey Elite and the Mexican State, 1880–1940.* Austin: University of Texas Press, 1988.

Scott, James. *Weapons of the Weak: Everyday Forms of Peasant Resistance.* New Haven: Yale University Press, 1987.

Scott, Joan. "Gender as a Useful Category of Historical Analysis." *American Historical Review* 91, no. 5 (December 1986): 1053–75.

Shelton, Laura M. *For Tranquility and Order: Family and Community on Mexico's Northern Frontier, 1800–1850.* Tucson: University of Arizona Press, 2010.

Sieglin, Veronika. "Agua, acumulación de capital, y burguesía en la región citrícola, 1910–1934." In *Agua, tierra, y capital en el Noreste de México: la región citrícola de Nuevo León, 1850–1940*, edited by Mario Cerutti. Monterrey: UANL, 1991.

———, ed. *Mujeres en el campo a finales del siglo XX: desarrollo rural y* género. Monterrey: Cuadernos del Topo Ensayo, 1996.

Silverblatt, Irene. *Moon, Sun, and Witches: Gender Ideologies and Class in Inca and Colonial Peru.* Princeton: Princeton University Press, 1987.

Snodgrass, Michael David. "Contesting Identities: Regionalism, Revolution, and Counter-Revolution in Monterrey." Paper delivered at the annual meeting of the Latin American Studies Association, Chicago, September 24–26, 1998.

———. *Deference and Defiance in Monterrey: Workers, Paternalism and Revolution in Mexico, 1890–1950.* Cambridge: Cambridge University Press, 2003.

———. "La lucha sindical y la resistencia patronal en Monterrey, México: 1918–1940." *Orgullosamente Bárbaros*, no. 17 (May 1996).

Soto, Shirlene. *Emergence of the Modern Mexican Woman: Her Participation in Revolution and Struggle for Equality, 1910–1940.* Denver: Arden Press, 1990.

Stoner, K. Lynn, "Directions in Latin American Women's History, 1977–1985." *Latin American Research Review* 22, no. 2 (1987): 101–34.

St. John, Rachel. *Line in the Sand: A History of the Western U.S.–Mexico Border.* Princeton: Princeton University Press, 2011.

Story, Victor O. "Genesis of Revolution in the Tamaulipas Sierra: Campesinos and Shopkeepers in the Carrera Torres Uprising, 1907–1911." PhD dissertation, University of North Carolina, 1991.

Tafolla, Carmen. "La Pasionaria." *Frontiers: A Journal of Women Studies* 24, no. 2–3 (2003): 233–36.

Taylor, Paul S. "Notes on Streams of Mexican Migration." *American Journal of Sociology* 36, no. 2 (September 1930): 287–88.

Thompson, E. P. *The Making of the English Working Class.* New York: Pantheon Books, 1963.

Thompson, Jerry. *Cortina: Defending the Mexican Name in Texas.* College Station: Texas A&M University Press, 2007.

Tiano, Susan. *Patriarchy on the Line: Labor, Gender, and Ideology in the Mexican Maquila Industry.* Philadelphia: Temple University Press, 1994.

———. "Women and Industrial Development in Latin America." *Latin American Research Review* 21, no. 3 (1986): 157–70.

Tinker Salas, Miguel. *In the Shadow of the Eagles: Sonora and the Transformation of the Border during the Porfiriato.* Berkeley: University of California Press, 1997.

Toscano Hernández, Mario Alberto. *Haciendas ixtleras en el cuarto distrito de Tamaulipas, 1877–1910.* Victoria: Museo Regional de Historia de Tamaulipas, 2003.

Tovar González, Ma Elena. "Extranjeros en el Soconusco." *Revista de Humanidades: Tecnológico de Monterrey, no. 8 (2000): 29–43.*

Truett, Samuel. *Fugitive Landscapes: The Forgotten History of the U.S.–Mexico Borderlands.* New Haven: Yale University Press, 2006.

———. "Transnational Warrior: Emilio Kosterlitzky and the Transformation of the U.S.–Mexico Borderlands, 1873–1928." In *Continental Crossroads: Remapping*

U.S.–Mexico Borderlands History, edited by Samuel Truett and Elliott Young, 241–70. Durham: Duke University Press, 2004.

———, and Elliott Young, eds. *Continental Crossroads: Remapping U.S.–Mexico Borderlands History.* Durham: Duke University Press, 2004.

Trujillo Bautista, Jorge. *Testimonios de la Revolución Mexicana en Tamaulipas.* Mexico City: INEHRM, 1992.

Tuñón Pablos, Julia. *Women in Mexico: A Past Unveiled.* Translated by Alan Hynds. Austin: University of Texas Press, 1999.

Tyler, Ronnie C. *Santiago Vidaurri and the Southern Confederacy.* Austin: Texas State Historical Association, 1973.

Van Young, Eric. "La pareja dispareja: breves comentarios acerca de la relación entre historia económica y cultural." *Historia Mexicana* 52, no. 3 (2003): 832–33.

Vargas, Zaragosa. "Mexican Migrant Workers in the Midwest." In *Major Problems in Mexican American History,* edited by Zaragosa Vargas. Boston: Houghton Mifflin, 1999.

———. "Tejana Radical: Emma Tenayuca and the San Antonio Labor Movement during the Great Depression." *Pacific Historical Review* 66, no. 4 (November 1997): 553–80.

Vázquez Juárez, Juan Antonio. "Joseph Andrew Robertson empresario norteamericano, inversor extranjero en Monterrey, Nuevo León (1890–1910)." VII Reunión de Historiadores Mexicanos y Norteamericanos, Oaxaca, October 1985.

Viotti da Costa, Emilia. "Experience versus Structures: New Tendencies in the History of Labor and the Working Class in Latin America: What Do We Gain? What Do We Lose? *International Labor and Working-Class History* 36 (fall 1989): 3–24.

Visión histórica de la frontera norte de México. Book 5, *De la Revolución a la Segunda Guerra Mundial.* Mexicali: Universidad Autónoma de Baja California Instituto de Investigaciones Históricas, 1987.

Vizcaya Canales, Isidro. *Los orígenes de la industrialización de Monterrey.* Monterrey: ITESM, 1969.

Walker, David W. "The Mexican Industrial Revolution and Its Problems: Porfirian Labor Policy and Economic Dependency, 1876–1910." Master's thesis, University of Houston, 1976.

Walsh, Casey. *Building the Borderlands: A Transnational History of Irrigated Cotton along the Mexico–Texas Border.* College Station: Texas A&M University Press, 2008.

Warman, Arturo. *"We Come to Object": The Peasants of Morelos and the National State.* Translated by Stephen K. Ault. Baltimore: Johns Hopkins University Press, 1976.

Wasserman, Mark. *Capitalists, Caciques, and Revolution: The Native Elite and Foreign Enterprise in Chihuahua, Mexico, 1854–1911.* Chapel Hill: University of North Carolina Press, 1984.

———. "Foreign Investment in Mexico, 1876–1910: A Case Study of the Role of Regional Elites." *The Americas* 36, no. 1 (July 1979): 3–21.

———. *Persistent Oligarchs: Elites and Politics in Chihuahua, 1910–1940.* Durham: Duke University Press, 1993.

Weber, David J. *The Mexican Frontier, 1821–1846: The American Southwest under Mexico.* Albuquerque: University of New Mexico Press, 1982.

———. *The Spanish Frontier in North America.* New Haven: Yale University Press, 1992.

Winn, Peter. *Weavers of Revolution: The Yarur Workers and Chile's Road to Socialism.* Oxford: Oxford University Press, 1986.

Yankelevich, Pablo. "Mexico for the Mexicans: Immigration, National Sovereignty, and the Promotion of Mestizaje." *The Americas* 68, no. 3 (January 2011): 405–36.

Yeager, Gertrude, ed. *Confronting Change, Challenging Tradition: Women in Latin American History.* Wilmington, Del.: Scholarly Resources, 1994.

Young, Elliott. *Catarino Garza's Revolution on the Texas–Mexico Border.* Durham: Duke University Press, 2004.

Zamora, Emilio. *Claiming Rights and Writing Wrongs in Texas: Mexican Workers and Job Politics during World War II.* College Station: Texas A&M University Press, 2009.

———. "Mexican Labor Activity in South Texas, 1900–1920." PhD dissertation, University of Texas at Austin, 1983.

———. "Sara Estela Ramírez: una rosa roja en el movimiento." In *Mexican Women in the United States: Struggles Past and Present,* edited by Magdalena Mora and Adelaida R. del Castillo. Los Angeles: Chicano Studies Research Center Publications, 1980.

———. *The World of the Mexican Worker in Texas.* College Station: Texas A&M University Press, 1993.

Zebadúa, María. "Género, política y vida cotidiana." In *Mujeres en el campo a finales del siglo XX: desarrollo rural y* género, edited by Veronika Sieglin. Monterrey: Cuadernos del Topo Ensayo, 1996.

———. "La lucha por la tierra en la región citrícola: cuatro ejidos." In *Agua, tierra y capital en el Noreste de Mexico: la región citrícola de Nuevo León, 1850–1940,* edited by Mario Cerutti. Monterrey: Universidad Autónoma de Nuevo León, 1991.

———. "Las Comunidades Campesinas durante la lucha por la tierra: testimonio oral; la región centro-sur de Nuevo León." In *Historia de la vida cotidiana en México, obra dirigida por Pilar Gonzalbo Aizpuru.* Book 5, *Siglo XX, campo y ciudad,* edited by Aurelio de los Reyes. Mexico City: Colegio de México, Fondo de Cultura Económica, 2006.

Zorilla, Juan Fidel. *Historia de Tamaulipas.* Victoria: Gobierno del Estado de Tamaulipas, 1987.

———. *La mujer en Tamaulipas.* Victoria, Tamps.: Instituto de Investigaciones Históricas, 1976.

———. *Tamaulipas: una historia compartida.* Victoria: Instituto de Investigaciones Históricas, Universidad Autónoma de Tamaulipas, 1993.

———, Maribel Miro Flaquer, and Octavio Herrera Pérez, eds. *Tamaulipas: textos de su historia, 1810–1921 II.* Mexico City: Instituto de Investigaciones José María Luís Mora, 1999.

Index